The Political
Economy
of
Romanian Socialism

The Political
Economy
of
Romanian Socialism

WILLIAM E. CROWTHER _____

New York
Westport, Connecticut
London

Library of Congress Cataloging-in-Publication Data

Crowther, William E.
  The political economy of Romanian socialism.

  Bibliography: p.
  Includes index.
    1. Socialism—Romania.   2. Romania—Economic
conditions—1945–   . 3. Romania—Politics and
government—1944–   . I. Title.
HX373.5.C76   1988   338.9498   87-29244
ISBN 0-275-92840-3 (alk. paper)

Library of Congress Catalog Card Number: 87-29244

ISBN: 0-275-92840-3

First published in 1988

Praeger Publishers, One Madison Avenue, New York, NY 10010
A division of Greenwood Press, Inc.

Printed in the United States of America

♾️

The paper used in this book complies with the
Permanent Paper Standard issued by the National
Information Standards Organization (Z39.48–1984).

10 9 8 7 6 5 4 3 2 1

CONTENTS

ACKNOWLEDGMENTS

Research necessary to the completion of this study was made possible by grants from the International Research and Exchanges Board, and the University of California at Los Angeles Center for Russian and East European Studies. I would also like to thank Andrzej Korbonski, Ronald Rogowski, Valerie Bunce, and Mary Ellen Fischer for comments and suggestions that were essential to its completion. Responsibility for remaining errors is entirely my own.

1 STATE-SOCIALISM IN EASTERN EUROPE

INTRODUCTION

This study focuses on Romania in the period since World War II as a case study of state-socialist politics.[1] Its primary purpose is to describe the organization of power following the inception of communist party rule, its social basis, and its evolution up to the present time. Its basic hypothesis is simply stated: the current Romanian regime and those of the other state-socialist countries can only be adequately understood when seen as integral elements in coherent political economies and located in the social histories of their particular countries. The synthesis of Leninist party organization and Romania's endogenous political legacy transformed the regime's original Marxist ideology and shaped its political strategy. Although the interpenetration of prerevolutionary political practices and postrevolutionary institutions is not limited to Romania (one need only review the recent histories of other contemporary state-socialist countries to appreciate the capacity of national traditions to reemerge in dramatically changed political circumstances), the Romanian Communist Party (RCP) differs from its East European neighbors in the extent to which it has drawn on a heritage of extreme nationalism and traditional authoritarianism. Bucharest's assumption of this posture is not simply an example of cultural determinism. Rather it constitutes a logical response to a particular set of economic and political constraints.

Before entering into a discussion of events specific to Romania, it is necessary to suggest a methodological approach that is useful in the analysis of political systems of the Soviet type. Therefore, this chapter begins by addressing the main theoretical concerns raised in the body of the following analysis, and sets out the

1

methodological principles to be employed in the course of the study. It seeks to sketch out in brief the characteristic dynamics of state-socialist society, the conflicts of interest that exist within it, and the logic which governs its progress. The evolution of postwar Eastern Europe is also outlined, in order to establish a basis of comparison for the analysis of Romania that follows.

Chapter 2 summarizes the salient characteristics of the prerevolutionary political system. The consolidation of the national state and political institutions are briefly discussed in order to establish a background for analysis. Next, Romanian attempts to develop within the prewar international capitalist economic system and the circumstances surrounding the emergence of fascism in the years between 1919 and 1940 are explored in some detail. Chapter 3 is devoted to the Stalinist period in Romania. It focuses on the revolutionary social/economic transformation undertaken under Russian tutelage, and the various factors that led the Romanian political elite to pursue at least limited national independence from the Soviet Union. Chapter 4 outlines the consolidation of the postrevolutionary political economy under the leadership of Nicolae Ceausescu during the late 1960s. It traces the various and sometimes contradictory policy strains of the period, and indicates why ambiguity was resolved in favor of an authoritarian nationalist renaissance. Chapters 5 and 6 undertake the analysis of developed "national communism." The pecularities of Romania's economic model are discussed, and the relationship among it, the evolution of Romanian class structure, and the nature of the party/state bureaucracy is evaluated. Chapter 7 explores the linkages between the international environment and contemporary Romania's domestic political and economic systems. Here the argument will be advanced that a complex two-way relationship has emerged. While the international economy has clearly had a potent impact upon Romanian domestic politics and economics, it is nonetheless true that the RCP's domestic political strategy has fundamentally shaped its behavior in the world market. Finally, a concluding chapter draws together the strands of the preceding argument and discusses the implications of the Romanian case for the study of state-socialist political systems in general.

THE METHODOLOGICAL ISSUES

Since the consolidation of the first communist party-state in the Soviet Union, countless attempts to explain this form of social/political organization have appeared, ranging from the implacably hostile to the eulogistic. Already difficult, the task of analyzing Soviet politics was vastly complicated by the emergence of a large number of states modeled (at least initially) on the Soviet Union and identifying themselves as "socialist." Otherwise diverse, these regimes share the common elements of control by a highly centralized single party, an ideological foundation in Marxism-Leninism, and effective, if not complete, nationalization of their economies. As becomes apparent when one reviews the literature, seeking to comprehend the nature of power relations under communist regimes, their structural characteristics, and the mechanisms through which they reproduce themselves, these systems present a considerable methodological challenge.

The difficulties of dealing with the politics of state-socialist countries have elicited varied and, to a certain extent, extreme theoretical responses among Western social scientists. In particular, a great deal of controversy was generated by the problem of identifying the locus of political power. Until recently, the majority of analyses had focused on a very limited number of political leaders who were assumed to be able to act virtually at will. The most influential expression of this view by far had been the totalitarian paradigm (Arendt 1958; Friedrich and Brzezinski 1956; Friedrich, Curtis, and Barber 1969. See also Cohen 1985; Lane 1982: 147-151; and Odom 1976). Like much of the social science literature on the topic of Soviet society that emerged after World War II, the totalitarian model took on an intensely anticommunist tone. Unlike most other efforts, however, it provided a comprehensive political analysis of state-socialism. At bottom the proponents of the theory argued that totalitarianism consisted of modern technology and organization mobilized in the service of a fanatical minority committed to the utopian transformation of society.

Totalitarianism's most distinctive trait as a theory of politics is that it locates all power in the institutions of the state. The possibility of countervailing power based in social classes, groups, or other institutions is rejected on grounds of the state's monopolization of economic processes, the means of communication, and the means of coercion. In its initial conception, authoritarian direction of virtually all dimensions of social behavior was a basic assumption of the model, which consequently took on a highly static quality and was for the most part restricted to explaining why such a phenomenon had come into being, how its various aspects were interrelated, and how it maintained itself. The impact of this approach on the study of state-socialist political systems was profound (see Cohen 1985 on this point). Numerous derivative models followed, all of which concentrated on the despotic nature of the new states and their violent programs of anticapitalist social transformation. Not unjustifiably, a majority of analysts attributed these common characteristics of the communist party-states to the related phenomenon of a foundation in Marxist-Leninist ideology and rule by communist parties.

In retrospect it appears that totalitarianism offered an adequate description of the particular phenomenon of Stalinism, but that its utility is confined to this limited (albeit crucial) historic period in the evolution of the communist party-states. The totalitarian model and its many offshoots based their analysis on extreme but relatively short-lived elements of these political systems, mistaking them for immutable patterns of behavior, and building them into a comprehensive model of state-socialism. Consequently they failed to consider adequately more fundamental and longer lasting characteristics of the state-socialist regimes. By locating all power within the state (particularly in its coercive apparatus), they failed to offer any sufficient account of how such a system could be dynamic, how it could be transformed, or the direction it would take (Hough 1972; Lane 1976: 44–63).

Faced with the challenge of explaining the post-Stalin changes in state-socialist politics, the shortcomings of the theory became obvious. The spectacle of previously conformist regimes moving off in new and dissimilar directions caused analysts to seriously consider a possible breakdown of state-socialist political systems on the domestic level, and the dissolution of the Soviet bloc internationally (Brzezinski 1966, 1967; Croan 1970). A heated debate arose among Western scholars concerning the coherence of the model once the element of "terror" and the central role of the personality cult declined, and also concerning the source of systemic change in state-socialism. As the prevailing theoretical consensus eroded, the continued utility of the totalitarian model came into question and a succession of new approaches intended to explain the shift in political conditions appeared (Friedrich, Curtis, and Barber 1969; Rigby 1972). Three directions were particularly evident in scholarship which emerged in years that followed. A first alternative consisted of the elimination of elements of the totalitarian model, such as the practice of terror, which no longer conformed with actual conditions, while maintaining the body of the theory substantially intact (see Kassoff 1969). This expedient, however, did little to redress the shortcomings of the earlier model. Second, many students of Eastern Europe and the Soviet Union turned to the more general field of comparative politics in search of appropriate models of political behavior. Thus modernization theory, for instance, became the basis of a number of studies of state-socialist politics. Finally, interest shifted away from whole system theories toward mid-level approaches and limited empirical studies (for a summary of these developments see Bunce and Echols 1979). This final course enabled researchers to avoid the problems associated with the previous period of "grand theorizing" and added tremendously to the body of information available on the communist party-states, but did little to increase our understanding of state-socialism as a unique form of political organization.[2]

More recently a growing number of analysts have sought to formulate alternative, but equally comprehensive, modes of analysis with which to replace the totalitarian model. These are intended to explain not just the revolutionary period, but rather the entire evolution of state-socialist societies, and to identify those factors that determine their development. Kenneth Jowitt, for example, contends that analysts have mistakenly treated "Leninist" regimes as an aberration, and failed to place them in their broader cultural historical context. In fact, he argues, they can best be understood as "a response to the 'arrested development' of dependent [status] societies" (Jowitt 1978). Similar to Jowitt in this regard, Rudolf Bahro argues from within the Marxist tradition that "state repression in these countries is in the last analysis a function of their industrial underdevelopment, or, more exactly, of the task of actively overcoming this underdevelopment" (Bahro 1978: 131). Economic transformation in the Russian context required establishment of a strong central political authority willing to use coercion in the cause of industrial development; among the Bolsheviks a large body of support existed for this course of action, event at the expense of early socialism's more humanistic principles. As Bahro aptly puts it, when the task of economic transformation was completed, the country was no longer guided by a political party, as previously conceived, but rather by "a political administration flanked by the organs of terror."

According to those who share this view of state-socialism, the product of the 1917 revolution and its Stalinist epilogue is not an unstable transitional phase, but a unique form of social/political organization, with its own dynamics and structural characteristics.[3] Despite their differences, the proponents of virtually all such models agree that it is impossible to understand state-socialism without reference to the crucial role played by the political bureaucracy. Unlike adherents of the earlier totalitarian model, however, they do not fix their analysis exclusively on the state's repressiveness and unrestrained coercion. Rather, they focus on its role in the society's productive relations, its sources of legitimation, and the "rules" which govern behavior within it. These theorists treat the state as the core element in a comprehensive form of social organization. Numerous attempts have been made to understand state-socialism in a manner consistent with this view (for example see Bahro 1978; Hirszowicz 1980; Horvat 1982; Rakovski 1978; Melotti 1980; Sik 1981). Similarly, for the purpose of this study the state is conceived of as the administrative complex through which political power is organized and social control is exercised. It will be assumed that the state, acting under the guidance of an executive authority, is capable of autonomous as opposed to class directed action (Skocpol 1979: 29).[4]

While the communist party bureaucracy may remain organizationally discrete, it is nonetheless an integral element of the state, as understood in this theoretical sense. The complex of hierarchical institutions organized around the communist party is at the center of the system of power in the political systems in question. The structural role of these institutions and the motivations of the political elite which guides their work must inform any useful analysis of state-socialism. Access to both political and economic power are monopolized by the party/state bureaucracy, and competition focuses not on profit as is the case in capitalism, but on avoiding risk and obtaining the "right" position within the administrative hierarchy. The state does not, however, act within a social vacuum. Interpretations of political events in contemporary state-socialist countries must therefore be sensitive not just to questions of institutional domination, but also to the role played by other less sharply defined social forces whose interests impinge upon those of the state.

If one accepts the idea that the actions of the communist party-states are increasingly constrained by other social forces, questions naturally arise concerning the nature of these forces, and how their influence is manifest. Several useful studies in this vein have appeared, employing group and elite theory to explore the state-socialist political system. Until recently less success has been seen in the direction of formulating a class analysis of state-socialism. In large part this lacuna is attributable to conceptual problems associated with the application of a class approach to social systems in which neither markets nor private property play a determinative role. Nonetheless, a substantial literature on the nature of class structure under socialism is beginning to emerge.

According to the official view of the CPSU and the other ruling communist parties, the revolution and dictatorship of the proletariat definitively eliminated the problem of class domination. The fundamental assumption of orthodox theorists is that under working class hegemony divergent social interests continue to cause social tension, but that antagonistic contradictions cease to divide those large social aggregates, class and nonclass, which persist under state-socialism. Differences remain between workers and peasants (on the basis of their divergent forms of property ownership), and the intelligentsia, which is categorized as a stratum of the working class (Ossowski 1963: 110-13), but these are "non-antagonistic" and amenable to mediation by the state (Wesolowski 1978: 47; Lane 1976: 25-28).

The growing complexity and differentiation occurring in all of the state-socialist societies in recent years have made the shortcomings of this characterization as anything more than an ideological smoke screen painfully obvious, even to its supporters. East European social scientists, faced with the everyday problems of describing and analyzing the structure of their societies, have increasingly turned to the concept of social stratification as a substitute for that of class structure (Szczepanski 1978; Yanowitch 1977: 3-22). This strategy allows them to proceed with the analysis of differences among groups of individuals at different locations within the system of production, while avoiding the forbidden questions of class formation and exploitation. The model of society based on this view resembles Western functionalists' treatment of the liberal political order (see for example Wesolowski 1979). Unfortunately the new stratification theory, like earlier official Marxism, avoids addressing the problematic issue of systemically generated antagonistic relations between strata and the nature of the relationship between various strata and the state (Szelenyi 1978).

Outside of the official Soviet view, contention over the class nature of socialist society is much greater.[5] One prominent group of theorists within the Marxist tradition (following Trotsky's lead) contends that those in control of the bureaucratic apparatus of the state constitute a new ruling class (Cliff 1964; Crompton and Gubbay 1977; Djilas 1966). Milovan Djilas, among the earliest and most prominent proponents of this view, argued that while party rule in the interest of the working class was real enough during the period of revolutionary upheaval, it was quickly replaced by the appearance of a new type of dominant class that rules through the party/state bureaucracy. Djilas contended that high level party functionaries collectively replaced the bourgeoisie with respect to control over property, and that they also assumed its repressive role with respect to the proletariat. Party leaders then began to form themselves into a class on the basis of their common interest in defending the institutions which allowed them to benefit. Thus: "The party makes the class, but the class grows as a result and uses the party as a basis. The class grows stronger, while the party grows weaker." (Djilas 1966: 39)

The nature and social basis of this hypothesized class is the subject of extended debate among those who develop their analysis along the general path outlined by Djilas. Within this general school Alec Nove is the strongest contemporary advocate of the view that a small and well defined group of bureaucrats at the peak of the institutional system constitutes a "ruling class." He concurs with Djilas that this class is rooted in the party/state administrative structure (Nove 1975, 1983). He goes on to argue, however, that the Soviet system represents a new and distinct mode of production, the evaluation of which demands a revision of the term class, based on a different criteria than simple ownership of property. Second, he contends that in an administered society the rulers are bound to be those who administer, and that the essential criteria of class must be tied to this function.[6]

Nove substitutes for the traditional Marxist concept an idea of class based on power, for example, the new rulers are "those who exercise control over resources and over people" (Nove 1983: 302). This methodological decision is defended on the grounds "that the term class in the conventional Marxist sense no longer applies under conditions of collectivization of productive property." Going beyond others who share this general perspective Nove attempts to identify the Soviet ruling class more concisely, relying on formal administrative limits as his guidelines. He points out that "the nomenclature of the central committee is the best available approximation to defining the 'class of rulers', the 'establishment'. . . where nearly everyone who is anyone holds official rank, membership in the nomenclatura of the central committee defines those whom the system itself recognizes as occupying posts of social, economic, or political significance" (Nove 1983: 298).

Thus the very limited stratum that dominates the central bureaucratic institutions is identified as the "ruling class" rather than the collectivity of administrative personnel. This type of analysis provides a valuable insight into state-socialist society and its workings. Employment of the nomenclatura criteria does, as Nove suggests, lead us to concentrate exactly on those individuals who the "establishment" itself considers to be of great importance, whether their particular institutional locations are in the sphere of economic production, culture, party organization, or elsewhere. The strength of his conception is its ability to draw the very relevant distinction between those who actually control the crucial administrative apparatus, and those who do not.

There is no doubt that members of the stratum identified by Nove as a ruling class play the role ascribed to them, and that they do share a common identity based on the positions they have secured at the summit of state-socialism's administrative hierarchy. Yet their power derives from their positions within particular institutions, and achievement of these positions is less a matter of ascription than of self selection into the world of the explicitly political. While heritability is by no means the crucial criteria of class formation, neither can it be entirely ignored. In the case of state-socialism, there is little evidence that the group in question is actually reproducing itself (Parkin 1971: 157).

Nove's approach and similar efforts arguably add to our understanding of the place of political leaders in the societies in question. But such analyses best reinterpret the status of top level figures who have been previously identified as the actual rulers of the communist party-state, without taking us any further along the road to comprehending the role of larger scale social aggregates and the constraints that these may place on the state and its masters. I would argue that it is analytically useful to distinguish between those who make the day-to-day decisions about the employment of political power, and social classes as more commonly understood. Hence the collectivity of these individuals who dominate the party/state bureaucracy can be more usefully conceived not as a class, but as a functionally based political elite. Following in the analytic framework suggested by C. W. Mills, such a "power" elite consists of those who "are in command of the major hierarchies and organizations of modern society" (Mills 1959).

If the class concept is to be gainfully applied to the study of state-socialism at all, it must refer to a social aggregate more broadly based than the narrow political group identified above. Richard Sklar (1979: 532; 1983: 190–91) uses the work of Polish sociologist Stanislaw Ossowski as the starting point for a power based concept of social class. This approach is particularly relevant to the question of class in socialist society (which was of course a primary motivation in Ossowski's original search for an alternative to Marx's focus on ownership of the means of production). Ossowski pointed out that not only in the case of socialism, but in modern industrial societies in general, "where changes of social structure are to a greater or lesser degree governed by the decision of the political authorities we are a long way from social classes . . . conceived of as being determined by their relations to the means of production or, as others would say, by their relations to the market." (Ossowski 1963: 184) He thus viewed changes in social organization resulting from industrialization as fundamental, and therefore argued that under the new conditions not just control over the means of production, but control over the means of consumption, and of compulsion, become the foundation of political power (Ossowski 1963: 185).

From Ossowski's comprehensive concept of political power there follows a notion of class that is not founded purely on common economic position, whether this is based on productive structure, or determined by the market. Rather, according to Sklar, if we are to build upon this perspective, class is better understood as an aggregation of individuals that forms (if at all) around a common position within the overall structure of domination within a particular society, including both its political and economic aspects (Sklar 1979: 533).[7] In state-socialist societies, just as elsewhere, class interests and opposition center on the appropriation and, very importantly in this case, the redistribution of surplus value. The fact that the state, a hierarchical and politically motivated formal institution, plays a determinative role in this process may shape and to a certain extent suppress the expression of class interests. It does not in any sense, as Feher, Heller, and Markus (1983: 106–33) suggest, negate the possibility of class formation.[8]

While the existence of a social division of labor and economic exploitation afford the possibility for class formation, classes only come into existence when individuals actually aggregate on the basis of their location within the extended authority structure and become differentiated from other members of the society. It is not necessary that such collectivities organize in an explicitly political manner, or that they develop explicit consciousness of their own class status. It is necessary that they share common values and common interests with respect to other actors in the society, and that they seek to promote these interests through various forms of social action (for a similar treatment see Becker 1983: 15). This conception of social class as an aggregation of individuals who are united by common interests that derive from their similar positions within the structures of domination and control within their society will be employed throughout this study.

State-socialist societies thus may be class societies, but they cannot be simply equated with Western industrial countries. As individual members of the population seek to maximize their personal well-being under the state-socialist regimes, new modes of aggregate political behavior consolidate around the opportunities and demands presented by postrevolutionary institutions (Jowitt 1983). Over time such "informal" behavior assumes a stable pattern and takes on an existence of its own. It becomes an integral part of the structure of society, which can be only effected marginally by central authorities without the risk of destabilizing the entire system of production. Once established such patterns of behavior are capable of reproducing themselves autonomously, without constant purposive state intervention. Thus, as in market societies, much of what actually occurs under contemporary state-socialism passes beyond normal administrative control.

But dynamics that emerge in political systems modeled on the Soviet Union differ in fundamental ways from those that govern the capitalist political economy. First, it is not the drive toward profit that motivates the economy, but the drive for accumulation (Bahro 1978; Sik 1981). More explicitly, economic decision makers at all levels seek to maximize the accumulation of resources under the control of the administrative apparatus (Feher, Heller, and Markus 1983; Kornai 1980: 189–215). This elemental fact defines much of state-socialist economic life. Economic competition becomes a struggle among sectors and particular enterprises to obtain resources from central planners, and among individuals for secure positions within the extended bureaucracy. As a consequence productivity is restrained, consumption is reduced, and the bureaucracy reproduces itself throughout the society.

While coercive power remains firmly in the hands of the political elite, which exercises control over the party/state apparatus, the broad stratum of skilled administrators, technicians, and the cultural intelligentsia (which will be referred to as a whole as the "extended intelligentsia"), also enjoys a special place in the post-Stalinist political economy (Konrad and Szelenyi 1979; Szelenyi 1978).

This group does not constitute propertied class as does the bourgeoisie under capitalism. Neither, obviously, is it a "ruling class".[9] I would argue, however, that as the normalization process proceeds it is in the process of forming itself into a "privileged class," whose members enjoy enhanced access to scarce resources as a result of their strategically important locations in the structure of material and social reproduction. Members of this class come into constant conflict with other social actors, most significantly the rulers of the socialist state and the direct producers, in a struggle to advance their collective interests.

A growing body of empirical research that is now becoming available in Eastern Europe is compatible with this view. Studies indicate the occurrence of increasing social differentiation within state-socialist societies and a decline in mobility between strata (Connor 1979; Cazacu 1974; Horvat 1982; Mathews 1972; Parkin 1971; Slomczynski and Krauze 1978; Yanowitch 1977). Most of these sources agree that state-socialist societies exhibit less differentiation between lower level white collar workers and blue collar workers than industrialized capitalist countries, but greater social distance between higher level white collar workers (managers), and both of the previous groups. The various authors of these studies are anything but unanimous in suggesting that these developments imply the occurrence of class formation. The data itself, however, indicate the consolidation of the professionals in the post-Stalinist era into a distinct and materially advantaged element within the society.

At the base of each of these social systems, deprived of the levels of consumption so obviously available in the West, and without recourse to autonomous bargaining units, are the workers and remnants of the peasantry. These direct producers, who are the presumptive heirs to the revolution, relate to their collective employers as an oppressive force (Haraszti 1978; Rakovski 1978). The political elite, and more recently, the privileged class of planners and managers who benefit from the existing state of affairs, are resented perhaps even more than under capitalism, since the link between the decision makers and the material results of their decisions is more directly visible, unmediated by market relations (Bahro 1978: 203-43; Bunce 1985; Pakulski 1986: 55-56).

CONSOLIDATION OF STATE-SOCIALISM IN EASTERN EUROPE

Prior to the Second World War socialist movements and parties failed to take firm root in the political and economic life of Eastern Europe, except, of course, for the deviant case of Czechoslovakia. Where tendencies in the direction of the left did exist, they did not survive the upheaval of the depression (Macartney and Palmer 1962; Janos 1970). Except for the case of Yugoslavia, where a powerful revolutionary movement was generated by domestic conditions, the new leaders who arrived back in their homelands with the Red army in 1945 thus took charge of government at the behest of their Soviet sponsors, not as the culmination of any internal dynamic (Brzezinski 1967). In the absence of any domestic base of support sufficient to explain their sudden rise to power, these postwar communist party elites can best be understood as the local agents of foreign power.[10] While the domestic response to the nascent regimes certainly varied, in no case during the early years did it constitute an integral element in a comprehensive ensemble of social structures, but was rather an expression of alien domination.

Between 1945 and 1956 Eastern Europe was subjected to a socioeconomic transition approximating the intensity of the Soviet experience of the 1930s. During this period of "socialist construction" extraordinary measures were taken to break down prewar institutions, where these posed a threat, and to eliminate active political opposition to communist party rule in Eastern Europe. Single party dictatorships undertook the first steps of state led industrialization and at the same time pursued social revolution organized and directed from above. The revolutionary states of the time have justifiably been characterized as dictatorial, and exclusionary; the sole embodiment of political power within their respective societies.

The ideological style, high levels of mobilization, and reliance on mass coercion characteristic of Stalinism were well suited to the immediate and very limited task of "breaking through" obstacles to development present in the prerevolutionary social structures (Jowitt 1971). Within five years after the end of the war private property in capital was virtually eliminated, and the replacement of capitalism as a mode of production was an accomplished fact.[11] Market relations were suppressed and replaced by centralized economic planning. The remnants of the bourgeoisie had either emigrated, been eliminated, or were absorbed into the new social structure. Bourgeois institutions were dissolved or remolded to serve the needs of the new regimes. Except for isolated cases, by the mid-1960s the peasantry was well on the way to extinction as well, at least as a landholding class, and its members were being transferred en masse into a mushrooming urban proletariat. Mass mobilization and state allocation of resources thus led the way through the first harsh stages of industrialization.

In a remarkably brief period the organizational infrastructure of communist party rule was constructed beneath the protective umbrella of Soviet support. Everywhere the new ruling parties' enrollment soared as individuals rushed to join, motivated either by conviction or by the possibility of quick advancement into positions vacated by the old ruling class. As administrative capacity increased, channels of control were extended into other institutional settings in a program of progressive bureaucratization (for an overview of this process in all of the countries in question see Brzezinski 1966; or Seton-Watson 1956). In essence, during this period of "anticapitalist transformation" the Soviet Union's political superstructure was reproduced throughout its new sphere of hegemonic influence and put at the service of the Soviet state (Abonyi 1978; Bahro 1978: 336–39; Bunce 1985). Accomplishment of this task was aided by the region's already existing tradition of bureaucratic rule, which was adapted to the exigencies of the new political reality (Mallet 1974; Janos 1970).

The harsh method of rule practiced in the postwar years did not, however, prove viable in the long term. By the mid-1950s Stalinism had shown itself ill suited not just to the needs of the general population in the subject countries, but also to the achievement of the more general interests of its originators. As Valerie Bunce suggests, "the combination of Stalinism at home and dependence on the Soviet Union abroad made Eastern European states highly vulnerable to public pressures" (Bunce 1985: 29). Stalinism thus failed to provide the Soviet Union with lasting stability in the territories it had taken upon itself to administer.[12] In addition to the inherent economic difficulties of overcentralization, which eventually led to reform in the Soviet Union, it became clear that in many cases industrialization itself created conditions more complex than could be accommodated by the Eastern European regimes (Korbonski 1972; Lane 1976; Johnson, 1970). The failure of the attempt to simply transfer Soviet practices to Eastern Europe was so great as to cause one recent commentator to dub the period one of "autocratic totalitarian inefficiency" (Sugar 1984).

In the years following Stalin's death the Soviet political elite was confronted both with questions of reform inside its own borders, and also with the problem of deteriorating economic conditions and increasing instability in Eastern Europe. In retrospect it appears clear that Soviet party chiefs arrived at a more or less explicit decision that rigid imposition of their own experience on dependent state-socialist countries was no longer a plausible course. Following the initial breakthrough in Poland in 1956 East European political leaders were provided with an expanded margin of freedom to develop political strategies more in keeping with their specific national conditions. In fact, under the guidance of the ascendant reformist Soviet leadership, fraternal communist parties were not just given the choice of seeking national solutions to their political difficulties, they were virtually compelled to do so. Thus in the decade of the 1960s experimentation with more flexible forms of rule became a predominant characteristic of East European politics.[13]

The shift in Soviet orientation compelled East European communist parties (some with more reluctance than others) to abandon their previous simple reliance on domestic coercion and external support (see, for example, H. Gordon Skilling's account of Czechoslovakia; Skilling 1976). No longer secure in the knowledge that Russian troops stood ready to defend them in the last resort, party leaders began seeking "political formulas" which were at least marginally compatible with their particular domestic situations (Gitelman 1970). In the short term this change in the political environment resulted in increased regime diversity (Skilling 1970: 233). In the longer term it produced a consistent pattern of "reform," that is, limited accommodation with domestic political forces (Abonyi 1979: 170; Rakovski 1978: 18). In general this has meant extending access to decision-making authority to a somewhat broader stratum of the population, increased levels of personal consumption, and decreased political intervention into normally nonpolitical aspects of social life (Bunce 1985; Bunce and

Hicks 1987; Feher, Heller, and Markus 1983). It has also meant searching out a new basis of legitimation for the state (while not violating the ideological limits imposed by the Soviet Union).[14]

The post-Stalinist transformation of Eastern Europe was thus comprised of a dual character. First, it marked the decline of direct Soviet political control over the political elites of dependent state-socialist countries, and a reduction in Moscow's commitment to specific representatives of those elites. If a particular set of party leaders failed to maintain domestic tranquility they could no longer be completely confident of Moscow's support in staving off challenges from intra-party rivals. Second, this change in the terms of Eastern Europe's relations with the regional hegemon combined with the reformist shift in Soviet domestic policy to necessitate adoption of a political strategy of limited state/society accommodation. Under the rubric of "developed socialism" the East European communist parties gave up mass mobilization for "social management" (Brus 1975: 134–48; Mlyner 1979: 116–43). The particular characteristics of the post-Stalinist regimes have varied widely from country to country, depending on both external factors and internal conditions; including level of development, the nature of the transition leadership, and the political legacy of the prerevolutionary period (see Gitelman 1970 for a more detailed exploration of this phenomenon).

While individual regimes met with varying degrees of success in their search for stable alternatives to Stalinism, the era of social upheaval and the purely exclusionary state passed almost everywhere in the Soviet sphere. The once omnipotent party apparat could not simply dictate; it became necessary to take into account the interests of competing forces that were beginning to coalesce in socialist society. The communist party-state may not have been limited by the rule of law but its actions were no longer entirely unconstrained. As Feher, Heller, and Markus (1983: 182–86) suggest, once the transition is made from "terroristic totalitarianism" to oligarchic rule party leaders must necessarily rely on nonpolitical elites to provide feedback from the society and to play a key role in the functioning of the system of production. The minimum level of support needed to gain their cooperation in carrying out these tasks has been secured through conciliation.

The growth of constraints on state action implicit in this process of accommodation has been widely commented upon. Stripped of the element of ideological evaluation, most accounts agree that the core of the process is to be found in the growing pluralization of the elite, a decline in the level of mass mobilization, and the appearance of "consumer communism." Variously termed post-Stalinist consolidation and postrevolutionary society, this complex of interrelated changes is inherent to the present phase of state-socialism in Eastern Europe, and represents a partial return to conditions of political "normalcy." While not entirely resolved, the societal discontinuities introduced as a consequence of the imposition of political regimes from outside the societies in question have been dramatically reduced.[15]

In Romania a significantly divergent pattern of interests and conflict has emerged. Bucharest's singular international behavior since the mid-1950s, interacting with domestic factors, set it off on a social trajectory very different from that seen in the rest of Eastern Europe. First, the RCP was able to secure the withdrawal of Soviet troops from Romanian territory, and to insulate itself from Moscow's interference in its internal affairs. Second, no reformist leadership in the Khrushchev mold came to power in Bucharest. Rather, the Romanians remained committed to rapid industrial transformation and tight political control. Although they were careful to avoid actions that might constitute a security threat to the Soviet Union, the added margin of autonomy that they enjoyed enabled Romania's leaders to pursue policies divergent from Moscow's to a far greater degree than was possible for the other East Europeans.

While other state-socialist regimes applied various methods of reform to their economies, moderated their goals, and increased consumption, Romania's development strategy remained hinged on tightly centralized planning and high rates of accumulation. Consequently the prerequisites necessary for elite co-optation (enhanced "privileged class" consumption and managerial autonomy) did not exist. No compromise was reached between the state and the extended intelligentsia, which was unable to consolidate itself as did analogous groups in the neighboring countries.

This divergent pattern of class/state relations fundamentally shaped Romanian political life. Having successfully excluded the managers from participation in political power and severely limited their economic privilege long after the conclusion of "industrial breakthrough," Romanian Party leaders were compelled to seek a political base different from those of other state-socialist regimes. The RCP took on an increasingly "populist" ideological tone, scapegoating intellectuals for abandoning revolutionary values and seeking to "remobilize" the masses within controlled channels. The Ceausescu regime based its legitimacy not on increased consumption, but on revolutionary populism and extreme nationalism. Finding themselves in worsening economic and political conditions, amd without a reliable source of external support, RCP leaders drew ever more heavily on the country's indigenous political traditions. The result has been Romania's transformation into an intensely authoritarian regime, strikingly similar to the "corporatist" state of the interwar years.

CONCLUSION

With the exception of historically brief periods of extraordinary revolutionary activism during which employment of extreme coercion becomes common (epitomized by the Stalinist experience), no large scale social organization, certainly not the entire activity of an industrial society, can be brought under the complete central control assumed by the totalitarian model and its theoretical cousins. When directed intervention by the state into the affairs of ordinary citizens recedes, individuals throughout the social system, even within the institutions of the ruling party itself, begin to respond less to ideological considerations (now bereft of compulsion), and more to the pragmatic conditions that confront them in their daily lives (Jowitt 1983). The "revolutionary break" thus leaves in its wake a new status quo in which mass behavior takes on an autonomous shape around the new institutions of state-socialism. Individual countries within this broad grouping make their inevitable national adjustments to the new reality, and must be interpreted as particular instances within a general mode of production, in the same sense that France and the United States represent variants of industrial capitalism.

With the advent of this increasing accommodation between state and civil society it becomes necessary to treat the East European countries as something more than "enslaved societies" if they are to be understood. They must be comprehended as unique social/political formations, as particular instances of the general phenomenon of state-socialism, each with its own limitations and potentials. Pursuit of an inquiry into the workings of these social systems requires a critical methodology, but one which is as free as possible from theoretical preconceptions. The remainder of this study shall employ the perspective of "political economy," following in general Karl Polanyi's interpretation of that concept (Polanyi 1957). Political economy explores "the way in which a surplus is extracted from the economy, how and by whom it is distributed, and for what purposes" (Chirot 1976: 2). Such an approach is useful in the study of state-socialism because it makes no presuppositions with regard to the class structure of the societies in question, or the social basis of power. It is in this regard identical to recent variants of the "critical" Marxist approach which have been fruitfully employed in the same task, and which also place the means of surplus extraction and redistribution at the center of analysis (see, for example, Feher, Heller, and Marcus 1983).[16] Like more traditional Marxist analysis, its utility consists of "combining analysis of structural divisions with *social dynamics*, so as to explore the conflicting interests of different groups and refer those interests to the economic and social mechanisms operating within the given type of society" (Hirszowicz 1976: 263; see also Hirszowicz 1986).

That the ubiquitous party/state bureaucracy occupies a fundamental location in state-socialist political systems is beyond dispute. Communist party leaders constitute a powerful functional elite, and exercise monopolistic control over the institutional mechanisms of domination. Yet the party-state's dominant role does not in itself represent a sufficient theoretical reason for excluding a priori the possibility of class formation within the state-socialist mode of production, along the lines suggested above. Members of the "extended intelligentsia" are the indispensable managers of socialist society. They are increasingly able to obtain stable access to sparse consumer goods, to successfully defend their interests, and to ensure that their children also will be admitted into the world of the privileged in their turn.

The political role played by the extended intelligentsia in contemporary state-socialist societies varies depending upon each country's prerevolutionary history, its experience during the revolutionary transformation, and the balance reached between it and other active social forces during the post-Stalinist transition. In particular, politics during the current phase is conditioned by the balance between the state (and the political elite that controls it), the workers and peasants, and the extended intelligentsia. In most of Eastern Europe the new status quo represents a compromise reached between the state and the latter group. While post-Stalinist reform varied according to national context, the general trend was toward limited decentralization of economic decision making to the level of upper and sometimes intermediate managers. "Liberalization," in the realm of ideology and culture policy, that is, the reduction of intellectual suppression, allowed the intelligentsia to indulge more freely in the cultural activities through which it seeks to express itself. Political power, however, remained the exclusive preserve of the party elite.[17]

The following chapters seek to show that Romania represents an extreme type within the general category of state-socialism. "Ceausescuism" is sometimes more than simply an extreme case of personal dictatorship. It is, rather, one expression of a complex of political, social, and economic policies which, taken together, comprise a coherent alternative to the development strategies pursued by the other state-socialist regimes in Eastern Europe. Exploration of the genesis of Romania's particular course, and its consequences, will add to our understanding of state-socialism as a whole.

2 *THE HISTORICAL SETTING*

INTRODUCTION

Like others who have won national autonomy late and under adverse conditions, the Romanian people attribute very great importance to the historic events and cultural traditions that set them apart from their neighbors. In the Romanians' case a national identity has been built around the mythos of Daco-Roman origins and the survival of their Latin traditions in a "sea of Slavs" (Kolarz 1946: 171-88). The territory of contemporary Romania was in fact occupied by Rome at the beginning of the second century A.D. and continued as a colony of the empire for approximately 170 years (Seton-Watson 1963: 1-16; Otetea 1970: 91-126). It was, however, the unenviable fate of the Romanians to occupy a geographical location spanning major invasion routes and separating peoples larger and more powerful than themselves. The desire to establish a barrier against barbarian invasion first led Rome to colonize the province, but, having concluded that the burden of defending it was too great, the Romans withdrew around the year 270. The Romanized agricultural population, left behind by this retreat and submerged by the successive waves of nomadic migration that repopulated Southern Europe, disappeared from the stage of history for nearly a millennium.[1]

Romanians first reappeared as political actors in the thirteenth century, under varying circumstances in the three regions that constitute the territory of the modern state: Walachia, Moldavia, and Transylvania. The last-named territory came under Magyar rule in the early eleventh century. Faced with constant pressure, first from steppe nomads following in the Magyars' own path, and later from the Ottoman Turks, the Hungarian monarchs populated this border province with Saxon, Szeklar, and Magyar military colonists, extending substantial privileges and grants of land to those willing to risk settling there. The ruling class of Transylvania was drawn from these three groups, while the Romanians (Vlachs) constituted a lower stratum of the population engaged in agricultural and pastoral pursuits.[2] The fortified towns founded by the German colonists, particularly Hermannstadt (Sibiu) and Kronstadt (Brasov), developed into centers of cottage industry and became the focus of trade between the Black Sea and Northern Europe.

Formation of political entities in Moldavia and Walachia proceeded on a different basis. Both areas avoided Hungarian domination as a result of the Mongol onslaught of the mid-thirteenth century, which checked the former power's southward expansion. In fact it was the increased stability and trade brought by the Mongols that initially encouraged state formation in the region. As the Mongols withdrew from southeastern Europe the commercial routes and customs system they had installed were taken over by the local leaders. Each of the new Romanian states was located astride a major trade route: Moldavia on the "Tartar" route to the Genoese trade centers on the Black Sea, and Moldavia on the path linking Northern Europe, by way of the German Transylvanian towns, to Constantinople (Chirot 1976: 28; Seton-Watson 1963: 25).

These early states derived income both from taxation of and participation in long range trade, and through the sale of local commodities to both the East and West.[3] While the princes and the upper nobility were active as merchants, the peasantry continued much as it always had, organized into free communities and only marginally implicated in the monetary economy that was becoming increasingly important at higher levels of the society. These nascent polities led an extraordinarily precarious existence on the frontier separating the political powers of Europe and the growing Ottoman Empire. To simplify a rather complex evolution of events, it appears that for as long as they held a key position on the trade routes from which to extract resources the Romanian Princes were able to hold their own against local contenders for power (see Chirot 1976 for a detailed account). At times they were forced to pay tribute to one or another powerful neighbor, but they always managed to free themselves, either through guile or force.

During the fourteenth and fifteenth centuries Ottoman power gradually advanced and disrupted the trade on which the Romanian Princes depended. By the beginning of the sixteenth century their resistance was clearly failing. This setback to their rulers was disastrous for the agricultural population of the principalities. The peasants suffered the effects of nearly continuous raiding and intermittent full-scale warfare as armies moved across their territory. In addition to external depredation, following the loss of trading income, their own states imposed continually increasing taxes on the local population. One highly visible effect of these conditions was a drastic demographic decline. According to Chirot (1976: 41), Walachia was inhabited by approximately 500,000 people at the beginning of the fifteenth century; by the end of the sixteenth century Turkish authorities estimated that this number had been reduced to between 150,000 and 180,000. The nobility's struggle to retain its position in this environment led to the imposition of serfdom, as it did under similar conditions of rural depopulation in Russia (Stahl 1980: 175).

From the sixteenth until the middle of the nineteenth century both Moldavia and Walachia were reduced to a state of semi-vassalage to the Ottoman Empire. Trade was resurrected, but now it consisted almost entirely of the export of domestic agricultural products moving in the direction of Constantinople. Control over commerce passed from the hands of the Romanian nobility to Greeks and Armenians who appeared in Romanian cities at the time, and who dominated trade through their connections with the Ottoman capital. By the 1700s it had become common practice for the right to occupy thrones of the Principalities to be purchased in Constantinople. Princes were generally no longer members of Romanian aristocracy but were selected from among the wealthiest (and presumably more loyal) Phanariot Greek trading families.

In contrast to Western feudalism, the landed Romanian nobles (*boieri*) were almost entirely dependent on the state. Not only were they at the mercy of the Ottoman military which the Phanariot Princes could summon if required (virtually no Romanian forces remained at the time) they were also heavily dependent on the central political administration for their material privileges. Even the right to claim membership in the upper aristocracy was not hereditary, but depended on obtaining office in the court of the Prince. The state's taxing authority provided a major source of nobles' income, and its agents were essential to maintenance of the rural order. During this "Phanariot period" tax collection took the form of tax farming with its associated evils. Rights of exploitation over particular villages were sold or leased to agents who managed the large estates as they saw fit. Ultimately it became necessary for the Turkish rulers to demand a reduction of the burden on the peasantry in order to avoid total depopulation of their Danube provinces. At their insistence serfdom was abolished in 1746, and freedom was guaranteed to any peasant who agreed to return to his village of origin. But the rural population remained bound to pay feudal dues in return for the right to use their land.

Transylvania experienced somewhat better progress (or rather suffered less decay) during these years. While Ottoman expansion lead to the near absorption of the two eastern principalities, it served the cause of releasing Transylvania from Hungarian rule. The semi-autonomous status of the third Romanian province dates from the battle of Mohacs in 1541, which transformed the Buda fortress from the symbol of Hungarian royal power into the site of an Ottoman Pashlik. After Mohacs, political authority in Transylvania was vested in a *Voivod*, elected by the three recognized estates: Magyar, Szeklar, and Saxon. While formal allegiance to the Hungarian crown was maintained, Transylvania became a protectorate of the Sultan. The *Voivod*, as representative of the noble order, was able to rule much as he desired with respect to domestic affairs, as long as required tribute was delivered to representatives of the Grand Porte.

During the course of the next century and a half Transylvanians enjoyed their only experience of self rule. This interregnum saw the consolidation of feudalism. The landed aristocracy continued to be largely Magyar, while the wealthiest German trading families constituted an analogous privileged stratum in the urban population. Despite peasant unrest associated with the consolidation of feudalism and occasional outbreaks of conflict between the ruling groups, relative tranquility prevailed domestically. During this period the established Romanian population was joined by an influx of their kinsmen from the adjoining areas under direct Ottoman rule. These newcomers were absorbed into the existing feudal structure as serfs, and continued to be excluded politically.

Like its two neighbors to the south, however, Transylvania was never really strong enough to stand alone when pressed by the competition of great powers. Even during its brief period of autonomy it was the site of recurrent conflict between Turks, Austrians, and Russians. When Ottoman forces were finally expelled after their final attempt to conquer Vienna in 1683, the province passed under Austrian rule (Pascu 1982: 96–130; Seton-Watson 1963: 120). Economically, Transylvania enjoyed substantial progress under the Hapsburgs. Large amounts of capital entered the province to develop its mineral potential. Manufacturing was encouraged, at least in sectors that produced materials needed by the Austrian economy. Agriculture expanded under the influence of the demand for its products provided by the Austrian administration. These economic trends set Transylvania off from the stagnation that settled over its eastern neighbors. Politically, the long term effect of Hapsburg rule was to undermine the local aristocracy in favor of centralized royal power (Pascu 1982: 130–49). The institutions of feudalism were eroded, and authority came increasingly to be vested in the state administration. Like their counterparts in the Principalities, members of the Transylvanian nobility came to rely on public office, to which their status entitled them, as a source of income (Vedery 1983: 158). Following a serious peasant uprising in 1784 serfdom was abolished by the Emperor. Little else, however, was done to improve the lot of the peasantry.

Thus by the beginning of the nineteenth century all of the territory occupied by contemporary Romania was under foreign domination. The two southernmost principalities were subjugated by the resurgent Ottoman Empire, while Transylvania fell under the control of the Hapsburgs. As a whole the region was plagued by continued military conflict, which retarded development. In all three territories the majority of the population was composed of peasants of Romanian ethnicity who were tied to the land as serfs. In the Turkish areas, increasingly cut off from the events of Western Europe, an oppressive officialdom extracted taxes which slowly drained the country; political and economic corruption became an established way of life. Under Hapsburg rule, Transylvania experienced limited progress, but the status of the Romanians continued to be that of politically excluded subordinates, socially deprived, and tolerated only in so far as they fulfilled the economic needs of the dominant nationality groups.

LINKS WITH THE WEST AND
THE EMERGENCE OF NATIONALISM

The course of the nineteenth century saw a dramatic shift in the direction of events; the birth of a movement to gain national independence, and the integration of the Principalities' domestic economies into the European-dominated world trading system. These phenomena were not unassociated. Emergence of the national movement can only be understood in relation to the ongoing struggle of major powers to dominate the region. As long as the international correlation of forces allowed the declining Ottoman Empire to employ military force to control its Balkan dependencies, the Romanians, who began to exhibit national aspirations at around the turn of the century, had no real chance of achieving their goals. Only after the Turks themselves met defeat at the hands of rapidly industrializing Western powers could national sovereignty be realized in the Balkans. The same dynamic growth that allowed Western Europe to supplant the Turks, however, rapidly transformed Romania into an economic colony.

The Romanian nationalists' failure to prevail on their own against foreign overlords is epitomized by the Tudor Vladimirescu revolt of 1821. In the expectation of at least passive Russian support, Vladimirescu raised a peasant army of 65,000 and in loose association with the Greek liberation (Etiaria) movement occupied Walachia (Otetea 1945; 1964: 894-99). His intent was apparently not to break completely the association with the Grand Porte, but rather to overthrow the Phanariot regime and replace it with one more amenable to Romanian (and peasant) interests (Djordjevic 1981; Fischer-Galati 1981: 81). Vladimirescu's forces were easily able to gain control of the nearly undefended country, but the Russian support that he expected would check Ottoman intervention failed to materialize. After a month of indecision the Tzar's government denounced the entire affair, the revolt collapsed, and the Ottoman military occupied both Principalities. But the tide of international politics in the Balkans had clearly turned, and the reoccupation proved little more than a postscript to Turkish rule. In the Grand Porte's declining years Russian expansionism emerged as a new threat. For over a century the Tzars had struggled to establish control of the Dardanelles and the mouth of the Danube, a goal requiring that Turkish influence be supplanted in the Moldavia and Walachia. This latter aim was finally accomplished in 1829 by the Treaty of Adrianople, which, while it left the official situation unchanged, gave Moscow de facto control over the internal affairs of the Romanian Principalities.

Russian influence was imposed on Romania during a period of military occupation lasting from November 1829 to April 1834. General Kiselev, acting as the Tzar's representative, reorganized the Principalities and introduced modern administrative practices to Romania.[4] Kiselev's political reforms, codified in a document known as the Organic Regulations (*Reglement Organique*), played a crucial role in the country's political development. While establishing the concept of constitutional rule for the first time, the *Reglement* had less laudable effects as well. Most importantly, it strengthened the position of the *boieri* as a landed class. Confronted with the problem of rationalizing Romania's particularly murky system of property rights, the Russian administration resolved the issue firmly in the favor of the aristocracy. Peasants' rights to use previously common land were restricted, the nobility's obligation to allow their tenants to raise livestock (traditionally the mainstay of their income) was reduced, and one-third of all property was reserved for the nobles' exclusive use. Corvée labor (*clacasi*) was set at 12 days per year, but "days" were translated into work norms that could typically be accomplished only in two or three temporal days (Otetea 1970: 332).

Recognizing that it would be unable to continue to control the Moldavia and Walachia directly, the Russian Empire established an indigenous administration designed to serve its purposes indirectly. Political power was placed in the hands of the high aristocracy, whose members were as a result tied to the Russian cause.[5] This upper stratum of the *boieri*, ranking as "full" nobles, amounted to only approximately 400 families in both principalities. Their status was not hereditary, but depended on securing high office in the state administration. This traditional practice encouraged constant competition for position within the elite. Just as under Ottoman administration, it also resulted in widespread political corruption at the highest levels of the society. It also strengthened the hand of the reigning prince, who controlled access to appointments (Chirot 1976: 105). At the opposite end of the scale large numbers of petty nobles were only slightly better off than the peasantry, despite the fact that they were exempt from taxation. Resentful of their poverty and exclusion from political power, this group became susceptible to counter systemic ideas and provided a fertile recruiting ground for the liberal cause in the mid-nineteenth century.

That the Principalities were not entirely absorbed into the Russian Empire was largely due to the countervailing interests of the other European powers. While the Hapsburg Monarchy was still very much concerned with limiting Russia's advance, this traditional rivalry was overshadowed in the middle of the century by the growing importance of the "Eastern Question," which led Great Britain into the fray. London's chief goal in the region was to retard any Russian expansion that might threaten its interests in the Middle East. In particular, this meant shoring up the faltering edifice of Ottoman rule. In addition to Great Britain's strategic concerns, West European states were also developing a growing commercial interest in the Balkans. The Treaty of Adrianopole broke the Turkish cereals monopoly in the Principalities and cleared the way for development of a thriving grain trade directed toward the West. Before the removal of Ottoman political constraints on trade such commerce scarcely existed, but by 1847 there were already 1,383 ships calling at the port of Braila, of which 418 were British.[6]

Improved administration and rationalized taxation coupled with this increased demand led to dramatic increases in grain production. The area under cultivation in wheat, for example, rose from only 249,102 hectares in 1837 to 1,509,683 hectares in 1890 (Stahl 1980: 97). Given the consolidation of aristocratic political power under the Reglement, it was virtually inevitable that this improvement in the market environment should redound to the disadvantage of the peasantry. Landlords clearly saw profits to be made in cereal production, and acted forcefully to consolidate their control over it. Rather than extending their own acreage, the general pattern up to the end of the century was for the *boieri* to induce peasants under their influence to give up other pursuits and turn exclusively to grain growing, both on their own plots and on demesne lands. Surplus was then extracted through taxation and through the nobility's control over trade in grain (Stahl 1980: 97; Chirot 1976: 98–104).

Increased economic activity transformed urban life as well. This was most visible in Hapsburg-ruled Transylvania. Disadvantaged with respect to the more developed Austrian provinces, Transylvanian manufacturers turned to the Romanian principalities as a source of raw materials and as a market for their products.[7] Industry in Moldavia and Walachia, other than food processing, developed less rapidly. The growth of international commerce, however, did transform the cities. Between 1831 and 1860 the population of Bucharest approximately doubled, and expansion of the Black Sea trading ports was even greater. Since relocation of the peasantry into cities was severely limited by feudal regulations, and educational institutions were virtually nonexistent even for the petty nobility until the middle of the century, much of the new commercial middle class was made up of foreigners. In the south the newcomers tended to represent a variety of nationalities including numbers of Greeks, Germans, French, and Jews. In the northern province Galatian Jews predominated, making up over half of the population of the capital, Iasi, by 1850.

The combination of changes in the international market and the political reorganization of the Organic Regulation thus dramatically reshaped conditions in the Romanian Principalities. As Daniel Chirot (1976: 89) suggests, it constituted a transition to "true" colonialism during which Romania became part of the periphery of West European capitalism. While both economic and political structures were modernized, power remained in the hands of the small landed aristocracy, and the gulf dividing the peasant majority and the dominant class actually grew larger. One striking element of continuity with the past was the degree to which the state played a fundamental role in underpinning aristocratic rule. While the Organic Regulations codified feudal land privileges and thereby laid the foundation for the latter transformation to capitalist private property, the upper nobility still controlled the countryside primarily through the agency of the state, and extracted much of its income indirectly through the state's taxing power. The stage was thus set for the degeneration of rural conditions that plagued the country from that time until the outbreak of the First World War.

1848 IN ROMANIA: ABORTIVE LIBERALISM

Romania's second attempt to establish a national state, in 1848, was a decidedly more serious affair than the 1821 Vladimirescu uprising. The social basis and intensity of the 1848 revolution differed widely from province to province. In Moldavia and Walachia it was led by, and to a large extent limited to, members of the *boieri* class. Beginning in the 1820s the sons of noble houses (especially those becoming economically marginal) began traveling to the West in substantial numbers to obtain their educations. Many congregated in Paris, where they became infected with the liberal revolutionary consciousness of the time (Janos 1978: 80). Seeing opportunity in the outbreak of liberal revolts in the West, they acted to realize their own demands. These were largely nationalist in nature, focusing on calls for the unification of the two provinces and an end to the Russian protectorate which underpinned the political monopoly of the upper aristocracy.

The liberal rebellion was weakest in Moldavia where, after a single demonstration in the capital, leaders were arrested and the movement was squelched practically overnight (Otetea 1970: 350). In Walachia the insurgents fared better. On receiving news of the Paris revolt, they formed themselves into a revolutionary committee and were able to seize power virtually without the use of force. In June they formed a new government and sought diplomatic support from France and Great Britain. This, however, failed to materialize. Autocratic Russia strongly opposed the spread of liberalism so close to its borders and encouraged Ottoman intervention. In late September Turkish and Russian armies jointly occupied the province. Lacking either a military force or widespread popular support for what was in essence a *boieri* affair, the revolutionary regime collapsed and its leaders went into exile.

The social base of the Transylvanian revolution of 1848 was fundamentally different from that in the Principalities; it was anything but a revolt of the nobility. Rather it constituted the combination of a Romanian national movement and a broadly-based peasant insurrection. The expression of Romanian nationalism came in response to the Hungarian revolution against the Hapsburgs. The Hungarian population, led by its nobility, fought for independence from Vienna and for incorporation of Transylvania into Hungary; the Romanian peasantry entered the conflict as a third force seeking to free itself from the Hungarian nobility and to secure national recognition (Vedery 1983: 184). When the military forces of the Hungarian rebels under Polish general Joseph Bem entered Transylvania in December, the Romanians, who were already engaged in warfare against the indigenous Hungarian population, retreated into the Western mountains. While negotiations designed to unite all Transylvanians against the Austrian forces dragged on indecisively, any chance of success was lost. In June 1849 Tzar Nicholas I, having reached agreement with the Hapsburgs for joint action against the revolution, dispatched a Russian army to Transylvania and suppressed all resistance.

Thus for a second time since the turn of the century foreign intervention acted to restrain Romanian national aspirations and at the same time retarded progress in the realm of social relations. Nevertheless, irreversible changes had occurred since 1800. In all three provinces national sentiment was growing, and in the wake of Ottoman decline the effect of economic progress was beginning to make itself felt as well. Links were slowly forming between the Principalities and the European world. Despite differences in Ottoman and Hapsburg administrations, in all three provinces commercialization of agriculture benefited the landed aristocracy, which retained its grasp on political power, while the majority of the peasants slipped further into poverty.

FORMATION OF THE ROMANIAN
NATIONAL STATE: 1850-1920

The international environment that had been so influential in retarding Balkan nationalism before 1850 proved more benevolent in the second half of the century. In particular, the Crimean War was pivotal in altering the balance of forces in the region; this time in a direction favorable to formation of an independent Romanian state. Russia's defeat was followed by peace talks in which Romanian representatives, many of them exiles from the 1848 revolution, argued strongly for unification and independence. The most steadfast opponents of this plan were Austria, which feared creation of a Romanian state that might act as a magnet to the ethnic Romanians living in its territory, and Great Britain, which was trying to create conditions in the Balkans conducive to a regeneration of Turkish power.[8]

The 1856 Treaty of Paris attempted to settle the Romanian question in a compromise. Russian occupation was terminated, but rather than being liberated, the Principalities were placed under the joint protection of the European Great Powers, including Turkey, which retained formal sovereignty. But no generally acceptable formula for political organization could be arrived at. Finally it was agreed that the Principalities should retain separate Princes and civil administrations, but share a high court and a "Central Commission" which would resolve questions of common concern.

Nationalist sentiment in both Principalities had reached such a pitch, however, that the plans of the guaranteeing powers were successfully circumvented. In the elections of 1859, orchestrated by "Unionists," the Moldavian and Walachian assemblies chose a single Prince, Ion Cuza. Cuza, a relative unknown whose family was of minor nobility, represented a compromise acceptable both to the liberals and to conservatives who justifiably feared that loss of their privileges would follow independence. The new ruler acted resolutely to achieve administrative unification over the objections of the Guaranteeing Powers, and gained international recognition of this accomplishment in December 1861.

The country's leaders then consistently (and for the most part successfully) pursued a policy designed to establish their homeland's full international status.

During the late 1860s "Romania" was recognized as the official name of the united Principalities, and its right to conclude treaties independent of the Ottoman Empire was established. The Romanian army was provided with an opportunity to show its abilities in 1877 fighting alongside the Tzarist forces in the Russo-Turkish War. Settlement of the conflict at the Congress of Berlin, however, proved disappointing. On the one hand, full national independence was finally and fully recognized; on the other hand, and in the opinion of Bucharest far outweighing any other gains, the entire province of Bessarabia was detached from Moldavia and turned over to the Tzar. The Berlin agreement both heightened traditional hostility to Russian interference and increased the Romanians' resentment at being made the pawn of great power politics.

Meanwhile, the conservative aristocrats' hope that Prince Cuza shared their views on domestic matters had proved overly optimistic. After his election Cuza's reformism, mild as it may seem by contemporary standards, brought him increasingly into conflict with the *boieri* who dominated the National Assembly.[9] He broke the political impasse that ensued by overturning the original constitution. In May 1864 a Royal proclamation was issued calling for a national plebiscite to broaden the franchise and increase his own power. In a pattern which later became standard for ruling political parties, he employed the resources of the state to mobilize popular support for his cause, and won the election by an overwhelming margin.

Having momentarily consolidated his position, Cuza pushed ahead with agrarian reform. Under the provisions of his reform act of 1864 peasants were given title to the land they cultivated, and remaining feudal obligations were abolished (Otetea 1970: 388). Landlords, for their part, were given outright title to forests, and to the demesne land that they had retained under the Organic Regulation. They were compensated by the state for the loss of labor services and the acreage turned over to the peasants. The cost incurred by the government was to be repaid over 15 years by the peasants (Seton-Watson 1963: 310). The impact of this reform was disastrous. In all, the state and the landlords retained fully two-thirds of all agricultural land (Otetea 1970: 389). Even the wealthiest category of serfs was to receive only 5.5 hectares of farmland per family. The less affluent were alloted progressively less, down to the lowest category, which obtained only their houses, along with 2.5 hectares. Under existing conditions of production, on an average a minimum of 5 hectares was required to support a peasant family. Based on this requirement it has been estimated that between 60 and 80 percent of households living on the plains and 40 percent of those in the more hilly regions received less than adequate holdings (Chirot 1976: 129-30). Hence the reform actually increased the dependency of the peasantry of landed proprietors.

However, before the dominant position of landlords could be completely reconsolidated under conditions of capitalist production it was necessary that their control over the state be reasserted. On the local level this had never really been seriously challenged. The overthrow of Prince Cuza in 1866 returned the central administration to their hands as well. Even many of Cuza's original supporters had considered the 1864 reform as dangerously radical from the outset. When peasant production of grain dropped by more than half in the year following its introduction (seriously affecting exports) liberals joined the conservatives in opposition to the Prince (Chirot 1976: 131). Left without any base of support (except possibly the peasantry which he never considered mobilizing), Cuza was forced from power in 1866. Unable to agree on a new prince chosen from among themselves, the representatives of the Liberal and Conservative factions jointly recruited the scion of a foreign royal family, Charles Hohenzollern, to rule the country.

Prince Charles (later King Carol I) and the leaders who brought him into the country set into place the regime that remained the foundation of Romanian politics up to the mid-1930s. The new momarch vastly improved the country's communications and civil administration, and reorganized its military on the Prussian model. The new government consisted of a parliamentary system in which elected upper and lower houses were to share power with the monarch. In theory the electoral system and a variety of civil liberties that were guaranteed under the new constitution insured that politics in Romania would be pursued on a democratic basis. In fact a limited franchise and complex system of four electoral colleges weighted in favor of the propertied classes insured that the parliament and cabinet remained the preserve of *boieri* and wealthy urban famil- ies (Seton-Watson 1963: 321). While control of the government traded periodi- cally between Conservative and Liberal politicians neither of the dominant parties established ties with the lower classes. The monarch played an important, and conservative, role in the post-1866 political system. The chief political asset of the ruler was control over the state administration and the patronage that this provided (Janos 1978: 88). The king was also empowered to veto legislation, and to call on the politician of his choice to form a government. Since the newly in- stituted government could then use the state apparatus to engineer elections, the monarch's support played a vital role in the alternation in power between the Liberals and Conservatives.

With the *boieri* once again at the political helm after 1866, domestic social conditions understandably came to reflect their interests. Rising grain prices on the international market substantially added to the demand for Romanian agri- cultural exports. In order to take advantage of this improved market following the division of their estates, the *boieri* began to conclude "labor contracts" with peasant communities that were little more than the resurrection of feudal rela- tions. Fulfillment of the peasants' contractual obligations was guaranteed by pas- sage of the 1866 Law of Agricultural Contracts, which gave landlords the right to use armed force (the national police were made available) to ensure compliance (Stahl 1980: 89). The state also imposed mandatory work loads on peasants to insure repayment of their land debts (Mitrany 1930: 63-92). The rapidity of rural deterioration under these conditions was striking.[10] In addition to the im- pact of much higher direct rents, peasants were burdened with a large increase in taxation, which doubled between 1885 and 1913 as the size and cost of state administration mushroomed (Weber 1965: 508). The plight of the peasantry was eloquently expressed by the fact that parliament felt itself obliged to pass a law in 1882 that guaranteed the peasants the right to work on their own plots for at least two days per week (Chirot 1976: 133).

Thus during the transition to capitalist agriculture the upper nobility retained its hold on the agricultural economy, and, in general, its traditional way of life.[11] By 1900 the proportion of agricultural land owned by large proprietors (more than 100 hectares) had risen to 51 percent from 33 percent at the time of the reform. Ninty-seven percent of peasant property owners with farms of less than ten hectares accounted for around 42 percent of all arable land (Chirot 1976: 147). Increasingly large landowners became absentees, living either abroad or in Bucharest (Roberts 69: 14). Their affairs were overseen by *arendasi*, who, as the tax farmers of old, leased the right to collect rents and oversee peasants on a given property.

Similar to the rural elite of many other societies drawn into the world market in the role of neocolonies, most members of the Romanian landholding class made only limited efforts to engage in commerce. A limited shift of capital from agriculture to manufacturing did begin to occur as a result of the drop in world wheat prices in the late 1870s. Landlords who responded to the international economic crisis in this manner focused their efforts on industries based on processing primary agricultural materials (Zane 1970: 168). But the general level of economic development remained quite low, offering few employment opportunities to those seeking escape from the countryside. Consequently, despite the formal abolition of serfdom, most peasants found it impractical to leave their villages.[12]

The few large-scale enterprises (for the most part in textiles and petroleum) established in Romania before the turn of the century were almost entirely controlled by foreign capital (Zane 1970: 169). In 1899 approximately two-thirds of all capital invested in industry is estimated to have been of external origin (Chirot 1976: 146). The population's consciousness of subjugation to outside forces was heightened by the fact that many of those active in commercial occupations continued to be non-Romanian. Increased commercial activity associated with the rise of international trade continued to attract large numbers of foreigners to the country's cities, where they filled jobs left vacant by the Romanian population, and came to constitute a major component of the minuscule Romanian "middle class."[13]

Meanwhile the Romanian petty nobility turned increasingly to the state administration as an alternative source of employment. Their attraction to officialdom can be at least partially explained by aristocratic attitudes according to which most commercial occupations were unsuitable to noble status. More pragmatically, their general lack of training put members of the lesser nobility at a substantial disadvantage in seeking commercial employment. Their widespread recourse to state service as a career alternative was amply demonstrated by the fact that, as Janos (1978: 92) points out, in 1885 Romania with a population of approximately 5 million boasted a larger number of officials than either France or Prussia. Financing a bureaucracy of this magnitude inevitably had serious consequences. In 1890, for example, government revenue amounted to $53.6 million, while government expenditures were more than three times that figure (Janos 1978: 93). Even this outlay, which contributed greatly to the perennial Romanian fiscal crises, did not provide a subsistence wage for the thousands of functionaries requiring support. In order to supplement their incomes low level officials turned to behavior typical of the country's Ottoman administration; resorting to the practice of "baksheesh," or informally accepted corruption.

The upper nobility similarly transformed their political status into a financial asset through the mediation of the state, though at an altogether more impressive level, which was also entirely in keeping with tradition. Manipulation of the national bank and the acceptance of personal recompense for awarding governmental contracts were notorious (Janos 1978: 92; Otetea 1970: 420). Beginning in the 1880s the utilization of tariffs to protect domestic entrepreneurs from foreign competition (an important new source of elite income enhancement) became a central concern of the Liberal Party, under whose influence the first of a series of protectionist measures was implemented (Spulber 1966: 21; Jelavich 1983, 2: 25).

The pattern of economic development that followed liberation from Turkish rule in the second half of the nineteenth century thus appears to conform with the neocolonialism experienced in other regions. The international market thoroughly penetrated and transformed the Romanian agricultural economy by 1900. Abolition of serfdom changed the form but not the essence of peasant oppression. Landlords did not make the transition to entrepreneurship, and foreign capital dominated the limited indigenous industry. The rough outline of the crisis that was soon to overtake Romania was thus already drawn, and was similar to that of its contemporaries on the margin of European development. The specific form of the crisis was further defined by two additional factors: the focal political role assumed by a massive bureaucratic state; and the increasingly vitriolic nationalism engendered by Romania's long and difficult experience with nation building, its growing subordination to foreign capital, and the movement of large numbers of non-Romanians into the commercial class.

BREAKDOWN OF THE LIBERAL POLITICAL ORDER

Despite its semblance of political stability, Romania's situation entering the twentieth century was becoming critical. One must look outside agriculture to the general economic orientation of the state and progress in the industrial sector to understand the causes of the rural crisis that overtook the country. As it grew older the Liberal Party shifted considerably away from its roots as the representative of *boieri* interests, and began to act in the interests of the small but influential bourgeoisie; an urban elite that relied on control of the bureaucracy and the financial institutions created by the state for its status. Peasants, not surprisingly, continued to suffer. Industrial growth could not be self financing in a country as impoverished as Romania at the beginning of the century. The Liberals attempted (unsuccessfully) to industrialize "on the backs of the peasants" through a system of increasingly protective tariffs and taxation that extracted four times more from the peasantry than from landlords (Mitrany 1930: 84).

Deterioration in rural conditions was brought into sharp relief by the peasant revolt of 1907 (Deac 1967; Eidelberg 1974). The uprising began as an anti-Semitic outbreak in Moldavia. Within days, however, it took on a more generalized antilandlord character and spread to other areas of the country, becoming more radical and violent as it gained mass support: land was seized, estates burned, and landlords assassinated. Soon the entire countryside was in rebellion. The insurrection was put down only with difficulty through a military campaign in which approximately 11,000 peasants, or 2 out of every 1,000 members of the rural population, were killed (Roberts 1969: 3).

Measures taken in the wake of 1907 ameliorated but by no means resolved the conditions that caused the revolt. Lease and rental agreements were regularized, a land office was established to buy estate property and transfer it to the peasantry, and rental cooperatives were established (Roberts 1969: 21). Any positive effect that might have been expected of these efforts was undermined, however, by the fact that their implementation remained in the hands of the *boieri*. Thus the 1907 revolt, while drawing worldwide attention to the plight of Romania's peasants, left them at least as badly off as before; their resistance broken, and at the mercy of the local gentry and officials.

Revolution in neighboring Russia and the government's dependence on an army of peasant draftees during the First World War made more fundamental change inevitable. In June 1917 King Ferdinand I announced that when the war ended estates would be limited to 500 hectares, and that the holdings of the monarchy and foreign and absentee landlords would be expropriated and subdivided among the peasantry (Seton-Watson 1963: 420). This expedient succeeded in its immediate political purpose of avoiding the spread of the Bolshevik revolution in Moldavia and keeping the peasant army in the field, but it ultimately did little to resolve the problems of rural poverty and economic stagnation.

The reform that followed the war could not be faulted on its breadth; it was the most extensive redistribution of land to take place in Europe outside the Soviet Union. A total of 14.8 million acres were expropriated, of which 9.6 million were distributed to 1.4 million peasants (Jelavich 1983, 2: 162). Redistribution was most extreme in Bessarabia, where land was seized by direct action of the peasants during the period from July 1917 to April 1918 (Roberts 1969: 34). Representatives of Bessarabia voted for union with Romania only on agreement that the Romanian state would uphold the expropriation. In Transylvania, where little progress had been made in rural social relations since the abolition of serfdom by the Hapsburgs, redistribution was complicated by the nationality issue. Conservative estimates suggest that 87 percent of properties over 127 acres were owned by Magyars. Thus in Transylvania expropriation of large estates and land owned by foreigners affected the Magyar population almost exclusively, and was enforced much more severely by the new Romanian rulers than in the "Old Kingdom" (Roberts 1969: 38; Vedery 1983: 287).

Redistribution, even on this scale, could not in itself ensure development of a prosperous peasant agriculture. Provisions were not made to provide agricultural credit, and little effort was expended to introduce modern production techniques. Consequently, in the years following the land reform agricultural productivity suffered serious decline. Between 1928 and 1932 Romania's wheat yield was lower than that of any other Balkan state except Greece (Roberts 1969: 57). Neither did redistribution encourage the peasantry to move off the land. The effect of administrative land division was compounded by continued fragmentation of peasant farms through inheritance. Ultimately 75 percent of all holdings were reduced to less than five hectares in size (Volgyes 1980: 102). If, as some suggest, the actual aim of the state was to allow market conditions to eliminate small holders to the advantage of rich peasants, it clearly failed.

On resuming power after the war Liberal Party leaders committed themselves wholeheartedly, as other East European rulers had done, to a strategy of industrial development intended to end Romania's backwardness and economic dependence (Janos 1970: 209-11). The methods that they employed to achieve this goal, however, ultimately proved self-destructive. In the prewar environment it might have been possible to milk the earnings of agriculture to feed industrialization; after the war and land reform this was no longer feasible. While yields declined domestic consumption had risen, reducing the surplus available for sale on the international market. The already substantial effect of depressed international grain prices was intensified by heavy duties imposed on grain exports that were intended to keep domestic food prices low. Wheat exports plummeted from 13,314,000 quintals between 1909 and 1913, to only 502,000 quintals in the 1921-1925 period, with the consequence that Romania dropped from fifth to tenth in rank as world exporter of cereals (Mitrany 1930: 343).

Other measures equally detrimental to the interests of the peasantry were promulgated as well. Peasants who had received land as part of the agrarian reform were pressed to repay their redemptions to the state ahead of schedule, and high import duties were imposed on agricultural implementes and textiles (Roberts 1969: 124). The combination of these measures drained away what little capital existed in the agricultural sector. Consequently, rural consumption of products from the urban economy was dramatically reduced, with much of the peasantry returning to subsistence farming.

Conditions in industry present a very different picture. Before 1916 manufacturing in Romania was led by food processing, followed by petroleum (exploitation of which had begun before the turn of the century), and lumber (Roucek 1932: 279). The First World War caused tremendous economic losses. Industrial production in 1921 was only 47 percent of the 1913 level, and it did not surpass that of the latter year until 1926 (Roberts 1969: 68). Conclusion of the war, however, laid the basis for the beginning of a new phase of development through the addition of the natural resources and more advanced industries found in Transylvania and the Banat to those already available to Moldavia and Walachia. Hence while food processing and petroleum continued to dominate industrial activity, by the late 1920s metallurgy, textiles, and chemicals were also beginning to play a growing role (Humphreys 1928: 23; Roucek 1932: 283).

Industry's relative success was in part attributable to the fact that domestic entrepreneurs, unlike members of the peasantry, enjoyed the full support of the state. Under Liberal legislation natural resources were nationalized to protect them from foreign exploitation, foreign capital was prohibited from exceeding more than 40 percent in any enterprise, and three-fourths of company director-ships were reserved for Romanians (Jelavich 1983, 2: 163). New tariff barriers were added to those already protecting domestic industry, and state subsidies were provided to enterprises employing more than ten workers (Otetea 1970: 500). Thus favored, Romanian industry began to advance.

The Liberal Party strategy, however, did nothing to alleviate the poverty of the vast majority of the population. Most of Romania's advanced enterprises were linked not to the domestic economy but to the world market. Protective tariff barriers merely induced foreign capitalists to increase direct investment in the Romanian economy; an effect that domestic ownership restrictions (as a consequence of widespread corruption) did little to reduce. As late as 1930 Romania's petroleum industry, which is of particular interest because of its importance in foreign trade, was overwhelmingly dominated by American, French, and Belgian interests (Roucek 1932: 264–71). One clear sign of the lack of integration among Romanian economic sectors was the fact that while industry experienced respectable rates of growth, the rest of the economy continued to flounder. While manufacturing employment grew at a rate of approximately 10,000 per year, the annual increase of excess agricultural workers has been estimated at between 100,000 and 200,000 (Roberts 1969: 70). Furthermore, the state's policy did nothing to reverse the decline in the standard of living, which for workers fell 53 percent below the prewar level and had dropped even lower among government employees (Mitrany 1930: 464–65). In addition to absorbing a preponderant share of national capital, industry, as it was organized, failed to provide an outlet for the growing rural labor surplus.

The pattern of Romania's economy in the first part of the interwar period thus appears familiar. Its depressed rural consumption, economic marginalization of much of the population, and extractive industry linked not to the domestic economy but to industrial consumers in more advanced nations, are also common to contemporary underdeveloped countries. Attempts to industrialize utilizing a protectionist trade regime failed, aside from enriching the commercial elite. The social/political correlates of this economic pattern, social polarization, and growing unrest ultimately created pressures beyond the capacity of the country's fragile new institutional structure to bear.

More immediate regional problems were at work as well. In removing Russia from the camp of the victors, the Bolshevik revolution had placed Romania in the enviable position of being able to claim territorial compensation from both winners and losers in the First World War. The Greater Romania that emerged from the Versailles settlement comprised the two prewar Principalities, with the addition of Bessarabia, Bukovina, the Banat, Dobruja, and most importantly both from a national and economic standpoint, Transylvania. The population of the new Romania was doubled, making it the second largest country in Eastern Europe. Expansion, however, brought with it the seeds of domestic political unrest. Despite the important social role played by minorities, the Old Kingdom's pre-1916 population was overwhelmingly Romanian. The largest minority was the Jewish community of around a quarter million, which constituted something less than 5 percent of the total population (Jelavich 1983, 2: 26). After the peace settlement the minority population grew to 28 percent, led by Transylvania's 1.7 million Magyars, followed by Germans, Jews, and Ukrainians.[14] Minority populations were concentrated in Transylvania and Bessarabia, each of which presented special problems of governance.

During this early phase of development education levels rose rapidly, which, ironically, caused considerable new difficulties.[15] The number of students enrolled in higher education more than quadrupled between 1915 and 1934, as the country's youth sought to use it as a channel of upward mobility (Janos 1970: 211). Even more striking, the proportion of law students ranged around 40 percent of total university enrollment, with the result that Bucharest boasted more lawyers than Paris (Rothschild 1974: 320). The attraction of the legal profession among students of the time was a clear indication of the continued appeal of careers in the state bureaucracy for those seeking to escape rural life.

For a brief but euphoric period the opportunity to advance through state service was quite real. Having decided on a centralized administration from Bucharest after the war, it was necessary for the political elite of the Old Kingdom to establish administrative control over its new provinces. As a rule, in the newly acquired territories the central government "simply evicted the members of the minorities from their positions and put their own men in their places" (Macartney and Palmer 1962: 217). In Transylvania this task was eased by the emigration of approximately 20 percent of the Magyar population. This exodus decimated the administrative structure of the province, which had been the almost exclusive preserve of the Magyar minority (Vedery 1983: 287). In Bessarabia and Bukovina establishing central authority was less complicated by minority issues, but was nonetheless formidable. In both areas large numbers of new Romanian officials were accommodated, but the new incumbents were deeply resented by the local populations, and in turn reacted with defensive hostility toward the minorities.

Within only a matter of years the state's ability to absorb excess talent reached its limit. Romania's domestic tax base proved unequal to meet the demands placed on it by the mushrooming bureaucracy, with the result that in the first postwar decade alone its international debt doubled (Weber 1965: 513). Despite the fact that the bureaucracy absorbed 56 percent of the governmental budget by 1934, 76 percent of those employed by the state earned less than $30 per month (Janos 1978: 108). Consequently an underemployment of crisis proportions struck the new thousands of graduates, who had sought an education because they were no longer satisfied to remain among the peasantry, but who were unable to achieve their aspirations for a more "modern" way of life. The increasing numbers of this marginal intelligentsia added greatly to the instability of the time. As economic conditions worsened its members became available for recruitment by the opposition parties, which offered patronage employment should they meet with electoral success, and later by radical movements of both the right and the left (Janos 1978: 109).

Under these conditions Romania's politically dominant urban financial elite faced ever greater difficulties in retaining control over the country, and responded by elevating the practice of election rigging to an art form.[16] Confronted with the possibility of a united opposition, in the mid-1920s Liberal politicians tightened their stranglehold on the electoral process by altering the constitution. Successive attempts by democratic opponents to supplant the regime were frustrated. On those two brief occasions when the opposition parties managed to achieve parliamentary power they proved impotent against the combined resistance of the monarchy, bureaucracy, and large financial institutions. In ever growing numbers Romanians lost faith in the constitutional system and turned to radical, or at least authoritarian, alternatives.

After decades of Liberal Party domination Romania experienced two disheartening years of governance by the opposition National Peasant Party before beginning its final slide into authoritarianism. This last effort exemplified the insurmountable difficulties confronting even those politicians committed to democratic norms. The National Peasants' most decisive action was taken in the realm of international trade. Having concluded that the domestic economy could not independently generate development, the Peasantists tried an approach that reversed their predecessors's policy of economic nationalism. In a move intended to reduce the financial burden on the peasants, foreign loans of over $1 million were solicited, and a major effort was expended to attract foreign capital (Roberts 1969: 131). The level of protection enjoyed by industry was reduced, and tariffs on consumer goods were for the most part eliminated (for a detailed account of the National Peasant Party's program see Madgearu 1930). Except for stipulations concerning employment of Romanians, restrictions on the participation of foreign capital in domestic industry were dropped.

Domestically the new administration's initiatives were more limited and less successful. Its leader, Iuliu Maniu, came to power committed to ruling strictly on the basis of law. Despite his best efforts this attempt failed. Members of Maniu's own party proved less incorruptible than the Prime Minister himself, and soon Bucharest was awash with its usual financial scandals. Nor was it possible for the Party's leaders to restrain the excesses of the military and police in their ongoing campaign to suppress subversive elements. Perhaps even more damaging in the long run, the National Peasant Party had, by 1928, lost much of its early political conviction. Its leaders settled on an agrarian program that compromised with the interests of urban elements that had been incorporated into the party, and offered little more to the rural population than had been provided by the Liberal regime.

The National Peasant government consequently found itself without widespread support when it was confronted with the crises of the 1930s. The onset of the depression, just as the government was proclaiming an open international stance to be the solution to the country's long-standing economic problems, was inopportune at best. Romania's balance of trade was not as badly hit as other East European countries by the international economic crisis because of its oil exports, which were increased despite the decline in world prices. Thus 1,953 thousand metric tons were exported in 1927 for earnings of 7,517 million lei, while nearly three times that amount, 5,885 thousand metric tons, were exported in 1933 for 7,838 million lei (Humphreys 1933: 37). According to Roberts (1969: 75), revenue from the oil industry provided the Romanian state with nearly one-third of its income during these years. Romania's undoubtedly welcome mineral wealth did little, however, to shield the rest of the economy from the effects of the depression. For the peasantry these were devastating. Grain exports, which were valued at 19,016 million lei in 1929, fell to 3,262 million lei by 1932 (Humphreys 1933: 27). Domestic grain prices dropped to 44 percent of their 1929 level, per-capita income was nearly halved, and even by 1937 had not yet regained its 1927 level (Roberts 1969: 81, 176). Such rapid decline fed the growing upheaval in Romanian society. Strikes and rioting broke out across the country, and apocalyptic rumors gained currency among the population.

THE RISE OF ROMANIAN FASCISM

Romania's "democratic" political system and the liberal philosophy upon which it was based were, by the 1930s, largely discredited. Even before the period of wholesale coercion and election rigging the Bucharest-based elite's ability to control events to their own advantage had been obvious. Except for a brief period of postwar recovery the living conditions of the peasant majority, never easy, continually deteriorated. The privileged minority, however, made substantial gains in the twenties and was largely untouched by the depression. This economic gulf dividing rulers and ruled was widened further by cultural factors. While the peasant majority remained close to its cultural traditions, among the upper classes conspicuous consumption and West European culture had become signs of distinction.[17]

Conditions specific to Romania's historical experience determined that its response to the trauma of the interwar period would take the form of radicalism of the right rather than that of the left. Among the most fundamental factors favoring emergence of right-wing extremism was the intense nationalism that had become a prominent trait among the majority of Romanians by the beginning of the twentieth century, and which culminated in an outburst of xenophobia in the 1930s. The roots of this tendency have been outlined above. Recent attempts by powerful neighboring states to "denationalize" the Romanians during their efforts at annexation, and the proximity of the struggle to establish an independent national identity were crucial (see the account of Turczynski 1971). The depression, continued international economic dependence, and the highly visible role played by members of non-Romanian ethnic groups in the domestic economy all served to intensify Romania's nationalist response.

Antipathy toward foreigners was manifest in the national culture long before the advent of an explicitly fascist movement. Many among Romania's most renowned literary figures were prominent in expressing it.[18] But as the twentieth century progressed, xenophobia became more widespread and more virulent. Its conservative strain was epitomized by the acclaimed historian, Nicolea Iorga, and the political economist A. C. Cuza. In addition to lending their intellectual abilities to the struggle against foreigners, these Iasi university professors joined together to form the Nationalist-Democratic Party. Through it they acted as the political mentors of a younger generation that was to lead the fascist organizations of the 1930s (Weber 1965: 510).

Resistance to the growth of fascism was weakened by the absence of any robust left-wing alternative among the Romanians. No politically decisive working class movement emerged in response to the depression. Nor could one have been expected, since the country's industrial base was still so weak. In 1930, approximately 80 percent of the population was rural. The large majority of urban workers were newly recruited from the peasantry, and retained a rural outlook on their social conditions. A nascent Social Democratic movement was in evidence, but it had only a limited following within the proletariat, and its strength was greatest among the German and Hungarian workers of Transylvania. Its attraction to educated Romanians (who were strongly represented within the right-wing parties) was quite weak. Because of their ideological and cultural predispositions, socialist organizations made little attempt to establish contact with the Romanian peasant majority, and remained cut off from events in the countryside. Hence, almost by default, the left drew its greatest support from among minority intellectuals who were excluded from participation on the political right because of the right-wing parties' attachment to the philosophy of ethnic nationalism (Janos 1978: 109).

The limited possibilities that did exist for socialism to gain popular support were undermined by the Bolshevik revolution. Following the formation of the Soviet Union, Romanian socialists came under increasing pressure from their own state because of the confrontation between it and the Soviet revolutionary regime. Attempts at reconciliation between the two countries were obstructed by the Kremlin's refusal to recognize Romania's postwar annexation of Bessarabia. In the following years the province was the scene of Bolshevik inspired subversion, and suppression by the Romanian state. Perhaps even worse, the Romanian Communist Party, subordinated to the dictates of the Third International, was compelled to adopt a policy of national self-determination that would have resulted in the breakup of the country. In light of the nationalistic climate of the time espousal of such a view was, at least in the popular perception, tantamount to treason.

With the left-wing thus constrained the field of political extremism became a virtual monopoly of rightist groups, which gradually gained coherence, forming two broad and mutually antagonistic movements. The first of these tendencies, radical fascism, took on a unique coloration of its own in Romania. Populistic, mystical, and rooted in the peasantry's Orthodox Christianity, radical fascism found its foremost expression in the Legion of the Archangel Michael, or the Iron Guard as it was otherwise known. Many within the conservative community were deeply attracted to fascism as well, but not to this radical version. They turned instead to Royal Absolutism (or so-called middle-class fascism), as an alternative to failing liberal political institutions. Although united in their opposition to democracy and their common anti-Semitism, the two wings of the rightist movement took shape partially in opposition to each other as well, and are best understood in this light.

In June 1930 Carol Hohenzollern, son of Ferdinand I, returned to the chaotic Romanian political scene from a period of exile imposed on him in the early 1920s as a result of his unsavory personal life. With his assumption of the throne (through the connivance of the National Peasant Party) the remnants of the political center began to erode, leaving in its place an increasingly violent conflict between polarized groups. Within weeks a confrontation developed between the King and the politicians who had engineered his return. Iuliu Maniu resigned his position as Prime Minister in a protest against Carol's arbitrary behavior. His action failed, however, to elicit any strong show of popular support, making the weakness of the democratic system manifest to all concerned. Carol not only remained in place, but established a degree of personal sway over the political processes that paved the path toward dictatorship (Fischer-Galati 1971: 113). In April 1931 the conservative nationalist, Nicolae Iorga, was called upon to form the first of a series of unstable right-wing cabinets that became the basis of government until 1938.

The coalition of forces that united around the monarchy in the 1930s was in many ways similar to that which had supported the Liberal Party governments of the 1920s. But by now both the international economic environment and domestic political conditions had greatly changed, and the policies of the regime shifted in response. Large-scale industrialists and financiers as well as high level administrators supported strong direction from a centralized state as the solution of the problems of economic underdevelopment. Under their influence protective tariffs were reintroduced, beginning in the depression years, 1930 to 1933, and the state intervened into the economy on an ad hoc basis in order to stave off total collapse. What began as a series of defensive measures, however, evolved in the second half of the decade in an explicit policy of economic nationalism.

The political philosophy that legitimated this strategy was formulated in the work of Mihai Manoilescu; father of the concept of corporatism and Carol II's first Minister of Finance. Manoilescu rejected outright the concept of comparative advantage and the idea that the exchange of raw materials for industrial commodities could lead to development. The failures of the late 1920s, coupled with the depression, convinced him and others that state-supported heavy industrialization was the only open route toward development. (See Chirot 1978 for a discussion of the neoliberal theorists of the time, especially Stefan Zeletin; and Nagy-Talavera 1970: 286.) The political implications of applying this strategy in the Romanian context are succinctly summarized by Henry Roberts:

The policy of extending protection exclusively to industry and not to agriculture—whatever its intrinsic benefits for the national economy—would mean increased costs for the agricultural sector, uncertain markets, and, at best, a forced transfer of personnel from agriculture into industry. Furthermore, if over three-fourths of the electorate belongs to the peasantry, it is difficult to see how such a process could be achieved within the framework of a representative government. (Roberts 1969: 197)

Manoilescu's preferred solution to this dilemma was abandonment of parliamentarianism in favor of *organized* society (Schmitter 1978: 125-31). He was supported by the King, who himself favored a form of royal absolutism. Consequently power passed ever more openly out of the electoral system, and into the hands of those who controlled the bureaucratic state. These included the select few financiers and administrators that made up successive "camarillas" centered on King Carol and his mistress, Madame Lupescu. Large new enterprises were founded almost exclusively by a small number of private industrialists (the King, Nicolae Malaxa, and Max Ausnit being the most notable), and private capital was displaced by the National Bank (under the direction of Manoilescu) and the state. Cartelization was encouraged, and monopolies and subsidies provided to favored concerns (Nagy-Talavera 1970: 286; Roberts 1969: 200).

The economic impact of this policy was considerable. Production of capital goods increased by 57 percent between 1927 and 1937; steel output more than doubled between 1933 and 1938 (Roberts 1969: 198). Much of this new production, however, relied on government contracts (particularly armaments contracts). In the case of the metallurgic industry, for example, 70 percent of output in 1938 was consumed by the state (Roberts 1969: 69). The program's effect on the peasant majority was much as might be expected. Romania was the slowest of the East European states to recover from the material declines of the depression. As late as 1940 the standard of living was estimated to be between 33 and 64 percent lower than in 1916. While the elite flourished as never before even in notoriously corrupt Romania, the peasantry and urban poor struggled merely to survive (for a firsthand account of conditions at the time, see, Barth 1979).

Even as the economic program of the Romanian national bourgeoisie progressed, plans for a change of a very different sort were taking shape among less exalted members of the population, where the old-fashioned nationalism of Iorga and his associates was no longer considered relevant to the country's problems. Here conservatism was supplanted by a radical Romanian variant of the fascism seen throughout Eastern Europe in the interwar period. From the beginning it was associated with Corneliu Zelea Codreanu, who became the movement's undisputed leader, and then its martyr.

Codreanu was born in 1899, the son of a vehement Romanian nationalist.[19] After an early education in military schools he entered the University of Iasi in 1919. His early political activities developed in the turmoil of the immediate postwar years. He organized nationalist workers' groups to counter strikes organized by the communist trade unions in Moldavia (Weber 1965: 518), and in 1921 formed a nationalist student movement that demanded limitation of Jewish enrollment in higher education. After expulsion from the university and a brief sojourn abroad, Codreanu returned to Romania in the winter of 1922 to participate in protests against stipulations of the new constitution which guaranteed Jewish civil rights, and to help Professor Cuza with the organization of the League of Christian National Defense (L.A.N.C.).

Codreanu's energies could not be contained within what was essentially a traditionally conservative organization. Disagreement with the older leaders of L.A.N.C. over the need for organizational discipline and violence led Codreanu to split off from Cuza in June 1927 and establish the Legion of the Archangel Michael as an independent group. Unlike its predecessor, the new organization, which viewed itself as "a militant religious order," was to be tightly disciplined and elitist. Its Orthodox Christian orientation clearly differentated it from other fascist movements, and gave it a base of support among the deeply religious peasant population.[20] Its ethos was obsessively focused on the need for self-sacrifice. Death in the service of the cause became a member's highest goal, and those who achieved it became objects of cult worship. For the rest, Codreanu rejected detailed policy in favor of maintaining a heroic ideal. As he himself stated his position, "[Romania] goes to pieces not because of the lack of programs but because of the lack of men. In our opinion the task is not to formulate programs, but to create men, a new kind of man." (quoted in Nagy-Talavera 1970: 267)

During its first years the Legion had to struggle merely to survive. Its appeal was strongest among the young, and in the provinces of Bessarabia, Bukovina, and Moldavia, where the Romanian Jewish population was largest.[21] Members were sent on training marches, and dispatched to the villages to aid the peasants in harvesting their crops and organizing public service projects. But with the onset of the depression the Legion experienced a sharp increase in popularity. Appealing for support in regions of the country where anti-Semitism was not an issue, Codreanu adopted Manoilescu's corporatist doctrine. In 1930 a recruiting drive in Bessarabia met with massive support and began the period of the Legion's expansion. In the same year Codreanu formed the Iron Guard, which was intended to serve as an activist vanguard within the Legion. Despite the fact that both organizations were disbanded by the Iorga Cabinet, Codreanu and his representatives were able to win over 73,000 votes and 5 seats in parliament in 1932 (Weber 1965: 545). Once in the national legislature Codreanu increased his notoriety by attacking prominent members of the elite, publicizing massive loans they had received from the country's major banks, and calling for the death sentence in cases of abuse of government funds (Nagy-Talavera 1970: 283).

The intense economic distress of the mid-1930s combined with dramatic changes in the international environment (the growing strength of Nazi Germany in particular) to create conditions in which extremist groups began to thrive. Professor Cuza, among others, formed a new and violently anti-Semitic fascist organization in association with the ultranationalist poet Octavian Goga. This National Christian Party, as they called it, attracted support from the urban middle class which felt itself threatened by Codreanu's radicalism. Its militant arm, the *Lancieri* (Lance Bearers), became equally active in anti-Semitic violence and street battles against the Iron Guardists.

By the early 1930s the strength of the radical right was such that it could no longer be ignored by leaders of the more conservative political establishment. The two forces were locked into a conflict that drove the latter to increasingly oppressive measures, and the former to intensified violence. Before the elections of 1933, I. G. Duca, chosen by the King to form a new Liberal Party government, ordered Codreanu's organizations dissolved. In the confrontation that followed, 18,000 Legionaries were arrested and many were killed (Nagy-Talavera 1970: 285). The Cuzists, far more acceptable to the King and the financial elite, were supported by the state and allowed to organize freely in the hope that they would effectively counterbalance the Iron Guard. In 1933 they won 18 seats in parliament, and were immediately invited to participate in government. The Liberals successfully dominated the elections in this manner, but only at the cost of dramatically escalating the level of domestic conflict.

The regime's tactics in fact did little to reduce support for Codreanu. The Legion continued to operate underground while the All for the Fatherland front (*Totul Pentru Tara*, TPT) was formed as a legal vehicle through which to contest elections. By 1937 there were still over 34,000 Legionary organizations active in Romania and over a dozen newspapers and periodicals (Nagy-Talavera 1970: 293). In the cities Legionary Workers Corps and cooperative enterprises were formed. Codreanu's open hostility to the country's financial capitalists and the weakness of alternatives on the left combined to create conditions in which the new urban groups flourished. In the elections of 1937 the TPT gained 16 percent of the total vote, making it the third largest party in the country.[22] At the same time the Legion's striking power was reinforced by the formation of suicide squads committed to silencing their leader's enemies. Their effectiveness was driven home when Codreanu's followers assassinated Minister Duca in retaliation for his role in the state's program of political suppression.

Unable to rely any longer upon the discredited Liberals, and unwilling to come to terms with either the National Peasants or Codreanu, the King turned to the substantially weaker National Christian Party to form a new government in December 1937. In addition to the national peasants the new government included three split offs from the National Peasants, and General Ion Antonescu, whose esteem within the army and reputation for political honesty added significantly to its strength. This so-called Goga cabinet was able to retain power for only three months. It was most notable for its unrestrained anti-Semitism, which both provoked a strong international response and created economic chaos in Romania (Polonsky 1975: 89). New elections were called, but as preparations were made to contest it, a virtual civil war broke out between the Iron Guard and the *Lancieri*. With the radical right clearly gaining strength the King was unwilling to risk a test of popular feelings. In early 1938 Goga was dismissed and a Royal dictatorship was proclaimed.

Carol's open assumption of dictatorial power resolved once and for all the tension between Manoilescu's authoritarian corporatist ideals and the democratic political structures inherited from Romania's nineteenth century liberals. Political parties were dissolved. Giving up the idea of forming links with the middle class extremists through intermediaries such as Cuza, the Monarch formed his own fascist organization, the Front of National Rebirth, complete with paramilitary formations and insignia. The heterogeneous Goga government was replaced by a National Unity cabinet responsible only to the ruler. This new government included the Orthodox Patriarch, Iorga, Armand Calinescu (who directed political suppression), and several other of the most influential old-guard conservative politicians in the country. General Antonescu was intially included as well, but was forced to resign his position as Minister of War in March 1938 as a consequence of his repeated clashes with the King over matters ranging from the former's relations with the Iron Guard to the latter's continued political interference in the running of the army.

The year 1938 saw the final polarization of rightist forces. Codreanu's radical populists, equally hostile toward the corrupt political system and toward capitalists who benefited from it, were entirely excluded from political participation. The middle class extremists, on the other hand, had become firmly attached to the industrializing elite organized around Carol's authoritarian regime. Convinced that German political ascendancy in East-Central Europe would ensure his ultimate victory, Codreanu was willing to accept the new state of affairs as a set back and wait for better times. The TPT disbanded and the Legionaries were ordered to withdraw from political activity. The King, however, now felt secure in his control of the army and police forces and decided to eliminate his competitors on the right, not least of all because they presented Hitler with a possible alternative to his rule. Codreanu was arrested and on November 29 he and 13 other Legionary leaders were murdered by their military guards (Weber 1965: 556). The directionless rank and file membership responded with a campaign of terrorism and assassination against both the Jewish population and the government.[23]

While monarcho-fascism continued its precarious existence for another two years by progressively giving in to German demands and continuing its bloody vendetta against the underground radical organizations, it could not survive the August 1939 Ribentrop-Molotov Pact. Codreanu's murder had enraged Hitler and, like Carol's continued flirtation with the Western powers, convinced the Nazis that his government could not be relied on to maintain stability in what was to them an increasingly important strategic location (Nagy-Talavera 1970: 301–2). It thus became expendable; more useful as a bargaining chip than as an ally. On June 25, 1940, the Soviet Union delivered an ultimatum demanding that Bessarabia and northern Bukovina be turned over to it within three days. Unable to resist such an adversary alone, Bucharest was forced to concede. Hungary also had old scores to settle, and was encouraged by the Soviets to join them in demanding retribution. Budapest's claims resulted in a much more serious blow, the loss of most of Transylvania through the Second Vienna Award.

The surrender of more than one-third of Romania's territory by a government predicated on nationalism was more than the population would bear. Acting in concert with leading politicians General Antonescu, who had been living under house arrest, demanded the King's abdication in favor of his son Michael on September 4, forcing Carol to flee the country shortly afterward. For a chaotic period of four months following this event the radical fascists realized their vision of themselves as heirs to the corrupt monarchy. A National Legionary State was formed with Horia Sima as Deputy Prime Minister, and the conservative Antonescu as Prime Minister. But by this time the Legion had been reduced to little more than a loose grouping of terrorists augmented by thousands of opportunists recruited after its success, and had virtually no positive program to implement. Once in power its negative and destructive impulses were given free reign. Legionnaires organized pogroms, looted, tortured, and murdered their political opponents.[24]

Unrestrained violence, however, conflicted with General Antonescu's desire to reestablish political stability, and also interfered with the interests of the Germans, who were far more concerned with uninterrupted oil production than the promotion of Romanian fascism. By the beginning of 1941 the impossibility of continued cooperation between the increasingly extravagant Legionaries and Antonescu's military was becoming obvious to both parties. The final chapter in the drama of Romanian fascism came when, seeing the writing on the wall, the Legion's leaders ordered a coup d'état on January 20. For three days the Iron Guardists occupied most of Bucharest except for military headquarters. While they rioted, Antonescu waited for an unambiguous signal of support from Germany. After receiving a direct request from Hitler that he restore order, the army entered the city, and the rebellion was put down within hours (Nagy-Talavera 1970: 326). With the final strength of the fascist movement thus extinguished, state power passed to Antonescu's military dictatorship, where it remained until the end of the Second World War.

CONCLUSION

Even in a world where harsh circumstances are the rule rather than the exception, Romania's experience with political and economic development before 1945 appears to have been unusually difficult. Constantly under pressure from neighboring great powers competing for control of the Balkans, the Romanian people spent most of their history under the direct or indirect domination of others. While more tranquil areas of Europe experienced significant progress, Romanian social and economic life stagnated. Romanian national identity was kept alive in the popular culture rather than through political institutions, which for the most part served the interests of foreign rulers.

Not until after the middle of the last century did Romania consolidate the majority of its population into an independent national state. By that time the region had been transformed by the spread of capitalism and was well on the way to becoming an economic semicolony of Western Europe. Commercialized agriculture turned almost exclusively to cereal production for export, and the peasantry was reduced to abject poverty. The nobility became increasingly a "rentier" class, more attuned to Western European than to Romanian society. Commercial and industrial activities, which enjoyed only moderate growth, came to be dominated by foreign capital and the ethnic minorities which constituted a disproportionately large segment of the country's middle class.

The combination of these circumstances proved decisive in shaping the reaction against national dependence that emerged before the turn of the twentieth century. Thousands of nationalistic (and under qualified) Romanians eschewed participation in the economy as a parasitic activity of aliens in favor of service with the state. Romanian officialdom soon grew out of any reasonable proportion to the country's real needs and did little to uplift the society other than providing a marginal living for its thousands of dependents. As social conditions deteriorated the state bureaucracy increasingly became a repressive force turned against the rural population.

As Romania progressed economically, the small nationalist bourgeoisie which emerged in the late 1800s became the driving force behind the dominant Liberal Party. Its members attempted to use the state simultaneously to promote Romania's national development, and to secure a better economic location for themselves at the expense of both foreign competition and the ethnic minorities. Their economic strategy, which placed a heavy material burden on the peasant population, was legitimated as a national imperative if Romania were to survive in a competitive international environment. This early Liberal theme was taken up by middle-class fascists during the 1930s. Confronted with economic collapse and growing social unrest the urban financial elite attempted to realize Manoilescu's vision of autarkic development by abandoning pluralistic institutions in favor of a corporatist state. In constructing the authoritarian regime they, like the earlier conservatives, cultivated the population's growing xenophobia in an attempt to establish solidarity within the population and to direct mass hostility elsewhere.

Given the presence of large numbers of unassimilated Jews in Romania and the country's history of difficult relations with Russia the growth of anti-Semitism and anticommunism is hardly surprising under these circumstances. Even more virulent than their middle-class counterparts, the radical fascists that joined in forming the Legion and Iron Guard made tremendous strides in gaining popular support during the mid-1930s. In an environment where no significant left-wing opposition existed, Codreanu and his movement became the central focus of populist opposition to oppression by the bureaucratic state and the urban elite that controlled it. The Guard established an increasingly strong presence among the peasantry (particularly after the decline of the National Peasant Party) and its appeal among urban workers was also significant.

But both the international and internal balance of forces worked against successful resolution of Romania's considerable developmental problems during the interwar period. While Manoilescu's formula produced significant industriali-zation it did not fundamentally alter Romania's position in the world economy; in fact dependence on Western Europe, and Germany in particular, substantially increased during the period of the country's greatest growth, while the condition of the population improved not at all. As for the right-wing radicals, their move-ment was abortive as well. Despite years of debilitating internecine civil violence and appeals to racial solidarity, they finally gained control of the state only to lose it again within months, having achieved nothing. These contradictions in Romanian historical evolution, which came so clearly to the fore in the turmoil of the interwar period, were to reemerge once again within decades, under the aegis of its postwar communist party-state.

3 *SOCIALIST CONSTRUCTION*

INTRODUCTION

The preceding chapter summarized the historical roots of Romania's twentieth-century social crisis, and the failed attempts to deal with it in the context of the prerevolutionary political order. Discussion now turns to the origins of the Romanian Communist Party and its early efforts to reshape society under Soviet tutelage. The major events of Romanian history occurring from the country's initial occupation by the Soviet Union until the beginning of Nicolae Ceausescu's tenure as General Secretary of the Romanian Communist Party (approximately 1945 to 1965) are well documented and require little additional discussion here.[1] My intent is thus not to provide an additional detailed account of the imposition of communist rule, but rather to explore those aspects of the period relevant to understanding the evolution of Romania's contemporary political economy.

Confronted with the German army's collapse on the Eastern Front in the spring of 1944 the traditional political elite in Bucharest began making plans to salvage what they could from the ruin of war. Their representatives entered the Allies into negotiations through the Romanian embassy in Cairo, seeking a formula for withdrawal from the conflict. On August 23, Marshal Antonescu was arrested and removed by King Michael. A provisional government representing the four prewar nonfascist parties was formed under General Sanatescu, leader of those military officers loyal to the King. The same day saw the beginning of the Romanian communists' experience with governance. Inclusion of RCP Central Committee member Lucretiu Patrascanu in the anti-German coalition as Minister of Justice represented a concession to developing political realities in the region (amply demonstrated by the rapidly advancing Red Army). After three years of intensive domestic and international political maneuvering this initial breakthrough was culminated in the RCP's consolidation of power and proclamation of the Democratic Republic of Romania in December 1947.

The brief span of two decades following inception of RCP rule saw Romania transformed from a poverty stricken nation of marginal peasant smallholders and ostentatiously wealthy financial magnates into a rapidly industrializing country. The following analysis focuses on two centers of intense activity during these years: state building and economic development. The former task presented nearly overwhelming obstacles, including the disrepute of the country's new leaders among the large majority of the population, the underdeveloped state of their party, and the low level of national administrative resources in general. In the economic sphere progress was retarded not only by wartime devastation, but by the depredations of early postwar Soviet economic policy and the switch from a market system to national planning under quite unfavorable circumstances.

Just as important, during the same two decades Romanian Communist Party chiefs, who were initially little more than the local pawns of Soviet rulers, were able to free themselves in large measure from Moscow's control. They managed to construct a cohesive leadership group and a local power base of their own. Taking advantage of the turmoil within the CPSU that followed Stalin's death and divisions within the international communist community that increased their bargaining power, the RCP leaders then maneuvered to increase their country's foreign policy autonomy. While cautiously avoiding actions that might constitute a security threat to the Soviet Union, the early Romanian leaders succeeded in establishing themselves as the most independent member of the Warsaw Pact. The margin of independence that they achieved was crucial in enabling their successors to diverge even further from standard bloc behavior.

THE PREREVOLUTIONARY ROMANIAN COMMUNIST PARTY

The RCP was at best badly prepared for the tasks facing it at the conclusion of the Second World War. Its prerevolutionary history promised anything but an easy transition to power. Following a stormy and generally unsuccessful existence within the Romanian Social Democratic Party, left-wing leaders (with Comintern advice) split off and officially formed a communist party in 1921. Indicative of the failure of Marxism to attract popular support in the Romanian social environment, the new party's membership never grew to more than 1,000 individuals at best in a population of over 20 million (G. Ionescu 1964: 119). In terms of electoral strength, the interwar vote for the Workers and Peasants Bloc (the Communists' legal surrogate) averaged approximately 2 percent of the total in all elections between 1932 and the end of the parliamentary system (Fischer-Galati 1970: 75). The RCP was, by most accounts, the least popularly accepted of any of the interwar East European communist parties. Its striking lack of accomplishment is attributable to a number of circumstances. The most basic among these were the low level of the Romania's industrial development and the concomitantly small size of its working class. By 1937 industry and mining produced approximately one third of national income and engaged less than 10 percent of the active population (King 1980: 20). Thus the most natural political base for the RCP was severely limited.

Furthermore, from its very inception the Romanian Communist Party was hindered by severe internal divisions. The party's founders were led by Constantine Dobrogeanu-Gherea (an unwilling emigrant from Tzarist Russia) and the renowned Balkan revolutionary Christian Rakovski. In the atmosphere of political ferment that followed World War I and the Bolshevik revolution, Romanian Marxists fragmented along a variety of lines. "Maximalists" argued for an immediate revolution in emulation of the Bolsheviks, while Party moderates held out for a more restrained approach. Divisions also arose over the question of the proper degree of subordination to Moscow.

As if this were not enough to contend with, the situation was further complicated by incorporation of new territories into Greater Romania. The addition of a Transylvanian branch into the RCP added greatly to the Party's strength. However, it also introduced an additional leadership faction that was coherent within itself, ethnically non-Romanian, and possessed of its own particular loyalties (for example, Magyar as opposed to Romanian nationalism). Incorporation of the Bessarabian party branch brought another strong force into the leadership. The Bessarabian organization, associated as it was with the Russian party during the prewar period, and involved in the revolutionary upheaval that occurred at the end of the First World War, not surprisingly proved both more militant and more closely allied with the new Soviet state than the rest of the Romanian party.

Separation from the Social Democrats failed to quell the internecine feuding among the left-wing Romanian leaders. The Comintern was forced to intervene repeatedly in attempts to restore order within the RCP. Between 1928 and 1930 two implacably hostile factions, both claiming to be the legitimate leadership of the Party, were formed. Divisions of this sort badly disconcerted the general membership, ultimately bringing all activity to a virtual halt. Finally, after a purge that removed several of the most prominent personalities of the preceding ten years, order was restored. The Party's Fifth Congress, in 1932, elected a new leadership which, while not conflict free, was at least sufficiently coherent to remain in control throughout the war. Along with surviving veterans a new group of younger leaders came to the fore during the 1930s whose members included much of the initial postrevolutionary political elite.[2]

The tremendous handicap presented by these internal divisions was matched by the international hostility that characterized the interwar period. Taking heed of the revolutionary ferment across its northern borders, the Romanian state acted decisively against its own radicals. Romanian maximalists and the Bolshevik regime unwisely aggravated right-wing reaction through their agitation and occasional terrorist activities. Consequently a state of siege was declared in Bessarabia, and the Romanian communists were outlawed in 1924. Several hundred of the

Party's organizers were arrested (400 in 1924 alone) and left-wing unions were broken up (Roberts 1969: 101). Less formally, but even more effectively, the government either sponsored or turned a blind eye to the illegal activities of proto-fascist groups such as Codreanu's early Guard of National Consciousness when these were directed against the left (Nagy-Talavera: 252-54). As a result above ground communist political activity became nearly impossible, and the Party's underground work was continually hampered by police infiltration and arrest.

Perhaps most importantly, the appeal of the Romanian communists was severely constrained by unfavorable popular perception of the Party. After 1917 communism was closely identified with Russia and the Russian national cause. This did little to endear it to the average Romanian, who was by all accounts among the most nationalist of individuals in an already quite nationalistic region of the world. A long history of Tzarist territorial aggrandizement made any Russian initiative, Bolshevik or otherwise, immediately suspect. The peasants' traditional mentality presented problems as well. Still a large majority of the population in the postwar years, peasants were strongly attached to the Orthodox Church, which played a central integrative role in village life. Hence the early communists' militant atheism could not fail to create obstacles to their organizing efforts among the poor peasants.

Collectivization of Soviet agriculture had a similarly negative impact. Like their counterparts elsewhere, Romanian peasants had a great deal of interest in agricultural reform insofar as this meant the acquisition of land, but had no use for schemes to expropriate existing holdings. The majority of Romanian peasants were not landless proletarians, but marginal subsistence farmers who augmented their incomes through sharecropping. Unlike their Russian neighbors, for most of them the tradition of a collective village life was long dead (Stahl 1980). To make matters worse word of events in the Soviet countryside beginning in the late 1920s could not help but filter through to the Romanian peasants, and no show of persuasive ability by communist organizers (who were at any rate not free to disclaim Soviet actions) could counteract the effect of such an example. The peasantry was thus left open to penetration by far right organizations such as the Iron Guard, which recruited actively among militant members of the rural population.

Finally, the question of nationality and nationalism constituted a continual source of difficulty to Romanian communists. Leftist organization in the Regat (traditionally Romanian Moldavia and Walachia) being comparatively underdeveloped, the leadership of the RCP not surprisingly came to be dominated by elements drawn from the Bessarabian and Transylvanian Party organizations. This established a strong Magyar and Ukrainian presence within the leadership, in addition to an already considerable representation from the country's urban Jewish population. Thus of 17 identifiable members of the first Central Committee only four were of Romanian ethnic origin (G. Ionescu 1964: 20). It was consequently a simple matter for enemies of the communist movement to label the

RCP alien and anti-Christian, a sinister foreign cabal, inimical to the traditions and interests of the Romanian People (Djordjevic and Fischer-Galati 1981: 221).

The credibility of this charge was immeasurably reinforced by the Comintern's insistence that the Romanian communists espouse national self-determination for the provinces up to the point of secession from the existing state. While the CPSU had the recovery of Bessarabia primarily in mind in its promotion of this policy, irredentist movements in Bukovina, Transylvania, and Dobruja were encouraged as well. Romanian nationalists, even within the Party, were necessarily taken aback by the call for such a massive partition of their newly won territory. For those already hostile to the left it demonstrated that their negative conclusions concerning the communists were justified.

FOUNDATION OF THE SOCIALIST STATE

The weakness of the Romanian Communist Party on taking power, its small size, lack of organization, and alienation from the population are quite understandable in light of the above circumstances. Its condition was further undermined by years of suppression and, beginning in 1940, by the military dictatorship. It was therefore probably a blessing that the Party enjoyed a breathing space before attempting to govern on its own. Participation, first within a real coalition, and then (following the formation of Petru Groza's National Democratic Front) within a manipulated one, provided RCP leaders with access to political and administrative resources far beyond their own means.

One crucial fault that hobbled the RCP's early efforts to rule effectively was severe internal party factionalism, which survived the Second World War. As in other East European communist parties a schism developed in Romania between those leaders who spent the war years inside their country and those who by one means or another reached Moscow. In the Romanian case this division was reinforced by two additional circumstances. First, the Moscovites were predominantly individuals with intelligentsia backgrounds, and were for the most part foreigners, that is, nonethnic Romanians.[3] The national communist faction that formed around the leadership of Gheorghe Gheorghiu-Dej, on the other hand, tended to be of working-class origin, and to be ethnically Romanian. Members of this group formed close personal bonds during their common incarceration by Antonescu during the war. These mutually exclusive experiences, discussed in detail by Jowitt (1971), served to consolidate the division between the two elements within the postwar leadership.

Even before the August coup d'état that brought Antonescu down and the Red Army's entry into Romanian territory, members of the Dej faction acted to strengthen their position by securing the removal of Stepan Foris as General Secretary and his replacement by Gheorghiu-Dej. The reconstituted Secretariat formed at the time included Dej supporters Iosef Ranghet, Constantin Parvulescu, and Emil Bodnaras, the latter two of whom had close ties with Moscow. This move, while undoubtedly unwelcome to the Romanian leadership group in the Soviet Union, cannot be interpreted as having been carried out contrary to the desires of the CPSU, since Bodnaras had himself just returned from the Soviet capital.[4] The hypothesis that he may have been conveying Russian approval for such an action is supported by the fact that throughout the following years Bodnaras was consistently to play the role of intermediary between the Soviet and Romanian leaders.

Accommodation between the internal center of authority and the Muscovites was achieved by the formation of a joint leadership in which both were represented. The Central Committee and Politburo named in October 1945 included the leading members of both groups, as well as representatives of a more moderate strain within the Party.[5] In addition to retaining Dej as General Secretary, the 1945 Party Secretariat included the three dominant Muscovites: Ana Pauker, Vasile Luca, and Teohari Georgescu. While it is not possible to judge with any real confidence the balance of power that existed in the leadership between 1945 and 1952, it does appear certain that Dej's authority was severely constrained by the other three Secretaries (G. Ionescu 1964: 118). As a result of this schism within the top leadership (and probably of the inability of either side to assert its interests within critical sectors of the new state against those of the CPSU's direct agents), the RCP was most remarkable during the immediate postwar years for its lack of internal cohesion. Policy implementation was confused and often contradictory, and the Party has been characterized as more a constellation of personalistic fiefdoms organized around particular leaders than a disciplined "organizational weapon" (Jowitt 1971).

Given its condition and the domestic political environment, the RCP plainly could have neither achieved nor held state power without the support lent it by the Soviet Union. Among the first actions taken following the August coup were measures directed at radically increasing the Party's administrative strength and ability to govern. The abruptness with which this process was begun is most evident in the membership drive initiated by Ana Pauker. From an initial underground base of less than 1,000, membership expanded to 35,000 by March 1945, the time of the installation of Petru Groza's National Democratic Front government. By mid-1946 717,490 recruits had entered the ranks of the Party, and early postwar membership strength peaked at a little over 800,000 in December of the following year.[6]

The rapidity of this influx suggests that the Party could not have been overly discriminating in admitting candidates. Three primary sources of new members can be identified. In the first year after the end of the war RCP leaders (particularly Pauker) were notoriously active in recruiting those who already possessed political skills that could be put to the RCP's uses. This pool of recruits included not only members of the traditional political parties and state employees intent on retaining their positions, opportunists and careerists as they later came to be called, but also former Iron Guardists. The latter element was encouraged to join the RCP because of its influence and organizational assets among the less affluent classes, which the communist leaders hoped could be transferred to themselves piecemeal. Many previous adherents of the fascist movement apparently accepted the victors' overtures as a means of avoiding scrutiny by the new security agencies that were soon busy isolating enemies of the regime.

Of much greater magnitude than this specialized recruitment, however, was the induction of large numbers of workers and peasants. Some among these undoubtedly chose to join the communists out of an aspiration to participate in the rapid advancement that was sure to follow formation of a new regime; a custom of long standing in traditional Romanian politics. But there is no reason to doubt that many peasants and workers, disillusioned with the prewar social order, also joined out of real ideological conviction. In addition to those mobilized for the first time many entered the Communist Party by way of earlier participation in the Plowmen's Front and the left-wing of the Social Democratic Party. Recruitment among the peasants was initially aided by the agricultural reforms of 1945 (discussed below). This postwar cohort of new members had substantial long term importance for the development of the RCP. Included within its ranks was the first wave of those who enjoyed upward mobility into the socialist professional class. This development was, however, a long way from realization in 1945.

The rapid expansion of the Party between 1945 and 1948 could not be accomplished without some degree of confusion and loss of cohesion. By February 1948 the number of basic party organizations controlled by the RCP had jumped to 21,850 (King 1980: 68-69). In addition to the demands imposed on a very limited base of trained cadres by their own dramatic increase, the communists were also burdened with an ever expanding role in administration of the state and a growing number of non-Party mass organizations.[7] Strengthening the RCP's internal organization thus represented a crucial task, and in the years following 1948 became the central policy field in which an increasingly intense leadership struggle was fought. At the elite level the problem of preparing for the task of governing was approached through the foundation of the Stefan Gheorghiu Party School in 1946, and by institution of eight-week political courses for specialists newly inducted into the RCP. Both measures were intended to raise the ideological level of high administrators (G. Ionescu 1964: 119). In 1948 a further step was taken with the establishment of the Zhdanov School (later a higher school of social sciences) for the ideologically correct preparation of instructors in higher education.

Simultaneously with this effort to mold a corps of top leaders, November 1948 saw the beginning of a massive campaign of verification intended to rid the general party membership of undesirable elements that had entered it since the overthrow of Antonescu. By 1950 this purge, carried out by an extra-party "aktiv," had removed in the neighborhood of 300,000 members, or nearly one third of the RCP's total strength (G. Ionescu 1964: 209; King 1980: 73). Overseen as it was by his closest supporters, the 1948-1950 verification campaign marks the beginning of Gheorghiu-Dej's consolidation as undisputed Party leader.

As Jowitt (1971: 138) points out, the aktiv not only undermined the power base of his competitors, but provided Dej with a "patrimonial apparatus within the regime and yet effectively beyond the Party's control."

The domestic political struggle that began with verification was followed by a series of maneuvers climaxing in the 'Muscovites' expulsion from the RCP. Changes beneficial to the General Secretary were occurring outside Romania as well. The growing anti-Semitism of Stalin's later years acted to weaken those ties between Moscow and Dej's rivals which had been the latter's greatest asset. The Jewish mass organization formed after the revolution was purged, with relatives of Ana Pauker being implicated in "Zionist" deviationism. Similar actions were taken against the Hungarian National Committee, an important base of support for Vasile Luca (G. Ionescu 1964: 209), with similar effect. Finally, elections held for leading Party bodies in 1951 strengthened the role of proven worker cadres, and thus of the Romanian ethnic element in the Party. The Muscovites' power having been thoroughly eroded in this manner, their removal followed almost as a matter of course. In the spring of 1952, Pauker, Luca, and Georgescu were each accused of right deviationism, then dropped from the leadership along with their chief lieutenants. (Luca, who resisted the charges brought against him, was immediately expelled from the Party.) Leading bodies were then further reorganized, greatly increasing the homogeneity of the political elite.[8]

The importance of this consolidation of the "national communist" faction from 1945–1952 for the country's future development can hardly be overemphasized. While differences remained among the Romanians involved at the highest levels of the Party, the core of a unified leadership was now firmly established. This group was no less wedded to Stalin and his political program than their defeated rivals: Dej proved himself time and again to be committed to rapid socialist construction through the employment of the coercive power of the state, and he showed little inclination to seek accommodation with class enemies. Yet the foundations of internal solidarity that enabled the RCP to successfully assert its interests against those of Moscow when differences did arise in the next decade were now laid.

WEATHERING THE STORM OF DE-STALINIZATION

Gheorghiu-Dej followed up his 1952 victory by tightening his grip on the Party rank and file. At the Central Committee Plenum held in August 1953, Dej complained of lax internal discipline and the Party's failure to establish close links with the population came under sharp attack. It was decided at the Plenum to form a new aktiv within the RCP consisting of 80,000 to 100,000 unquestionably loyal and qualified members.[9] Final accomplishment of this task in 1955 provided the central leadership with a completely loyal internal apparatus through which its policies could be implemented. In addition to creation of the new aktiv, general recruitment was reopened in 1952, but on a more cautious basis, and with an emphasis on enlarging the number of workers in the Party and raising the level of the membership's ideological commitment to radical change.

As a consequence of these measures the Romanian General Secretary was, in comparison with the majority of his East European neighbors, in a very favorable position to face the political convulsions that followed Stalin's death. Initially, the RCP appeared to shift its course in conjunction with the rest of Eastern Europe. Implementation of an economic "New Course" in 1953 slowed industrialization and eased the strain on consumption. This, however, may have been merely an example of good tactical politics taken in the belief that access to external support was about to be reduced, rather than a change in strategic orientation. At least on the surface Party and state administrations were separated and a collective leadership was formed in emulation of the Soviet example. In April 1954 Gheorghiu-Dej resigned as General Secretary, while retaining his position as Premier. Dej's Party post was divided among four members of a collective Secretariat which included Ceausescu, Mihia Dalia, Ianos Fazekas, and Gheorghe Apostol.

Behind the scenes steps were taken to see that reform did not cut too deep. Before acting on Party reorganization Lucretiu Patrascanu, who had been held in prison since 1948 as a national deviationist, and who in his political position if not his person represented a moderate alternative to the ruling faction, was summarily tried and executed. Following this salutary example reorganization proceeded, with the most formidable remaining Dej competitors being demoted in the reshuffle. Old stalwarts were eliminated from membership in the reconstituted Secretariat, and younger figures, more thoroughly loyal to Dej, appeared in their places. Nicolae Ceausescu was placed at the head of the political administration within the armed forces and named to the Politburo. Similarly, Alexandru Draghici was made Dej's watchdog over security affairs.

Despite these measures Dej lacked the confidence to convene the Party's Second Congress, originally scheduled for March 1954, until December 1955, when it could be brought together without fear of intractable disunity (King 1980: 75). In his address to the Congress Dej once again called attention to the feebleness of links between the Party and the masses, and the negative effect that this state of affairs had on the RCP's overall program. The fallen Muscovite leaders were sharply attacked for previous failures in the realm of collectivization and economic development. In an ominous note the delegates were warned that "every deviation from the party line jeopardizes the very existence of the party, and that the fight for the purity of its ranks, for its monolithic unity is the supreme duty of all members" (quoted in G. Ionescu 1964: 242). Those attracted to the new climate in Moscow were thereby put on notice that their room for maneuver was restricted.

The Second Congress left the Romanian leadership well prepared to contend with Khrushchev's denunciation of Stalin at the 20th Congress of the CPSU. In a special plenum of the Central Committee called to discuss the revelations of the Soviet Congress, Dej laid out the position that he was to retain tenaciously until his death in 1965. Stalin's contribution to the progress of world communism was very great, but marred by the excesses of the end of his regime. Within Romania there had been mistakes as well, but these were the work of Pauker, Luca, Georgescu, and their minions. These unhealthy elements had been expelled by the current ruling group, and their supporters rooted out in the course of the RCP's verification campaign. Romania had thus "de-Stalinized" as early as 1952, well before others even recognized the existence of the problem.[10]

Entrenched as he was, Gheorghiu-Dej did not weather the storm unchallenged. His obvious complicity in the affairs of the RCP between 1944 and 1953 necessarily left him vulnerable to attack by those leaders desirous of a more substantial policy reorientation. Most prominent among these was Miron Constantinescu, a Politburo member and head of the State Planning Commission from 1949–1955. Constantinescu, a moderate, apparently with good connections among the new leaders in the Kremlin, took advantage of the upheavals of 1956 to confront Dej directly at the Plenum. Ironically, his only open support at the leadership level came from Iosif Chisinevischi, a committed Stalinist closely associated with the purged Muscovites (G. Ionescu 1964: 260). These ill-matched dissidents failed to muster sufficient support to carry the day or even to publicize their charges widely. But neither, on the other hand, did the dominant faction feel sufficiently secure to expel them immediately from the leadership.

Among the most decisive factors in the Romanian Old Guard's success in preserving itself was Dej's ability to maintain stability during the crucial period of the Polish and Hungarian crises. The impact of these upheavals on the Romanian population was substantial. Among workers, particularly the railwaymen, demands surfaced for better living conditions. University students, on the other hand, demonstrated against continued Russian presence in the country. Finally, and certainly not unexpectedly, the large population of Transylvanian Magyars was deeply moved by events across the border in Hungary and showed strong support for their co-nationals. While disaffection with the regime was thus widespread it was also fragmented, and therefore it failed to develop into a national mass movement of the sort evidenced in Poland and Hungary. In part the failure of the opposition to achieve popular unity can be attributed to the absence of a dissident Romanian intelligentsia in the forefront of the unrest. Just as surely, however, it was a tribute to the effectiveness of the repressive apparatus molded by Dej in preceding years, and its successful response to the demands placed on it.

Having increased his political capital in Moscow by proving the ability of his regime to keep unrest in hand in 1956, Dej moved against his remaining domestic rivals. In June 1957, shortly before Soviet leadership acted against its own antiparty group, Constantinescu, Chisinevischi, and Constantine Parvulescu, who apparently supported the demands of the first two, were purged. The fallen leaders were accused of Stalinist deviations and of attempting to deflect attention from their errors by guiding the Party in the direction of liberalization following the 20th CPSU Congress. This, according to their accusers, would have resulted in an outcome similar to that in Hungary or Poland.[11] Despite the drawback of being patently contrary to the facts of the case, this exposition had the substantial benefit of being consistent with the ideological line being taken in Moscow, and of bolstering the Dej faction's claim to represent the forces of de-Stalinization.

With this last act in the drama, consolidation of Romania's nationalist leadership was virtually complete. No serious rival to Dej's leading role or representative of a competing policy orientation remained within the guiding bodies of the post revolutionary party-state. The regime that emerged after more than ten years of internecine struggle has justifiably been characterized as sultanistic. Gheorghiu-Dej's personal authority, based on relations of individual allegiance between him and subalterns in control of critical components of the state apparatus, surpassed the importance of Marxist-Leninist norms of behavior and party discipline. Thus even as Romania was in the throes of a massive socialist transformation the Soviet institutional model was subtly altered, and the traditionalistic character of prerevolutionary Romanian politics began to reemerge.

POSTWAR INDUSTRIAL TRANSFORMATION

In all likelihood the survival of a Stalinist leadership in Bucharest was not entirely welcome in the Soviet Union of the "thaw," but it was an outcome that appeared to bode well for continued stability. In the wake of Poland and Hungary Dej's presence clearly must have appeared preferable to anarchy that might follow a more meaningful effort to expunge Stalin's legacy in Bucharest. But differences between the two parties that went well beyond questions of personnel were already in the making by the late 1950s. In particular, divergence in the area of economic policy led to a clash of wills on fundamental issues, and ultimately to the open split of 1964.

Romania was among the most underdeveloped of European nations prior to the Second World War. Its 1937 per capita national income was less than half that of Czechoslovakia and was followed only by those of Yugoslavia and Bulgaria among the East European states (Berend and Ranki 1977: 99). Despite an extensive natural resource base prewar governments did not achieve appreciable industrialization. While autarky and state intervention did result in the creation of some heavy industry, the policy did not fundamentally alter the structure of the economy. Approximately 80 percent of the pre-1945 population was employed in agriculture (Dobrescu 1973: 164). The yield of its labor-intensive agriculture made up 64 percent of Romania's exports, and manufactured goods accounted for less than 2 percent (Spulber 1957: 8).

The overall pattern of Romanian economic development can therefore justifiably be typified as peripheral, in the same sense which applies to the economies of contemporary Third-World countries in their interactions with the industrialized West.[12] Furthermore, at the inception of communist rule Romania was at an economic disadvantage not only to the capitalist West, but also to its more developed northern neighbors within the Council for Mutual Economic Assistance (CMEA), that is, Czechoslovakia, the German Democratic Republic, and Poland.

In the early postwar years Romania's economic behavior was neither remarkable (except perhaps for its confusion) nor problematic in comparison to the pattern in the rest of Eastern Europe. Like the other members of the new Soviet bloc it suffered substantial physical damage during the war, and like them its recovery was complicated by the burden of reparations payments and the loss of substantial economic resources to the Soviet Union through the establishment of joint companies similar to those formed in other East European countries.[13] Once underway its socialist transformation was rapid and at times harsh. Initially, however, little progress was made by Bucharest. Romania lagged behind for a variety of reasons, not least of which was a severe drought in 1945 and 1946 that reduced agricultural output to less than 60 percent of the 1934–1938 average (Roberts 1969: 315). Agitation among the urban workers, coupled with the communists' struggle to assert their political authority, disrupted industrial production, and a foreign exchange crisis led to a severe shortage of materials and spare parts. As a result of all this, as well as the general lack of organization of the postwar years, 1947 production was reduced to 75 percent of that achieved in 1938 (Montias 1967: 24).

While some improvements occurred in late 1947 due to increased harvests and monetary reform, meaningful advances only began to be seen in conjunction with liquidation of the coalition government and the communist political offensive of 1948; from that point on matters proceeded quite rapidly. In June 1948 the new legislature, the Grand National Assembly (GNA), passed a nationalization law that resulted in the socialization of almost all of the country's industrial production in the course of the next two years.

Concomitant with nationalization central planning was introduced with the one-year plans of 1949 and 1950. These established the groundwork for the more comprehensive First Five-Year Plan initiated in 1951. The beginning of planning also marked the start of a program to commit massive resources to industrialization. Gross fixed investment in the socialist sector increased from 1.5 billion lei in 1948 to 7.5 billion in 1950, with industry absorbing more than 48 percent of total investment in the latter years (Montias 1967: 25–26). A similar pattern was evident in the course of the five-year plan. According to Montias's figures (1967: 27) investment rose from 7.5 billion lei in 1950 to 18 billion in 1953, when the plan was abandoned. During the same period the ratio of investment to national income rose from 19 to 34 percent.[14]

The majority of these new inputs were absorbed by industry and construction, which together accounted for over half of total investment during the first plan period. Agriculture, on the other hand, was allocated only around 10 percent and housing was almost entirely neglected, with 3.2 percent.[15] Within the favored sector planners focused on establishing the foundation for further development of heavy industry. Electric and thermal power, fuels, ferrous and nonferrous metallurgy, machine-building and chemical industries received over

78 percent of industrial investment during the first plan (Dobrescu and Blaga 1973: 30).

In the countryside, the drive for development signaled a more determined effort to achieve agricultural collectivization. In March 1949 all large holdings remaining in private hands after the agricultural reform of 1945 were seized, and their owners charged with economic sabotage and relocated by the militia. The approximately 1 million hectares thus obtained were either turned over to state farms or transformed into collectives. At the same time a renewed effort was made to induce small farmers to enter collective farms. The brutality with which this program was implemented gave rise to widespread resistance and sporadic violence in the countryside. According to a report made by Gheorghiu-Dej in 1961 more than 80,000 peasants were arrested and 30,000 were subjected to public trials in order to coerce their fellow villagers into compliance (G. Ionescu 1964: 201).

At a purely pragmatic level, however, the state simply did not possess the material basis necessary to carry out successfully a complete transformation of agriculture. The number of tractors and other mechanical implements was insufficient to meet the demands of large scale production. Neither were there trained administrators and technical personnel to manage the new units. By late 1951 the negative effects of accelerating the pace of agricultural transformation had become so evident that the RCP's Central Committee was forced to conclude that substantial errors had been made, and to order a retreat. Rather than pressing for immediate inclusion of private peasants in collective or state farms, state policy called for cooperativization, in which peasants retained their individual property. In order to ensure an adequate supply of food to the cities and a surplus for export, compulsory deliveries were imposed as a proportion of each peasant's production. In addition to its stated purpose, the quota system was employed by the state to punish "kulaks" and others among the rural population who were active in resisting the RCP's agricultural policy. Because the required deliveries were unrealistically high, thousands of peasants were forced to give up their land and join the growing migration to the cities. This pressure, combined with the attraction of employment created by new industries, resulted in a decline of agriculture's share in the total labor force from 74.1 percent in 1950 to 69.5 percent in 1955 (*Anuarul Statistic* 1980: 112).[16]

The impact of the initial surge of postwar development was substantial. In the three years between 1950 and 1953 gross industrial output increased by 68 percent, while employment in industry and construction doubled. Between 1948 and 1956 the urban sector mushroomed from 23.4 to 31.3 percent of total population, as thousands of peasants entered the industrial labor force. The strain of maintaining this pace, however, could not be borne indefinitely. Throughout Eastern Europe the drive for industrialization produced severe imbalances. In Romania, where consumption had been restrained even more severely than elsewhere, conditions were so much the worse. Thus it is probable, as Montias (1967: 38) suggests, that even had Stalin's death in 1953 not altered the regional political situation, Romania would have been forced by its domestic circumstances to undertake economic redirection.

Whatever its impetus the policy reversal that occurred in 1953 was dramatic. The sharp investment increases of preceding years were followed by a decline of 11 percent between 1953 and 1954, which was not regained in the following year (Montias 1967: 42). Funds were diverted into housing and consumption, and steps were taken to end rationing. Retail sales were increased, and new initiatives were taken to mollify the peasantry. Exports of raw materials dropped off, both because of their diversion into domestic consumption, and because of limits reached in the extraction of fuels and timber. Consequently the previously high rate of machine goods imports had to be restricted, exacerbating the slump in the pace of industrial growth. Blame for the decisions that had made such concessions necessary was laid at the door of the deposed Muscovites (particularly Vasile Luca), and the Party was exhorted to form firmer links with the working people so that such difficulties could never again develop unnoticed.

Despite the slowed pace of industrialization in 1953, there is little evidence that the Dej faction, which was in the process of consolidating itself at the time, had altered its basic intentions with regard to development strategy. Some of the worst abuses of the preceding period were rectified, and a period of recuperation and taking stock was provided so that previous gains could be consolidated; but the basic structure of investment shifted only slightly. Fuels and heavy industry remained the linchpins of the national economy, with other sectors playing a secondary role. The validity of this assessment is underscored by examination of the initial version of the Second Five-Year Plan, covering the 1956–1960 period. Its goals for production and investment strongly indicated that a renewed industrial drive was intended. State investment was slated to increase by 21 percent, with 56 percent of this amount allocated to industry (G. Ionescu 1964: 250-52; Montias 1967: 52).

In light of the crises of 1956, however, the RCP prudently elected to reduce its actual investment to approximately half of the planned level, and to extend new concessions to the population in an effort to head off unrest. Compulsory agricultural deliveries were abolished, and workers' wages were increased by 15 percent, with the result that the years between 1956 and 1958 were among the best experienced by Romanians since the end of the war. But while events in Hungary and Poland may have cut renewal of the industrialization campaign short at its inception, the respite thus produced was short-lived. Once assured that the domestic situation was under control, planners reverted to their initial strategy. In contrast to more moderate goals in the rest of Eastern Europe, the policies announced by the Romanian Central Committee at its November 1958 Plenum resumed the 1948-1953 pattern of forced industrial development, signaling the initial stirrings of Romanian particularism. After falling off in 1957 total investment increased by 10.92 percent in 1958, and 16.23 percent in 1959 (Gilberg 1975: 143). Particular attention was devoted to expanding those sectors necessary to establishing an autonomous industrial base. Ferrous and nonferrous metallurgy, machine building, and chemical industry all received priority treatment (*Anuaral Statistic 1980*: 392; Montias 1967: 54). The RCP's orientation was further underscored by the fact that industry's share in overall investments, which fell from approximately 53 percent in the first plan period to 44 percent in the second, began edging up once again, to consume over 46 percent of national investment during the Third Five-Year Plan (*Anuarul Statistic 1980*: 382).

Perhaps an even more definite indication of the Dej faction's tenacious commitment to their pre-1953 strategy for social change was the resumption of agricultural collectivization. While Romania had not experienced a widespread reversion to private cultivation such as occurred in Poland, a definite slackening of the pace of rural transformation occurred in the early 1950s. Beginning in 1955, however, peasants were again being pressed to enter into collective production; and after the decisions of the 1958 Party Plenum a second full-scale campaign to socialize agriculture was initiated. The number of households engaged in private agriculture fell from 88.5 percent in 1955, to slightly under 7 percent in 1962, at which point the socialization of the countryside was declared complete (Montias 1967: 93). The decision to undertake such a momentous task without the support of the CPSU (and quite likely counter to its express wishes) represented a clear signal to the Khrushchev leadership (intended or not) that the Romanians were no longer to be considered mere subordinates.

ROMANIAN DEVELOPMENT AND THE
DRIVE FOR NATIONAL AUTONOMY

Bucharest's post-1953 New Course quite clearly appears to have been intended to maintain the essence of a Stalinist economic model, if in a somewhat rationalized form. This fact in itself is by no means unique; neither the leaders of Czechoslovakia nor those of the German Democratic Republic (GDR) were overly forward in implementing reform. For the Romanians, however, not just the avoidance of reform, but the continuation of large-scale industrial transformation became a focal issue. The amalgam of relatively more advanced northern tier economies and less industrialized southeastern European countries that characterized the Soviet bloc in the mid-1950s generally suited the CPSU's plans for CMEA development, and was actively promoted by the more developed bloc members. But cutting off the Stalinist strategy of state-led industrial breakthrough for all of Eastern Europe would, in the RCP's view, have frozen the Romanians in a subordinate position. For as long as Stalinist industrialization was consistent with Soviet aims, it was not a source of tension between the two leaderships. But following the defeat of the Soviet antiparty group in 1957, Khrushchev was well positioned to press forward with a program of economic coordination and reformism that was precisely the inverse of the course preferred by Romania's unreconstructed "metal eaters." This meant that Romania's leaders could only realize their commitment to national development in the face of Soviet opposition.

The breach separating Romania from the Soviet Union and other CMEA members was thus intimately related both to consolidation of the faction around Gheorghiu-Dej, and to Romania's continued commitment to a Stalinist development strategy while the CPSU shifted to advocacy of a more moderate approach to industrialization and economic socialist internationalism. The decision to pursue an independent course had profound ramifications for Romania's future evolution. Once underway, it shut off one whole range of policy alternatives (which could only be undertaken in concert with the Soviet Union), and impelled the leadership to undertake new initiatives that in all probability it would not otherwise have chosen.

While an ongoing disagreement surrounds the date at which the beginning of the Soviet/Romanian split can best be placed, it is clear that by the late 1950s areas of stress existed.[17] Such policy tensions obviously need not be transformed into open political conflict. In the Romanian case, however, serious differences developed concurrently with opportunities for their expression. Stalin's death and the leadership struggle that it precipitated in the U.S.S.R. severely weakened Moscow's leverage in dealing with Eastern Europe. Simultaneously Romania's success in maintaining domestic stability, and its useful role in restoring order at the time of the Hungarian uprising, added to Bucharest's bargaining power. Finally, the Sino-Soviet dispute provided opportunities for diplomatic maneuvering that would not have existed otherwise.[18] The confluence of these factors presented possibilities for the RCP to assert its independence just as differences with the CPSU were beginning to emerge.

The first substantial evidence of differentiation between the RCP and other members of CMEA came in the form of withdrawal of Soviet troops from Romanian territory in 1958. This occurrence, which has been the subject of substantial controversy, was in all probability neither purely the result of Bucharest's forcing the Russians to withdraw, nor of a unilateral Soviet decision to remove their troops for reasons of their own.[19] Rather, the breakthrough was possible because of circumstances that made Romania a good risk from the Soviet perspective combined with the application of diplomatic pressure on the part of the Romanians. The advantage presented to Romania by the growing Sino-Soviet schism and the utility of Chinese support first became manifest in regard to this issue. Indeed, according to Fischer-Galati (1967: 70), "The determining factor [in securing the withdrawal of the Russians] was . . . a combination of Rumanian pressure exerted in conjunction with the Sino-Soviet controversy over the role of national armies in the nuclear age and Chinese support of the Rumanian position."

Continued Chinese backing, expressed in the form of an ongoing exchange of visits between the two countries, by China's public praise of Bucharest's renewed industrialization effort, and in the declarations of both communist parties concerning the necessity of maintaining the proper relations between all socialist states, proved invaluable in the growing controversy over Romanian domestic development and international economic relations. Russian dissatisfaction with the continued rapid growth of Romanian heavy industry (symbolized by Moscow's failure to provide any material assistance for the construction of the keystone Galati steel complex) met with surprisingly firm resistance in Bucharest, where development was portrayed ever more explicitly as a national goal. Propaganda building on this theme was undertaken to rally popular support to the RCP as the legitimate representative of Romanian interests.

Since Soviet economic assistance could no longer be relied upon, Romania moved at an early date in its dispute with Moscow to reduce its vulnerability in foreign trade. Beginning in 1959, a concentrated effort, including the dispatch of high level delegations to several European capitals, was initiated to establish better trade relations in the West. Between 1958 and 1964 the Soviet Union's share of total imports dropped off from 57.7 to 37.7 percent, while exports to the U.S.S.R. declined from 50.2 to 39.8 percent. Trade with the developed West, on the other hand, increased dramatically, with imports nearly doubling, from 21.5 to 39.9 percent, and exports climbing from 24.9 to 32.8 percent during the same 1958-1964 period (Montias 1967: 164). Planners' intentions seem perfectly clear in light of the composition of their growing Western trade. By 1965, according to Montias's calculations, the West certainly accounted for 42 percent, and may have supplied as much as 50 percent, of Romanian machinery and equipment imports, as the Romanians sought to establish a stable alternative source of the material required to proceed with their industrialization program (Montias 1967: 169). In exchange for industrial supplies, Bucharest diverted its growing agricultural surplus and other raw materials from its Eastern trading partners to the West. These efforts allowed industrialization to proceed on the basis of a foreign trade regime that freed Romania from unilateral dependence on the Soviet Union.

Bucharest's failure to respond positively to signals to restrain itself did not go unnoticed in Moscow. Beginning in 1961 Kremlin leaders and the Romanians moved toward open confrontation. Two developments were particularly salient in bringing matters to a head. First, the long brewing controversy over supranational planning and industrial specialization within CMEA was exacerbated by the Soviet shift in mid-1961 from a position of relative noncommitment to one of strong support for Czechoslovakia and other CMEA members who favored centralization.[20] Second, and probably not unrelated to the decision to pressure Romania into accepting closer integration into the socialist community, was the renewed assault on Stalinism during the October 1961 Twenty-Second CPSU Congress. As part of his report to the Congress, Khrushchev attacked not only Stalin, but Stalinists remaining in leadership positions in the communist parties.

Khrushchev's anti-Stalinist onslaught could hardly have been viewed positively by Dej, considering has status as an outstanding survivor of the old order. His immediate response was a firm reassertion of previous statements to the effect that Romanian de-Stalinization had been completed with the ouster first of

Pauker, Luca, and Georgescu, and then with the removal of the antiparty group, that is, Constantinescu and Chisinevischi. This time, however, Dej placed considerable emphasis on the Stalinists' Muscovite background, in contrast to the Romanian origin of his own ideologically sound workers' faction. In a further implicit thrust at the CPSU, his denunciation of Stalin focused on the dictator's improper interference in the affairs of fraternal parties, thus bringing into question Khrushchev's own attempts to impose order within the communist international community.

This interchange clearly set the two nations on a collision course. Khrushchev intensified the pressures on Bucharest to fall into line, apparently even up to the point of seeking Dej's overthrow from within the RCP and considering military intervention (Jowitt 1971: 218; Fischer-Galati 1970: 178). In reaction the RCP redoubled earlier efforts to insulate itself against Moscow's maneuvering. Further measures were taken to garner mass support, including the gradual Romanianization (elimination of practices introduced under the influence of the Soviet Union) of the educational system and extension of an amnesty to political prisoners. While agricultural collectivization was completed on schedule in 1962, substantial concessions were made to the peasantry with the intent of reducing their antipathy toward the regime. Finally, after a period of membership stagnation, the Party was reopened for recruitment in April 1962, and restrictions that banned participants in the prewar bourgeois parties were dropped. As a result of this policy between 1962 and 1965 the RCP was strengthened by 600,000 new members, many of whom were motivated by the leadership's implicitly anti-Soviet stance. Many, too, were drawn from the new socialist intelligentsia created by the industrialization drive of the preceding decade (King 1980: 79; Jowitt 1971: 216).

At this critical juncture in Soviet/Romanian relations fate intervened on the sides of the RCP in the guise of the Cuban Missile Crisis. The failure of Khrushchev's 1962 venture undermined the Soviet leader's ability to control the communist movement, and encouraged the Chinese to step up their attacks on the revisionist leadership of the CPSU, thus greatly increasing the Romanians' ability to maneuver without risking an absolute break with Moscow. When the Soviets attempted once again in early 1963 to impose supranational integration within the framework of the CMEA, the Romanian Central Committee felt sufficiently secure to issue a public statement (supported by the Chinese) that economic relations should be governed by the "observance of national independence and sovereignty, of full equality of rights, comradely mutual aid and mutual benefit."

This clash was followed almost immediately by Romania's formal rejection of Soviet domination. The final breach was opened by publication of Mao's "twenty-five points" criticizing the CPSU's foreign policy in June 1963. Alone among the East European bloc members, Romania resisted coming to Moscow's support and took up a position critical of both of the major parties. This obstruction of the CPSU's efforts to expel China from the world communist movement provoked a sharp escalation of the Soviet's anti-Bucharest offensive, which included calling into question the status of Transylvania as a legitimate part of Romanian territory (Fischer-Galati 1970: 178–79). Rather than coercing RCP leaders into compliance this threat merely impelled them to take further steps to extricate themselves from Moscow's control. Measures to establish links with the West were increased, and in April 1964 the RCP Central Committee issued its noted "Statement on the Stand of the Romanian Workers' Party Concerning the Problems of the World Communist and Working-Class Movement."[21] The Statement addressed itself directly to the key debates of the time, rejecting categorically the right of the CMEA to carry on activities that limit the autonomy of its members, and opposing Soviet attempts to call a conference that did not include representatives of all communist parties (that is, rejecting the practice of "excommunicating" particular parties from the World Communist Movement). It is most remarkable for asserting clearly and firmly the national sovereignty of Romania, and the "exclusive right of each party independently to work out its political line, its concrete objectives, and the ways and means of achieving them" (see Griffith 1967: 269–96 for an English translation of the text).

CONCLUSION

The RCP 1964 Statement epitomized the character of Romania's political evolution from the beginning of its revolutionary transformation until the death of Gheorghiu-Dej, less than a year after its publication. The country had emerged from the Second World War materially devastated, and politically subjugated by the vastly stronger forces of the Soviet Union. Its fortunes appeared to be at their lowest ebb since unification of the Principalities nearly 100 years previously. From this base of social exhaustion the previously weak and obscure Romanian Communist Party, employing the support of the Soviet occupying forces, began a program of economic and political transformation that fundamentally altered the social fabric of the country in less than two decades.

Industrialization, once it got underway, proceeded at a faster rate than in any other East European country. The mobilization of resources that went into the effort was truly massive. Between 1950 and 1965 investment in the economy grew by 748 percent (*Anuarul Statistic 1980*: 202). Between 1950 and 1965 the industrial labor force increased from 12 to 19.2 percent of the working population, while the agricultural labor force declined from 74.1 to 56.5 percent. According to Romanian figures, industrial production responded by showing an increase of 649 percent between 1950 and 1965 (*Anuarul Statistic 1980*: 138–39), with priority sectors, such as machine building, performing at an even higher rate. Even if actual growth was somewhat less than official figures indicate, most sources agree that the pace of economic growth was impressive. As a consequence of the RCP effort, by the end of the third plan period the traditional pattern of the economy had been broken. Romania was no longer simply a dependent sup-

plier of agricultural commodities, but was well along on the path toward industrialization, producing a substantial proportion of its own machinery needs, and
exporting increasing amounts to its trading partners.

The social impact of forced industrialization was equally significant. The expanded educational system turned out thousands of new graduates; new professionals and skilled workers replaced the prerevolutionary middle class and filled
positions created by the growing economy.[22] On the other hand, urban areas
were starved of funds for construction, and their inhabitants suffered overcrowd-
ing and a critical lack of services. As a result of the RCP's diversion of all available resources into investment the level of consumption, while increased in
absolute terms, remained relatively the lowest among the East European state-
socialist countries in virtually every category.

Fundamental events occurred in the international environment as well. Identifying a single cause among the many variables that set the Romanian communist leadership on a course at odds with that of the Soviet Union is a problematic
task at best. The leaders that emerged from the postwar RCP power struggles of
the late 1940s and early 1950s were thoroughly committed to ending their country's relative backwardness through a program of heavy industrial development
and rapid agricultural collectivization, even at the expense of straining their relations with the Soviet Union. Romania's insistence on the priority of national
goals over the principle of specialization within the CMEA conformed with this
outlook. By the early 1960s, however, continued insistence on this position
may well have been equally motivated by a desire to insulate the unreconstructed
Dej leadership from Khrushchev's openly revisionist intentions.

The faction that formed around Dej in the early postwar years was, as others
have noted, more firmly grounded in Romanian cultural traditions than its competitors for control of the RCP. It is unlikely that these leaders' nationalism,
such as it was, would have been sufficient in itself to cause the rupture with
Moscow. Yet it certainly did shape the course of events once strains began to
appear. On the elite level it can be said to have colored the political sensibilities
of the Romanian leadership, establishing a basis of common understanding of
the problems that had to be faced, and of methods for their resolution. On the
level of the general population, nationalism, when it could be plausibly appealed
to (and this almost necessarily meant appealed to in opposition to the Soviet
Union), provided a powerful set of symbols that could mobilize mass support for
the RCP. Once set into place, an increasingly nationalist variant communism,
along with the commitment to industrial development, became fundamental
aspects of the Romanian political order.

4 *THE CEAUSESCU TRANSITION*

INTRODUCTION

The leadership transition that followed Gheorghe Gheorghiu-Dej's demise was fundamental to Romania's further socioeconomic evolution: During the second half of the 1960s the RCP leaders who survived Dej were faced with a series of critical choices, both domestic and international. Nicolae Ceausescu's successful effort to replace Dej as the dominant figure in the RCP was crucial in determining how these choices were resolved, and the future direction of the country. By the end of the decade the new General Secretary's position was sufficiently secure to allow him to exercise substantial personal influence over the political system. With his authority firmly established he launched a concerted drive to remold Romania to conform with his particular vision of "the radiant future." Yet as Marx's frequently quoted but nonetheless accurate phrase suggests, no one (not even a Ceausescu) can make history just as he likes. It might well be added that his dictum holds especially true for those, like the Romanians, who inhabit militarily weak countries with powerful neighbors, and whose ambitious plans are matched by access to only limited material resources.

The following discussion focuses on the struggle of the post-Gheorghui-Dej political elite to consolidate its position, to negotiate a difficult societal transformation, and to implement its chosen political program in a hostile domestic and international environment. After a brief description of Ceausescu's struggle to gain control of the RCP, analysis of the transition period begins with an evaluation of the domestic social/economic environment confronting Party leaders in the mid-1960s. By this time economic development in Romania had reached a stage at which significant redirection was called for if the Party's plans for industrialization were to proceed. Furthermore, increasing numbers of skilled professionals had appeared on the scene, and were beginning to form a distinct social stratum and to differentiate themselves from the rest of the society.

In the course of describing the transition years I will seek to show that, while the opportunity to do so clearly existed, and that a significant body of opinion favored such a course, the new Romanian political leadership resisted reforms that would have led in the direction of civil/state accommodation. The choices made by the group which consolidated itself around Ceausescu, particularly the decision to continue along the economic track laid down under Dej, foreclosed the possibility of evolution along the accommodationist lines that were becoming apparent in other East European countries. Similarly, the decision to reconfirm Romania's policy of national autonomy limited the RCP's access to Soviet support (either material or ideological), which could have been used to sustain the regime. The Romanian political elite was thus impelled to look inward for a solution to its problems. By the close of the transition period RCP leaders were feeling their way toward a uniquely Romanian political strategy; one which differed significantly from those of the other East European state-socialist regimes.

CEAUSESCU AND THE 1960s LEADERSHIP CONSOLIDATION

The selection of Nicolae Ceausescu to succeed as RCP General Secretary was surprising only with respect to the new leader's relative youthfulness (47 at the time of his accession to the top party position). In fact, having spent his entire adult life as a revolutionary activist, he was by 1965 a veteran Party leader with wide organizational experience and was well placed to carry out a successful campaign to consolidate his new position. The uneducated son of poor peasants from the region of Oltenia, Ceausescu had arrived in Bucharest at the age of 11 seeking to support himself as a shoemaker's apprentice. He first entered the RCP youth organization, the *Uniunea Tineretului Comunist* (UTC), in 1933 at the age of 15, and rose rapidly to membership in its guiding bodies. After arrest for underground activity and imprisonment in Doftana prison (where he came into contact with Gheorghiu-Dej and other incarcerated members of the highest communist leadership), he emerged in 1938 to become UTC First Secretary. In August 1940 he was once again arrested by the Carolist regime and jailed in Jilava, Tirgu Jui, and other prison camps where he remained throughout the war years.[1]

On his release from custody in 1944 Ceausescu began his ascent within the Romanian Communist Party. He immediately resumed his position as First Secretary of the UTC, and was elected in October 1945 to the RCP's first postwar Central Committee. From then until 1950 he worked in the Dobrogea and Oltenia provincial Party committees on agricultural affairs, and in the Ministry of Agriculture (as a Deputy Minister) during the 1948–1950 collectivization drive. Having apparently proven himself equal to the demands of high level positions, Ceausescu was subsequently assigned to head the Higher Political Department of the Army and simultaneously was made deputy Minister of Defense. Although he retained this latter position until 1954, he was soon afterward also appointed to the RCP Orgburo. In April 1954 Ceausescu was named Party Central Committee Secretary with responsibility for organizational work, and by 1957 he had replaced Miron Constantinescu in charge of cadres policy. His decade-long tenure as a key figure in personnel selection for the central apparatus during the crucial period of postwar party building, as well as his connections with the political department of the Romanian military, and the UTC, were clearly pivotal in providing Ceausescu with a strong base of support for his later struggle to gain control over the RCP.

Despite the advantages which this career path obviously afforded him, Ceausescu was not without serious rivals in his quest for the top leadership position. The most serious of these appear to have been members of the old guard Dej generation of leaders (particularly Gheorghe Apostol); and Alexandru Draghici, Minister of Internal Affairs, and the most obvious alternative to Ceausescu among his own contemporaries. Nearly five years of constant maneuvering were required between the time of Dej's demise and the emergence of an undeniably Ceausescu regime in control of Romanian politics. The general pattern of elite politics during this period has been most fully analyzed by Mary Ellen Fischer (Fischer 1977, 1980, 1983). As she has argued, the period from his election in 1965 until late 1969 were marked by "personnel manipulation" (that is, bureaucratic infighting within the party and state apparatus) and policy ambiguity, as the new General Secretary felt his way toward a viable political formula.

Efforts in the former area began in 1965 with a reorganization in which the size of the Party's central bodies was increased, allowing Ceausescu to strengthen his voting support, but at the same time avoiding recourse to dismissals until his position was better established. Thus between 1965 and December 1967 virtually no top leaders were removed from their positions, and the membership of the RCP Executive Committee nearly doubled (Fischer 1980: 219). In a similar 1968 maneuver administrative reforms were introduced that increased the number of territorial units directly subordinated to the central government from 16 (provinces) to 40 (*Judets*), providing strategically important positions between the center and the local apparat that were filled by supporters of the new leader. Simultaneously with this "packing" of the RCP's executive organs a party statute was introduced that forbade the accumulation of multiple leadership positions. This tactic was used most effectively against Draghici, who was removed from his position as Minister of Internal Affairs and thereby cut off from direct control over his power base within the secret police. Draghici's removal from the Secretariat in December 1967 and final expulsion from the Party in April 1968 signaled Ceausescu's intention to take the offensive, and marked the beginning of the displacement of his other rivals from key positions.

With the exsecurity chief's ouster secured, the 1965 ban on holding multiple leadership positions was reversed and Ceausescu began his unprecedented accumulation of Party and state offices; becoming (in order of succession) President of the State Council, Chairman of the Socialist Unity Front, Chairman of the Defense Council, and Supreme Commander of the Armed Forces. In sharp contrast to the pattern of the preceding four years, members of the pre-1965 leadership were precipitously eliminated from the new inner circle.[2] During the crucial years of 1968 and 1969 over half of those elected to the Party's guiding bodies before 1965 were removed. They were replaced by newly selected Ceausescu supporters, many of whom were recruited from among those who had been advanced into mid-level leadership as a result of the General Secretary's support during his years as a cadres administrator (Fischer 1980: 219). By the opening of the Tenth Party Congress in August 1969 the initial leadership crisis had been negotiated, and Ceausescu was established as the leader of the RCP. Earlier pretenses at collective leadership were then dropped, and the General Secretary emerged as the dominant force in Romanian policy formulation.

The nature of elite politics during the transition period is thus straightforward; nor is it out of character with the experience of leadership transitions in other state-socialist countries. Despite his initial appearance of caution and conciliation, behind the scenes the *nominal* leader carried out a bitter and shrewd administrative campaign to consolidate *actual* control over the mechanisms of power. Members of the new ruling group which he installed differed from their predecessors in a number of specifics. First, the preponderance of technical specialists within the leadership was increased (Fischer 1980: 214–15).[3] This innovation at the center was matched by an effort to improve the qualifications of Party activists at all levels. Second, the number of ethnic Romanians in top Party bodies increased, intensifying the process of homogenization that had been apparent under Gheorghiu-Dej (Fischer 1980: 215). Finally, as will be shown in the following chapter, power at the top of the party-state became even more concentrated than during the Dej period, when secondary leaders often achieved the status of semiautonomous bureaucratic chieftains. Unlike their predecessors, Ceausescu's lieutenants were clearly complete subordinates of the General Secretary. They were rarely permitted to establish any stable base of personal support, and consequently remained much more dependent on retaining the good graces of their patron. The tradition of intense cohesion within the top political leadership thus survived the leadership transition, and became one of the fundamental characteristics distinguishing Romania from the other East European regimes.[4]

THE SOCIAL/ECONOMIC SETTING
OF THE CEAUSESCU TRANSITION

Even before the demise of Gheorghiu-Dej a variety of indicators suggested that the Romanian development model had begun to encounter difficulties requiring fundamental decisions by the leadership. Romania had undeniably made tremendous strides toward economic development since the inception of the socialist regime. The most recent wave of industrialization, unleashed by Dej in

1958, completed the collectivization of agriculture and dramatically altered the structure of the economy. In the ten years preceding Ceausescu's assumption of power total industrial production more than tripled, and during the decisive 1958-1963 period net industrial output increased at approximately 14 percent per year (*Anuarul Statistic* 1980: 142-43; Montias 1967: 52). The direction of development continued along the lines laid down in the earlier postwar phase of intense industrialization. Priority was ascribed to basic industry, particularly extractive industry, metals, machine building, and chemicals, in which the rate of growth was even higher than the national average. By 1965 industry had achieved a predominant position in the economy, accounting for 57.3 percent of national income. But in the final years of the industrialization campaign there were unmistakable signs of impending difficulties (*Anuarul Statistic* 1980: 92).

Romania's classic extensive development was fueled by a combination of massive labor, and equally large capital, inputs. Before the completion of collectivization both grew at moderate rates. As the transformation of the rural sector proceded, however, the rate of labor transfer from agriculture to industry necessarily slowed appreciably. The decline on this side of the input equation was accommodated through acceleration in the rate of capital formation. The rhythm of industrialization was thus maintained only by dramatically expanding the proportion of national income dedicated to accumulation (up to 24.3 percent in 1960-1965 from 16 percent in the preceding five-year period) at the expense of consumption (Tsantis and Pepper 1979: 82). By the first half of the 1960s this strategy appeared to have overburdened the Romanian planning system with more new investment than could be effectively accommodated (Jackson 1981a: 266).

The effect of having pushed the economic system to its limit in this way was evident in sharp declines in the rate of increase of capital productivity, and of investment efficiency, beginning in 1962 (Montias 1967: 58-59; Spigler 1973: 15). Agriculture presented a second source of difficulty. The effects of too rapid collectivization, and the insufficient capital investment following from the regime's focus on industry resulted in very low levels of growth and productivity. As the development plan advanced agricultural deficiencies were added to the problems already facing planners, and began to have a retarding effect on the rest of the economy. The combined impact of these negative developments forced central decision makers to reduce sharply the pace of economic advance, and enter into a period of reassessment. Investment in the economy, which had risen at 23 percent per year from 1959 to 1962, was cut back to 9 percent per year increases from 1963 to 1965 (Montias 1967: 66).

Romanian social structure had, by the mid-1960s, undergone a transformation as extensive as that seen in the economy, and one which was becoming equally problematic for policymakers. The most powerful demographic tendency in evidence was rapid migration from rural communities to the growing industrial centers, particularly Bucharest, and the shift of the labor force from agricultural to industrial occupations (Sandu 1984). These associated changes were motivated both by the increasing gap between the rural and urban standards of living (the draw of better paid industrial work in the cities) and by the desire of peasant producers to escape the effect of collectivization in the countryside. Thus between 1955 and 1965 the population occupied in agriculture declined from 69.5 to 56.5 percent, and in approximately the same period (1956 to 1966) the urban population increased from 31.3 to 38.2 percent (*Anuarul Statistic* 1980: 45, 112–13). This transformation was particularly pronounced in the years from 1954 to 1962, then dropped off as the country entered a period of economic retrenchment and policy vacillation lasting until the final years of the decade (Sandu 1984: 116–31).

The population shift indicated by the data above presented complicated challenges to the Party. On the positive side, the massive movement from underpaid rural occupations into marginally more lucrative industrial jobs was one significant factor in the steady increase in the standard of living experienced by most of the population since the mid-1950s. The continuing employment shift permitted improvements to occur despite the high accumulation rate, and without increasing the wage scales within particular job categories. But at the same time the brute flow of population into the cities in and of itself placed a massive strain on the Romanian economy, overburdening the service system, the supply of housing, and infrastructure in urban areas.

The social effects of such an intense population shift were just as severe. Rural immigrants very quickly came to outnumber established city dwellers (Measnicov, Hristache, and Trebici 1977: 66–73). The influx of poorly educated and disproportionately young male immigrants apparently had a significant negative impact on efforts to socialize the urban population in the ethics of the socialist working class. Fear that the established proletariat, such as it was, would be swamped by newcomers was (and is) expressed in frequent comments about the "peasantization of the working class." The political leadership's preoccupation with the problems of successfully integrating such large numbers into new occupations and into the urban social milieu was expressed both in official statements, and in the appearance of a substantial sociological literature on the subject in the mid-1960s (Sandu 1985; Teodorescu 1985).

Simultaneously, a second important consequence of the industrial transformation made itself felt at a higher level of the social structure in the presence of increasing numbers of highly skilled technical, administrative, and cultural elites. The cultivation of these groups was an essential element in promoting continued economic progress, and was treated as a priority issue by the RCP. The importance attributed to improving the skill level of the work force was emphasized in numerous statements by the leadership, and confirmed by the substantial investments allocated to education at all levels, along with a steady increase in the number of graduates (*Anuarul Statistic* 1980: 536–37; 548–49; Gilberg 1975a: 99–118).

Like rural-urban migration, elite growth and diversification were intrinsic to economic modernization. But this presented an even more troublesome political challenge, as was recognized by the Ceausescu leadership. The broad outlines of the phenomenon's genesis are clearly indicated by a variety of statistical data which was beginning to accumulate at the time. The proportion of the active population employed in occupations classified as intellectuals and officials had reached approximately 13 percent by the early 1960s (Traistaru 1975: 64). The total number of those who had achieved higher education climbed to 328,241 by 1966, an increase of 58 percent in only ten years (Measnicov 1977: 170). The number of students enrolled in universities had in the meantime more than doubled, from slightly over 53,000 in 1950 to over 130,000 in 1965 (*Anuarul Statistic* 1980: 544–45). According to census data over 289,000 of these personnel with higher education were employed in the national economy by 1966, and the number of those with intermediate levels of qualification had risen even more rapidly (*Recensamintul* 1966: 722).

A more detailed evaluation of the implications of this postrevolutionary societal transformation is possible on the basis of data provided by Honorina Cazacu's large-scale analysis of intergenerational social mobility, carried out in 1969 (Cazacu 1974).[5] The study, which provides the only available detailed information on mobility in Romania for the period in question, traces the occupational status of individual families through four successive generations; that is, the respondents' grandparents, the respondents' parents, the respondents, and finally the respondents' children. This research strategy allowed Cazacu to capture an image of the social mobility pattern at three very different points in Romania's evolution. Data on all three generational transitions for the sample of active Bucharest respondents are summarized in Table 4.1. Among the first generation (respondents' grandparents), for example, the great majority, 72 percent, were either peasants or farm workers (Cazacu 1974: 91). Structural mobility (that is, social mobility associated with changes in the occupational structure from one generation to the next) from the first to the second generations was 32.4 percent. Total social mobility between the first two generations was 57.7 percent, but was limited primarily to movement from the peasantry into the working class (Cazacu 1974: 91–93).

The following generational transition (to those actively participating in the economy in 1969 from their parents) experienced the main force of the revolutionary transformation. Structural mobility increased to 53.6 percent, and total mobility to a remarkable 83 percent (Cazacu 1974: 94). Over half of the children of skilled and nonskilled workers in this generation moved upward in the occupational structure, while the places which they previously held in the urban working class were filled by new recruits from the countryside. If one considers only this generation, over 43 percent of the occupants of upper level positions in the economy originated from the working class, and approximately 25 percent were of peasant origin. But only 14 percent of those holding such positions came from intelligentsia family backgrounds themselves (Cazacu 1974: 94).

In the final generational transition analyzed, that between the urban respondents and their children, who were entering the work force as members of the

Table 4.1

Intergenerational social mobility of four generations within the same families of Bucharest respondents. Sample taken during 1969 among actively employed male heads of households over the age of 25.

	Gen I/ Gen II	Gen II/ Gen III	Gen III Gen IV
Total Mobility	50.7%	83.0%	60.0%
Structural Mobility	32.4%	53.6%	27.2%
Social Mobility (non-structural)	18.3%	29.4%	32.8%

first postrevolutionary generation, a clear decline in the pace of social mobility is evident. Total mobility dropped back to 60.2 percent, and structural mobility declined to 27.4 percent, indicating that the initial peak in the socialist transformation of Romania had passed, and that the social structure was beginning to stabilize.[6] This phenomenon is evident in Table 4.2, which provides a summary of the percentage of social self-reproduction (the percentage of respondents in a particular category whose parents were of the same social origin) among peasants, workers, intermediate level cadre, and intellectuals (for example, personnel in positions that required higher education), for each of the three transitions.

Cazacu (1974: 130) points out that throughout the transition, those with occupations requiring higher education have had the greatest success in passing on their status to their children. Thus as structural mobility declined, the rate of social mobility *into* intellectual occupations (while it remained relatively high) began dropping off as well. This finding conforms with Connor's (1979: 170) conclusion that inheritance of elite status is as common in the socialist countries as a group as it is among their Western counterparts. The decline of the flow of worker and peasant children into higher level occupations was partially attributable to normalization of the elite recruitment process. In particular it resulted from the decline of rapid social advancement based on political criteria common during the height of the revolutionary transformation.

As economic transition advanced, the demand for skilled personnel increased, and formal educational credentials necessarily became a crucial factor in determining entrance into high status occupations. This change in recruitment criteria is borne out in Cazacu's data. For the two groups in her sample most affected by the socialist transformation (respondents who had retired by the time of the survey in 1969, and the parents of currently active respondents), the rate of social mobility is significantly greater than the rate of educational mobility. Social mobility for the retired population was 69.4 percent, and educational mobility was 55.3 percent. The parents of respondents experienced an extremely high rate of total social mobility, 83 percent, and a somewhat increased level of educational mobility, 69 percent, as well. The distances between the two mobility figures for the groups are 14.1 and 14.0 percents respectively. But in the case of the children of the respondents analogous mobility rates were 60.2 percent for social mobility, and 56.7 percent for educational mobility. The gap between the two figures had declined markedly, to only 3.5 percent, indicating the increasing role played by educational attainment in social mobility (Cazacu 1974: 188).

Similar conclusions concerning the growing tendency of social reproduction at the upper levels of society in Romania through the mechanism of the educational system are indicated by other researchers as well. In a nationwide study of students carried out in 1969, sociologists noted that while peasants and workers made up over 85 percent of the active population, their children filled only 47 percent of the positions available for students in universities. Intellectuals and officials, on the other hand, constituted only 7 percent of the general population, but their offspring made up 22.8 percent of the university student body. Thus while upward access remained open for the most able of the worker and peasant children, downward mobility for the offspring of the intelligentsia was obviously quite limited. Additionally, students with intelligentsia backgrounds

Table 4.2

Social self-reproduction of peasants, workers, the intermediate cadre, and intellectuals, for three generational transitions (combined urban and rural samples).[7]

	Gen I/ Gen II	Gen II/ Gen III	Gen III Gen IV
Peasants	96.16%	95.95%	58.62%
Workers	19.38%	26.99%	45.71%
Mid-level Cadre	70.00%	20.30%	52.31%
Intellectuals	26.09%	14.61%	32.99%

were found to be concentrated in the most prestigious universities and faculties while those of worker/peasant origin were relegated to the academic periphery (Cinca et al. 1973: 44-45, 51). Thus it appears clear that, as Lane (1982: 115) suggested following his survey of data concerning the state-socialist countries as a whole, "[t]he educational system to some extent operates to negate the political ideals of equality."[8]

Despite the fact that this new socialist intelligentsia was spawned by its own policies, the Romanian Communist Party leadership was uneasy with the emerging situation. Its anxiety was undoubtedly increased by the rapidity with which the new professionals assimilated the attitudes and customs of the pre-revolutionary intellectual elite. In prewar Romania, as in the rest of Eastern Europe, extraordinarily high prestige was attributed to the members of the cultural intelligentsia; philosophers, historians, writers, and artists. This tradition continued to be characteristic of the postrevolutionary generation, as did their predecessors' disdain for manual occupations, regardless of the needs of the national economy and the ideological predisposition of the new rulers toward more technical professions. Consequently, the new intelligentsia (even those who were themselves occupied in technical or administrative positions) attempted both to replicate the cultured life-style of the old elite and, whenever possible, to place their offspring in humanities faculties, which would legitimate their status as members of "better" families.[9]

Thus by the middle of the 1960s members of the population occupying technological and professional roles were both reproducing themselves in increasing numbers and also emerging as a distinct element within the society. As the comparative research suggests, this pattern of consolidation among the professional strata was by no means anomalous among state-socialist countries as a whole (Connor 1979; Horvat 1982: 70-83; Lane 1982). According to Connor's study Romania is most remarkable for its significantly lower rates of downward mobility from the intelligentsia into other social categories. Connor argues that this phenomenon is not immediately explicable on the basis of any peculiarity of Romanian society, and suggests that it is probably attributable to the nature of Cazacu's sample data (Connor 1979: 127-29). While these reservations are warranted, it also appears likely that Romanian elite parents' success in transferring their status is a consequence of the extraordinary effort they bring to bear on preparing their children to face the selection process. Although no conclusive data on the question is available, informal discussions suggest that the higher rate of status transferal is also partially the result of mores which are quite accepting of informal corruption. This permissive environment enables higher status Romanians to circumvent the formally impartial selection process with greater ease than their colleagues elsewhere in Eastern Europe.[10] In light of the corroborating evidence provided by data on access to the educational system and discussions with Romanian researchers familiar with the topic, it therefore seems safe to accept the general validity of the picture presented above.

During the leadership transition of the mid-1960s, then, Romania was entering the first stages of a developmental crisis already in evidence in more advanced socialist countries. An overburdened central planning mechanism and the lack of production incentives to workers, an inevitable side effect of extremely high rates of accumulation, were causing the country to drift into stagnation. Meanwhile, privileged class formation along the lines described in Chapter 1 was beginning to occur as well. The attitude of the RCP leaders toward this new social force, recruited to carry out the tasks of industrial development, which they themselves promoted as a crucial national goal, was at best one of ambivalence. The political strategy formulated by the Ceausescu leadership and designed to meet these twin challenges proved to be a crucial determinant of the future evolution of the entire political system.

THE IDEOLOGICAL ROOTS OF NATIONAL COMMUNISM

During his early years as RCP leader, Nicolae Ceausescu acted consistently to create for himself the ideological coloration of a reformer with strong liberalizing (in the East European context) tendencies. A concerted effort was made to curry the favor of the intelligentsia by indicating publicly that under his leadership the creative autonomy of artists and academics would be respected. The most renowned statements of this sort were made in meetings with writers and artists held in 1965. The same attitudes were clearly expressed in Ceausescu's report to the Ninth Congress of the Romanian Communist Party in July 1965, and in an interview given to a group of Italian journalists in June the following year (Ceausescu 1968: 92-95; 488-89). In addition to these more or less symbolic actions, a variety of concrete steps were taken to redress abuses by the security services that had occurred under his predecessor. As early as May 1965 purge victims began to be rehabilitated, and they continued to be returned to their homes over the next several years.

The liberal strain in Ceausescu's behavior reached its apex at the time of his attack on Gheorghiu-Dej in April 1968 for deviation from Party norms during the Stalin years. Open renunciation of the Dej legacy first occurred during a discussion of the rehabilitation of purged Party members, which led up to Ceausescu's main offensive against his political opponents (Ceausescu 1969 3: 163-95). While one may doubt that these moves had any more substantial motive, they did create an image of Ceausescu as a moderate leader and served to distinguish him from the old guard. This facade afforded obvious advantages in his confrontation with Draghici, who was vulnerable as a result of his role in the security apparatus during the Dej years, and also with leaders of the generation that had participated at the highest decision-making levels during the Stalinist period. In addition to clearing Ceausescu's own record with regard to persecution of fellow communists (at least as far as the official Party history is concerned) the denunciation also served to repudiate any link between the new leadership and the foreign policies pursued by Dej during the period of Romania's subservience to the Soviet Union.

A second tendency which appeared early in Ceausescu's career was the promotion of mass participation, if not mass democracy. Unlike the short-lived liberalism described above, this populist stance proved quite durable, and has since evolved into one of the constituent elements of the contemporary Romanian ideological system. Ceausescu became very active in carrying out tours of inspection to all parts of the country. Through these "flying" visits he apparently sought, with some success, to establish personal links between himself and the rank and file of the population. This tactic also enabled him to check directly on actual implementation of centrally mandated policy at the local level, indicating a distrust of mid-level party and state administrators that was to become more pronounced in later years.

The new General Secretary's statements on the desirability of mass participation within the socialist political order differed sharply from the "vanguard party" attitude of his predecessor, and raised the citizenry's hopes that the regime would undergo a basic change under his direction. In particular he called for more openness to criticism of shortcomings at all levels of the Party. The following statement, made at the time of the inauguration of Romania's revised constitution, is typical of the attitudes he expressed.

In Socialism the masses participate in the activities of leading the affairs of the state. As we progress along the path of perfecting the socialist construction the participation of those who work in the resolution of problems of social life is expanded, and socialist democracy increases. There has developed in the activity of the Party and state a practice of popular consultation on the most important problems of domestic and international policy, in the elaboration of the national economic development plan, of support for all actions undertaken on the creative initiative of millions of working people. This is a proof of the force and vitality of our socialist system, of the close relations between Party and people.

Beginning with the growing role of social and public organizations in our society, the constitution assures the citizen's right of association in unions, in cooperative, youth, womens' and social cultural associations, in creative unions, and in scientific and technical associations. The state supports the activity of mass and community organizations . . . it assures the broad participation of the masses in political, social, and economic life, and in the exercise of public control. It mobilizes them in the struggle for the perfection of socialist construction. ("Raport Cu Privire La Proiectul De Constitutie A Republicii Socialiste Romania," Ceausescu 1968: 126–27)

Various concrete steps were taken to increase the appearance of popular participation. Among other organizational innovations the role of the Grand National Assembly (GNA) and its Standing Commissions was enhanced with the intention of increasing popular input in legislation (Fischer 1977: 226). Similar alterations were made in the Popular Councils at the *Judets* and local levels in order to open new channels of communication between the population and the state. In party affairs, the Ninth RCP Congress in 1965 saw admission requirements dramatically eased in an attempt to broaden the social base of the membership (Congresul al IX-lea 1966). In addition to these changes in the country's political institutions, a major reorganization of the economy was introduced which, like other reforms at the time, was depicted in part as an attempt to enhance local autonomy with respect to central planners, and to strengthen collective decision making at the enterprise level (see Ceausescu's "Report Concerning the Measures for Perfecting the Management and Planning of the National Economy," 1969: 471–571).

The extent to which the putative commitment to popular democracy symbolized by these and similar measures has since been realized in Romanian social life is questionable at best. The fact remains, however, that such ideas were welcomed by the populace in the late 1960s and taken as a serious indication of intent. Ceausescu's pose as "champion of the common man" gained him widespread appeal throughout the transition period and afterwards. Populism thus represented a significant feature in Ceausescu's overall political strategy from early in the transition years and, unlike his flirtation with other reformist ideals, appears to be one to which he had some genuine, if limited, attachment.

A final area of ideological activity in which Ceausescu carried out significant initiatives during this period concerns revision of the Party's theoretical interpretation of the nation, and its attitude toward Romanian national independence. In contrast to his break with the Dej pattern in espousing liberalization and increased participation, in this sphere his predecessor's policies were intensified rather than contradicted. Ceausescu opened his renationalization campaign on the symbolic level almost immediately after assuming office in May 1965 by rechristening the Romanian Workers Party to the present Romanian Communist Party, followed by changing the name of the state from the Romanian People's Republic to the Romanian Socialist Republic in July of the same year. Both modifications were intended as a signal (to both internal and external audiences) that the RCP was claiming a status for Romania essentially equal to that of the Soviet Union. At approximately the same time the preamble to the Romanian Constitution was amended to include a strong statement of national sovereignty. In public speeches made in the course of his extensive tours of the country Ceausescu took an unprecedentedly antagonistic tone toward the U.S.S.R., and his attitude encouraged others to do likewise (Ceausescu 1968: 426-31; Shafir 1985: 52). The intent of these and similar innovations was clearly to indicate to the population that their new leader would pursue a strategy designed to enhance Romania's independence from the Soviet Union.

In addition to strengthening Dej's policy of implicit national independence, under Ceausescu the RCP almost immediately began to break new ground in its theoretical statements concerning the nature of the nation. The General Secretary's May 1966 address on the occasion of the 45th anniversary of the founding of the Romanian Communist Party included a series of statements on the relationship between socialism and nationalism, typical of the Party's new position, and sufficiently significant to deserve reproduction in some length:

Socialism carries forward the process of national development begun in the bourgeois epoch, it creates conditions in which the national life of the people can be completely affirmed. The socialist revolution, the construction of the new social system unfetters all the creative energies of the people. It constitutes in the life of every country an epoch of national reawakening, of vigorous affirmation of the patriotic sentiments of the broad masses. The slogan of multilateral flourishing (*infloririi*) of the socialist fatherland, formulated by the communist party, mobilizes the strength of the working people, it constitutes a significant factor in the progress of the people. Without doubt the nation will still for a long time continue to constitute the base of development of our society in the entire period of building socialism and communism. (Ceausescu 1968: 397)

Socialism and communism are not a rigid scheme, a pattern in which the reality of social life is compelled to enter. The superiority of the new, socialist, system exists in the fact that it is constructed on the basis of the highest science, which begins from the knowledge of objective laws of social development, from the demands of each stage of social life, from the national particularities of each people and each country, taking into account the different conditions in which each nation was formed and developed. The construction of socialism and communism is the expression of the will of each people, of their vital interests and aspirations—in this is constituted the invincibility of the new system, its strength and durability of granite.

National and international communism do not exist; communism is at the same time national and international. Socialism is not an abstract notion; it has become a reality in 14 countries, and other people are moving toward socialism. Each people constructing socialism, fulfills a national task and at the same time an international task, contributing to the general progress of humanity toward socialism. Communism is not directed against a single people. Communism is opposed only to capitalism, not to peoples who will arrive early or later at communism. (Ceausescu 1968: 402)

Life shows that no one can understand economic relations, the rapport and disposition of the class forces in one country or another, the internal and international political situation, and the evolution of these, better than the communist party, the revolutionary and patriotic force of the respective country. Therefore the right to formulate a political line, the revolutionary strategy and tactics of the working class, the methods of struggle, applying in a creating way the general truths of Marxism-Leninism belongs exclusively to [the Communist Party of the country in question]. This right cannot be the object of any dispute, each communist party being responsible to the working class to which it belongs, and to its own people. (Ceausescu 1968: 407)

This reinterpretation of orthodox Soviet Marxism was something that Gheorghiu-Dej, because of his long and undeniable commitment to Stalinism, had been unable (or unwilling) to undertake. Ceausescu, for his part, proved much less restrained. In these and similar statements he explicitly linked the Communist Party with the fulfillment of *national* aspirations through the construction of socialism. The RCP was shown to be the highest expression of the Romanian national tradition, and the General Secretary went so far as to appeal in speeches to the authority of such unorthodox figures as the nineteenth century liberal hero, Nicolae Balcescu. After 1965 the RCP began to be consistently represented in official communications as a vehicle of Romanian popular self-affirmation. As George Schopflin has argued, Romanian Party leaders recognized that "Marxism-Leninism alone had been insufficient to mobilize the creative energies of the nation fully; but coupled organically with nationalism, with the two ideologies reinforcing one another, the Party was thereby placed in a remarkably powerful position to mobilize the nation more intensively than any of its predecessors" (Schopflin 1974: 93). Given the intensity of Romanian nationalist sentiment, its lack of fulfillment in the interwar years, and its total frustration during the Stalinist period, such an appeal inevitably struck a responsive chord in a large segment of the population.

The post-1965 RCP strategy of promoting a new rapport between the communist state and the society on the basis of nationalism was particularly expedient because of its highly integrative character. The new wave of Romanian patriotism was regarded as an attractive development by virtually all social strata. It appears to have been perceived by Ceausescu and his supporters as a mechanism which could be employed to unite disparate social forces more or less automatically without the need for any intense manipulative effort on the part of the state (Chirot 1978: 490-91; Jowitt 1971: 273-92).

The more open culture policy of the late 1960s was thus pursued on the presumption that members of the intelligentsia could be enlisted wholeheartedly in the Party cause on the basis of a patriotic appeal, and would of their own volition limit themselves to supportive activity. By merely encouraging them to create works expressing the patriotic sentiments of the Romanian people, Ceausescu made significant headway in his approach to the intellectuals (Ceausescu 1968: 93). When one considers that not many years previously, the mere singing of the prerevolutionary national anthem could be punished by a long term of imprisonment, it becomes understandable why this change in attitude was perceived as an important advance. Ceausescu, as Jowitt (1971: 285-92) suggests, deliberately linked promotion of nationalism with liberalization in an attempt to assimilate technical and cultural elites on the basis of their attachment to the national cause. Substantial credibility was added to this reconciliation attempt through the simultaneous introduction of a campaign to bring large numbers of the intelligentsia into the RCP, without the previous concern shown for possible bourgeois background; and through efforts to increase the intellectual standards of the existing membership (King 1980: 80, 104-5; Shafir 1985: 88). According to data collected by Fischer (1979: 10), through both recruitment and politically motivated recategorization, the number of intellectuals within the Party was increased from 145,000 to 330,000 just between July and December 1965.

The regime's appeal to the peasantry and rapidly growing worker/peasant population in the cities was much more direct. A massive propaganda campaign was introduced with the unmistakable intention of establishing a firm link in the popular consciousness between support for the RCP and hostility toward the nation's traditional foes. Among the most widely noted (and eloquent) of the methods employed for this purpose were staged meetings at public festivities between Ceausescu and actors portraying the most admired of Romania's legendary heroes, Michael the Brave and Stephen the Great (Shafir 1985: 52). The identification between the current heroic leader and those of the past could hardly be missed by even the most unsophisticated spectator.

Telling as they are in themselves, such reenactments are but one aspect of a much more widespread effort enlisting the services of all of the country's institutions of mass socialization. Other Party activities included the en masse "rehabilitation of historical and cultural figures associated with the struggle for independence," and a nearly unmatched process of historical reinterpretation designed to capitalize on preexisting popular attitudes concerning Romania's past. The intensity of popular response to the post-Dej nationalist renaissance was apparently even greater than its initiators anticipated. The upwelling of xenophobia that it provoked was sufficiently disturbing to elicit unwelcome comparisons with the interwar years among those who followed Romanian affairs, causing the RCP to moderate its efforts following 1968 (Brown 1969: 14).

The role played by Ceausescu's response to the 1968 Soviet occupation of Czechoslovakia in shaping this ideological redirection can hardly be overestimated. At the same time, it serves to epitomize the ideological developments of the transition period. In the months preceding the crisis Romanian leaders attempted to play a conciliatory role between more hard line communist parties and Czechoslovak reformers. Like Tito, Ceausescu traveled to Prague to show support for the Dubcek government. When mediation efforts failed Romania was the only Warsaw Pact member that refused to participate in the August 20 invasion. Ceausescu denounced the Soviets' action in the strongest possible terms, referring to the incident as "a shameful moment in the history of the workers' movement" (quoted in Cioranescu 1969: 2). In a massive Bucharest rally he denounced the occupation as a "flagrant violation of the sovereignty of a fraternal socialist country" and intimated that faced with a similar situation, the Romanians would fight to defend their independence (Ceausescu, 1969 3: 382-85). Amid widespread rumors of Soviet troop movements on the border peoples' militia units, the Patriotic Guards were reestablished and regular army troops were placed on alert.

This single public act in defense of national independence by Ceausescu was worth more than a thousand words could have been in less trying circumstances. Whether a serious threat of Soviet intervention in Romania actually existed in the wake of August 1968 is questionable. There is no doubt, however, that the vast majority of the population perceived the threat as being real and believed that Ceausescu's policy of open defiance was crucial in averting a renewed Soviet occupation of their homeland. This show of resolve added a necessary element of "content" to the nationalist "form" which had become evident in the Party elite's propaganda efforts, and played a vital part in convincing the population of the credibility of the RCP's nationalist appeal.

Party leaders were quick to follow up on the opportunities thus presented by driving home their message of social solidarity. New mass organizations (including the Socialist Unity Front) were created, and efforts to enact the participatory reforms of the previous years were intensified. Consequently the popularity (or at least popular acceptance) of the RCP attained a postwar peak. Perhaps just as importantly, the experience of 1968 appears to have convinced Ceausescu of the nationalist appeal's efficacy not just in the service of the Party as an institution, but as a means of legitimating his own unique role as the leader of the nation. The identification of a strong ruler with the will of the people was entirely in keeping with the tradition of Romanian popular culture. Combined with the added attraction presented by the image of a determined (one is tempted to suggest regal) leader standing between the threatened people and their external enemies, it became nearly irresistible, even for those who otherwise had no sympathy for the RCP's system of government.[11]

The early Ceausescu years were thus characterized by flirtation with several (sometimes contradictory) ideological themes. The RCP's reformism was analogous to similar tendencies exhibited during leadership transitions in other East European states, and was clearly designed to attract the support of nonparty elites during a period of relative leadership insecurity. Liberalism and populism both appear to have been intended to appeal to select audiences; the growing technical and cultural intelligentsia, and the previously unrepresented worker and peasant masses, who had for the past two decades been little more than the objects of the RCP leaders' developmental program.

The generally positive and hopeful impression created in Romania and abroad by the initiatives undertaken in the late 1960s is epitomized by Stephen Fischer-Galati's evaluation at the height of the transition period:

Ceausescu's "New Romania" is the Romania of a representative but all-powerful Communist Party. . . . The rejuvenation of the Party apparatus, the rendering of the principle of democratic centralism into a meaningful political process, and, perhaps most significantly, reconciliation of all social and national groups in the construction of a sovereign, prosperous, and respected Romania, albeit under the strict direction of the Communist Party, represents the quintessence of Ceausescu's political philosophy. (Fischer-Galati 1967: 115–16)

Yet, quite the contrary to this outwardly positive trend of events, forces were already at work within the society that precipitously altered the outlook for a progressive social evolution in Romania. In the struggle to contend with the domestic and international challenges facing it, the political leadership that consolidated around Ceausescu during the transition period selectively eliminated several of the progressive tendencies noted above. Others, which proved most compatible with policy directions pursued by the Party, were reinforced and emerged as the ideological foundation of the established Ceausescu regime. In order to understand better the nature of the transformation which occurred during these years, it is necessary to turn now to the question of Romania's economic direction in the late 1960s, and its relationship to the country's political system.

THE ECONOMIC CHOICES OF THE LATE 1960s

The initial post-Dej policy decisions in the economic realm appear to have been intended to serve a dual purpose. First, the RCP elite committed itself to retain, or even strengthen, the primacy of heavy industry as the unchallenged leading economic sector, and to continue to direct activity through the established central planning mechanism. Repeated statements to this effect were utilized to create a sense of continuity with the development policies of the late Dej years. This served to reassure mid-level party and state administrators that their positions and perquisites would remain unimpaired, and was characteristic of the coalition building tactics of the transition period. (See, for example, Ceausescu's address to the IXth Congress of the RCP on these topics, in Ceausescu 1968: 20-31, 56-58.)

While the fundamental direction of development was thus reaffirmed, steps were also undertaken to expand the base of support for the Party and its policies among those favoring reform. Ceausescu opened the way for debate on the possibility of making adjustments within the existing framework, in order to improve the lot of previously disadvantaged groups. Initially discussion focused on suggestions for moderating the pace of growth and rectifying the sectoral balances within the economy in favor of consumer goods and agricultural production (Ceausescu 1968: 31-43; Montias 1967: 79; Spigler 1973: 7). The envisioned alterations in priorities would have ameliorated difficulties created by the previous years of taut planning and facilitated an increase in the level of consumption. It can therefore be assumed that they were generally welcomed by the population, if not by industrial managers and central planners.

Along with discussion of macrolevel adjustments in the national economy, the political leadership also held out the possibility of significant (and long overdue) institutional innovations.[12] In particular, reformers called for improvement of the system of plan indicators, for limited administrative decentralization, and for more emphasis on collective decision making by managers at all levels of the industrial structure (Ceausescu 1968: 56-58, 510-45). This facet of the transitional policy mix, introduced in conjunction with Ceausescu's liberalizing reforms in the political sphere, constituted a clear appeal to members of the mid-level technical elite which constituted a significant element of the emerging privileged class. Had the reforms been enforced such individuals would have achieved more independence and enhanced possibilities for material gain.

After nearly two years of debate and popular anticipation the reform program finally saw the light of day in late 1967 (*Directivele* 1967). As initially proposed, the Central Committee's 1967 Economic Directives were most notable for their plan to create very large semiautonomous industrial associations (*Centrale*). These institutions would assume much of the decision-making authority previously wielded by the nearly omnipotent central economic ministries. Furthermore, the RCP Central Committee was slated to be removed one step from direct control over plan formulation, which was to be left under the guidance of the Council of Ministers. Party leaders were henceforward to restrict themselves to large scale and long term planning. Other rationalizing measures called for in the Directives included significant improvements in the wage and banking systems intended to improve production incentives, the consolidation of plan indicators, and improvement of the provision of material supplies to enterprises through decentralization of the existing supply system (Smith 1980: 38–40; Spigler 1973: 39–43).

In essence these efforts amounted to a technical modification of the central planning system similar to those implemented in the GDR and the Soviet Union (Borstein 1977: 112). If successful, they may have constituted a first step for Romania in surmounting the well known dilemma of making the transition from extensive to intensive growth by increasing managerial initiative (for a discussion of the problems involved see Brus 1975). Had the promise of increased managerial autonomy and institutional pluralization evident in the reform program been fulfilled, it is quite likely that the Romanian political economy would have evolved in a direction more consistent with that seen in the other CMEA nations. It did not, however, live up to expectations.

From their first introduction, the measures proposed by the RCP in 1967 were subject to stiff opposition from at least two powerful forces in Romanian society. Not surprisingly, those in control of the Central Economic Ministries were quick to perceive a threat to their interests in the proposal to establish the new economic associations. They labored to the extent of their abilities to restrain implementation of the program. Second, Party hard-liners, despite the fact that they showed little sympathy for their colleagues in the state administration, were skeptical concerning the reforms for reasons of their own. In particular the devolution of even limited authority to mid-level elites which would almost necessarily accompany a program of economic decentralization was a key focus of their concern.

Ceausescu himself appears to have supported merely technical reform insofar as this promised to improve administrative efficiency and to spur industrial development. But once reform was perceived as a move toward relinquishing the central leadership's direct control over the economy to the benefit of nonparty elites, his attitude became increasingly hostile. By the end of the decade the General Secretary was clearly moving toward the position of Party dogmatists. Thus even as the final effort was unleashed to overcome ministerial resistance and implement the economic reorganization, Ceausescu was simultaneously initiating the first of his many attacks on the intelligentsia and remolding the reform program into a weapon against the administrative elite.

Consequently, as they were finally introduced in 1969 (at which point the reform was already two years overdue) the industrial associations were little more than an intermediary administrative unit implementing instructions whose formulation remained firmly in the hands of the central ministries (Borstein 1977: 133-14; Spigler 1973: 53-71). In each of the other areas of proposed reform only those changes which did not undermine existing power relations were ever actually implemented. The partial or complete abandonment of material balancing that would have to accompany any fundamental reorganization of the economy was never even openly considered. Thus despite some reorganization, and continual propagandistic statements concerning the progress of the new system, the Romanian economy remained one of the most tightly controlled among the socialist states. Furthermore, the beginning of the 1970s saw de facto abandonment of reform, and initiatives toward increased, not decreased, centralization.

Even while this flirtation with limited planning and administrative reforms was taking place, a more general debate was underway within the RCP concerning the pace and direction of development. This ultimately proved decisive for the economy, and to a certain extent reduced innovations in the former areas to irrelevance. It was of critical importance that, as the 1960s came to a close, the dispute over economic strategy was resolved in favor of a new readjustment of sectoral balances that benefited heavy industry, and precipitous resumption of the development drive which had been allowed to slack off in the preceding plan period. This unexpected change in direction was presaged by upward revision in mid-1966 of 1966-1970 production indicators that had been established only the year before. The scope of plan increases was substantial. According to the revised directive the average yearly industrial growth rate was to be 11.6 percent instead of an initially projected 10.5 percent, while that of agriculture was increased from 3.5 to 5.9 percent (Montias 1967: 79-80). Decision makers' confidence in the economy was such that the newly mandated production increases were to be carried out concurrently with a sizeable hike in the standard of living, including increases in the consumption fund and in the level of retail sales above those called for in the plan (already substantially increased in the original 1964 draft).

In part the political elite's conviction that the pace of industrialization could successfully be escalated to this degree was linked to unexpectedly large increases in agricultural output experienced in 1965 (Spigler 1973: 7; Montias 1967: 80, n. 190). Substantial gains in grain production in that year were apparently attributed to the success of initiatives undertaken to improve conditions in the rural sector since the completion of collectivization in 1962. This windfall, if it had proved constant, would have provided a welcome increase in available resources. But given the equally dramatic decline in production in the succeeding year it clearly would have been more prudent of planners to credit farmers' successes to the vagaries of the climate, at least until a more definite pattern was established. One can assume, however, that a policy change as extensive as that of 1966 was not undertaken exclusively on the basis of one year's agricultural output alone. It is far more likely, particularly in light of events of the following several years, that forces supporting intensification of the pace of industrialization were already at work within the leadership, and that the fortuitous bumper crop was employed as the rationale for pursuing a policy course which was already favorably regarded.

Whatever their motivation, the decisions concerning the rate of industrialization undertaken in 1966 had definite ramifications with respect to the structure of the economy as it evolved through the remainder of the six-year plan period and afterward. In essence, the economy was thrust back into the syndrome of high rates of investment and overly taut planning, which had characterized the previous phase of extensive growth (see, for example, the data compiled on long-term economic trends by Tsantis and Pepper 1979: 77–87). The leaders who formulated Romania's renewed development drive proposed to increase industry's capability to such an extent that it could efficiently supply the technical inputs necessary for rapid and simultaneous expansion of agricultural production. The added margin of agricultural output would then be employed both to increase the standard of living (providing higher production incentives for workers) and to supply the foreign exchange necessary to pay for technology imports required to spur further industrialization (Montias 1967: 81).

By the end of the plan period this strategy had run into serious difficulties, primarily (but not entirely) due to underfulfillment in agriculture. Yet the setbacks experienced by managers as the plan progressed were not allowed to diminish the growth rate called for in the high priority producer goods sector. In fact, far from faltering like the rest of the economy, by the end of the period the so-called Group A industries had overfulfilled their performance target, exhibiting an annual growth pace of approximately 12.7 percent instead of the 11 percent originally called for (*Anuarul Statistic* 1980: 88; Montias 1967: 80). In order to achieve this feat planners offset failures in productivity by boosting the level of investment. During the course of the plan period the rate of accumulation (which the Party leadership had originally committed itself to moderating) was increased to over 30 percent, in contrast to the 28.5 percent called for in the already accelerated version of the six-year plan (Spigler 1973: 9, 25). Other less favored areas necessarily had to bear the burden of decreased investment. Neither consumer goods production nor the standard of living rose according to plan projections.

It is apparent from the nature of these decisions that, despite its rhetoric of social accommodation, as the end of the 1960s approached the RCP leadership was already recommitting itself to an essentially Stalinist economic strategy, well before analogous tendencies became visible in its political program. As problems developed in the over ambitious 1966–1970 plan alterations were consistently made in favor of heavy industry at the expense of both light industry and consumption. Resolution of the controversy surrounding initial formulation of the 1971–1975 Fifth Five-Year plan, which apparently became the focus of opposition to the Ceausescu leadership's overall strategy, confirms this supposition.

According to the directives laid down in August 1969 at the RCP's Tenth Congress the pace of industrialization was not only to be maintained, but accelerated. Investment rates were once again slated to rise and the priority of producer goods was retained despite the contradictions already becoming apparent in the 1966–1970 plan. Wages and retail sales, however, were assigned a slower rate of growth than in the preceding five year period (Tsantis and Pepper 1979: 87-88). The trend toward "remobilization," as Marvin Jackson has termed the Romanian economic course of the 1970s, thus became increasingly obvious as Ceausescu consolidated his political position and gained control over the policy process, bringing the transition period to a close.

CONCLUSION

The 1965–1970 period of leadership consolidation was critical to the evolution of a divergent Romanian variant of state-socialism. The available evidence indicates that by the mid-1960s the country was facing a transition crisis of the sort seen in virtually all of the East European CMEA countries at analogous points in their development. Whether the determinant factor in these crises is considered to be political (Johnson 1970; Gitelman 1970) or economic (Brus 1975; Borstein 1973; Hohmann 1979; Bunce 1985), there is growing agreement among analysts that the process of state-socialist development in itself generates social tensions which impel restructuring that has both economic and political implications.

In Romania the aging of the revolution was evidenced by changes in both the economic and social environments. Even before Dej's demise industrialization had begun to falter as the marginal return on new inputs into the economy declined. The problems facing RCP leaders by the mid-1960s were to a certain extent more severe than those of the other East Europeans as a consequence of the intensity and duration of their development campaign, and their relatively weak and unsophisticated planning facilities. Concurrently with the onset of this economic slowdown, the RCP was confronted with the political complications of increasing social complexity induced by modernization. Development meant not just massive expansion of the urban industrial work force, but also the emergence of a diverse stratum of technicians, managers, and cultural professionals. Recruited from a variety of sources, this first generation of this new socialist intelligentsia was clearly beginning to undergo a process of consolidation, and to successfully pass its newly won status on to a successor generation. While as yet inchoate, its members potentially formed the basis of a privileged class similar to that which was emerging under similar conditions in other parts of Eastern Europe.

Initially Ceausescu and his supporters cautiously avoided taking steps to deal with these problems which might have destabilized the domestic political environment. Until their initially tenuous grip on the Romanian state was more firmly established, they pursued a course of policy compromise. In particular the population was led to believe that moderation of the pace of industrialization and reforms in the spirit of the more advanced socialist economies were in the offing. Ceausescu made a concerted effort to appeal to the extended intelligentsia, criticizing the RCP's past dogmatism, and calling for more open cultural expression.

It is evident in retrospect that this posture was little more than an expedient subterfuge designed to counter the appeals of more genuine moderates within the Party, and gain the time needed to consolidate control over the levers of power. As this was accomplished changes began to appear in Ceausescu's policy orientation that were to become more pronounced in the succeeding period. The shape of things to come was most evident in the direction taken by economic policy. The early promise of relaxation faded into memory as plan indicators were ratcheted upward through a succession of decisions by high level Party leaders. When increasing output proved incompatible with reform, reform was sacrificed, and the possibility of a strategy of political accommodation collapsed along with it.

Thus the RCP leaders' commitment to the pursuit of an essentially Stalinist developmental course by the end of the 1960s cannot be seriously questioned. As the transition period progressed, the contradictions among the various incompatible policies espoused by Ceausescu during his consolidation struggle were consistently resolved in favor of remobilization. Accumulation at the levels required by a renewed industrialization foreclosed the possibility of a policy founded on increased consumer legitimacy. Effective utilization of the massive new capital investments that were deemed necessary to construct the foundation of multilateral development demanded tighter central control, not devolution of authority to either enterprise managers or workers councils. Consequently the opening of the new decade saw Romania not on the path to developed socialism, but rather entering the "Ceausescu Epoch."

5 NATIONAL COMMUNISM IN ROMANIA

INTRODUCTION

Pervasive party-state control over nonstate institutions and actors is considered, among Western analysts, a nearly axiomatic element of state-socialist political systems. Even in the literature focusing on the post-Stalin period a high degree of central political direction is assumed, and discussion proceeds from the perspective of a state-centric model. How, then, can it be argued that the Ceausescu regime differs significantly from its neighbors on the basis of its dominant role in the society? The answer to this question lies not just in the fact that the RCP is currently more repressive than other ruling communist parties, but in the nature of the relationship between the state, whose core it forms, and Romanian society.

Among other state-socialist countries a pattern of authoritarian politics has emerged in which party domination is combined with co-optation and limited representation of the interests of nonpolitical elites. This model, which preserves the role of final arbiter for party leaders, at the same time opens the way for partial depoliticization, and has become the basis of a formula for stable communist party rule. Under Ceausescu the Romanian political elite has thus far resisted taking a similar course. On the contrary, during the 1970s the circle of those sharing political power became increasingly restricted. Once this was accomplished, the RCP single-mindedly pursued an extensive development strategy that generated increasingly stressful conditions of life for a large part of the Romanian population. These parallel developments in the political and economic spheres are inextricably intertwined, and in fact cannot be adequately understood independent of one another.

REINFORCING PARTY/STATE HEGEMONY

During the early 1970s a variety of measures was employed to ensure the General Secretary's domination of all essential policy domains. Efforts to consolidate control over party and state institutions were typified by the introduction of cadres rotation and leadership unification. The practice of rotating Party leaders at all levels, initiated in February 1971, was utilized to shift personnel between central and local Party institutions, and from the Party to governmental administration. While ostensibly a measure to increase individuals' experience with various aspects of administration (*Scinteia* April 25, 1972; July 20, 1972), another prominent and hardly unintended consequence of recurrent rotation at the top of the political system has been to keep Ceausescu subordinates from amassing too much power through long term affiliation with any single institution. As a result of the introduction of this policy several strong figures close to the General Secretary in the early 1970s political constellation were removed from the center of power. King (1980: 96) links this initial period of reshuffling specifically to elimination of resistance within the administrative bureaucracy to the implementation of the 1971-1975 Five-Year Plan. But rather than abating once this was accomplished, extensive leadership reassignments under Ceausescu have been nearly continuous, and have occurred most rapidly during periods of political instability. According to data collected by Fischer (1980: 220-21) only five of 33 occupants of positions of ministerial rank remained unchanged between 1969 and 1973; and at least 13 central Party leaders were transferred from Bucharest to local posts between the formal announcement of the rotation program in 1971 and the end of 1973.

Institutional reforms were also employed to achieve concentration of authority at the summit of the Romanian political structure. In March 1974 plans were made to replace the Central Committee's Standing Presidium with a new and larger mixed party/state Buro. As originally described, this body was to include as ex officio members the RCP CC secretaries, and several high state officials. By the time of the 11th Party Congress in November 1974, however, a new alteration was decided upon. All members of the Buro were to be selected by, and from among, the membership of the Executive Committee (renamed the Political Executive Committee), a leadership body somewhat larger than the Standing Presidium and placed between it and the Central Committee. Ultimately only five individuals, all of them loyal adherents of the General Secretary, were actually chosen for the new ruling body (Fischer 1977: 224; Shafir 1985: 74). This combination of moves replaced the old Party Standing Presidium with a much smaller party/state body which could be more readily controlled by Ceausescu.

Similar party/state unification, or blending (*impletire*) in the Romanian political lexicon, at all levels of administration represents a second method utilized to enhance the Party elites' control over policy implementation. Blending has been carried out through two primary means; "plurality of office," and the creation of joint party/state administrations (King 1972). The widespread introduction of plurality of offices was presaged by Ceausescu's ascension to the post of President of the Council of State in 1967. At that time it was decided that the head of each *judets* (county) Party Committee should also hold the post of President of the *judets* Peoples Coupcil, and that similar unification of functions should be carried out on the local level. In 1972, not long after the inception of cadres rotation, party/state unification became more generalized, and in some cases was extended to include mass organizations as well.

The blending process was deepened through formation of joint party-government (and indeed party-government-mass organization) institutions. This aspect of the policy has been hailed as a significant ideological contribution by Romania for the promotion of the "organic integration of the party in social life," and was formalized through a directive of the National Conference of the RCP in July 1972 (Popescu 1983: 136–38). Unifying party and government activities was presented as a method of reducing administrative parallelisms and enhancing the efficiency of policy implementation, while the melding of mass organizations into the state was justified in theory as a means of increasing direct "unmediated" democracy. Among the most important of such combined party/state organizations are the Supreme Council on Socioeconomic Development (responsible to the State Council and the Council of Ministers), the Central Council for Workers Control of Economic and Social Activities, the National Council for Science and Technology, the Defense Council, and the Committee for Problems of Peoples Councils (King 1978: 495; S. Popescu 1983: 137–39).

Fusion of previously separate party and state hierarchies in this manner undoubtedly did reduce duplication of functions to a certain extent as indicated by Romanian commentators, but it just as certainly increased direct party control over formally nonparty organizations. As subsequent developments have amply demonstrated, its ultimate end was consolidation of party dominance over the state, and over public organizations (*organizatii obstesti*) and mass organizations. In essence, the combination of this blending with the cadres rotation policy has meant that RCP leaders directly held the top positions in all state institutions to a much greater degree than is the case in any of the other East European countries. Even by early 1973, 26 of the 54 highest government posts were occupied by individuals who were concurrently serving in the Party's guiding bodies (Gilberg 1974: 32).

Simultaneously with the restriction of the ruling circle by these means, a second institutional transformation, extension of the Party's penetration into the society, proceeded apace. The Romanian Communist Party's notable weakness during the interwar period, for example, its small size and lack of ties with the ethnic majority population, was substantially rectified during the Dej period. The early membership drive and subsequent purge of unreliable elements established a base membership comparable to that in the rest of Eastern Europe. Following the decision to diverge from the Soviet Union, however, membership began to increase anew as the leadership sought to enhance its legitimacy through more extensive popular participation. In particular, the early 1960s and the period immediately following the Czechoslovak crisis saw large influxes of new members. Despite some tapering off in the rate of admissions, the RCP continued to grow under Ceausescu even after 1968. The proportion of Romania's adult population enrolled in the Party increased from 13 to 20.9 percent between 1965 and 1975. By the mid-1980s over 15 percent of the total population (32.91 percent of the employed population), and 55.67 percent of workers were members, making the RCP the largest (proportionately) of the ruling communist parties (Nadelea 1985: 10). Comparative data collected by White (1986: 474-75) suggests the proportion of the RCP's membership drawn from the working class was matched only by the GDR, and further, that 80 percent of the RCP's new recruits were drawn from among the workers.

As the Romanian Communist Party grew during these years, it underwent a significant transformation. According to its own ideological conception, the RCP has ceased to be an organization of a few chosen and committed political operatives and has become "a party with a solid mass base, implanted organically in all of the cells of social life" (Ceausescu 1979: 68; Moldovan 1982: 178). It diverged significantly from the Soviet model common to the rest of Eastern Europe in this sense. In order to sustain such a large membership individuals in social catagories considered important by the leadership had to be "influenced" to become communists regardless of the actual sincerity of their political commitment. Consequently the Party can hardly be considered a vanguard institution any longer. Rather, as Fischer (1979: 16) has suggested, the contemporary Romanian Communist Party can best be understood as a hybrid of elite and mass institutions, and it has suffered from a certain amount of internal tension as a result of this mixed character.

CEAUSESCU AND THE MILITARY

Bucharest deviated from the East European pattern in the organization of civil/military relations as significantly as it did in other institutional realms.[1] This fact is hardly suprising, since maintaining control over the military and armed units of the Ministry of Interior is a more complex problem in Romania than elsewhere in Eastern Europe, and constitutes an area of special concern for the Ceausescu regime. Divergence from the Soviet Union left RCP leaders more dependent on the capability of their domestic armed forces than the rulers of any of the other CMEA countries. The nature of their predicament is twofold. First, ever since invasion of Czechoslovakia in 1968 there has been a widespread, but publicly unstated, agreement that the primary threat to Romania's independence derives from the Soviet Union, and that the army's primary defensive mission is to counter that threat. Far from being able to rely on their Soviet counterparts to intervene on their behalf, Ceausescu and his supporters clearly harbor grave doubts of their security in office should Soviet forces enter the country for any reason. Thus the RCP must ensure that the Romanian armed forces are prepared to carry out a defense role that is, to say the least, unique within the Warsaw Pact.

A second element of insecurity is caused by the RCP's self-imposed isolation from the country which is, realistically, its only likely source of support in case of domestic unrest. Romanian Party leaders are in no sense less resented than their counterparts elsewhere. They, however, must depend entirely on domestic repressive capabilities to contain internal dissent. The Romanian army and security forces must be prepared to suppress any counter regime manifestation on the part of the population without the expectation of Soviet assistance.

In order to meet their external mission and these internal security demands, the forces of the Ministries of Defense and Interior must be provided with sufficient personnel and equipment, and their morale must be maintained at a level adequate to ensure that these will be effectively deployed should the need arise. Yet the Romanian leaders face a serious dilemma, for while disengagement from the Soviet Union requires them to retain a strong coercive apparatus, it also leaves them more vulnerable than other East European elites to extraparty opponents with access to the means of physical violence. The RCP leaders must therefore retain a tight grip on possible adversaries within the military/security establishment who might under some circumstances be tempted to seize power through a coup d'état, particularly should they conclude that such action would be met with approbation from Moscow. They must also avoid the development of the armed forces into an institution powerful and influential enough to rival the role of the Communist Party.

In reaction to this situation Ceausescu acted consistently and in multiple directions to exert personal control over the crucial military and security bureaucracies. His potential for dealing with the Ministry of National Defense was greatly enhanced by the fact that he had served as Chief of the Higher Political Department from 1950 to 1954. In this capacity he served as the Party's highest representative in the armed forces, and played an important role in their postwar restructuring along Soviet lines. Beginning in 1965 a series of personnel changes were introduced which significantly increased the General Secretary's influence within the military. In August 1966 long time Minister of Defense Leontin Salajan died, leaving the top position in the armed forces open to be filled by a candidate amenable to the new Party leader. Salajan's position fell to Ion Ionita, whose relations with Ceausescu, if his record of promotion over the next several years is any indication, were quite congenial. Ion Gheorghe, who had close personal ties to Ceausescu, was made Deputy Minister of Defense and Chairman of the GNA Commission on Defense problems in March 1965, then named Chief of Staff of the Romanian Army in 1966.[2] Similar steps were taken to extend control over the Ministry of the Interior. Ceausescu's early rival for power, Alexandru Draghici, was replaced as Minister by Cormel Onescu in 1965. In 1967, Olt Judets First Secretary and Ceausescu familiar Ion Stanescu was moved into the Ministry in the key position of Chairman of the State Security Council.

A second direction taken by the new leadership to ensure the reliability of armed forces was the renationalization of the Romanian military. This process was in itself multifaceted and actually began under the influence of Dej, but it became most evident in the late 1960s, particularly as part of Ceausescu's response to the Soviet invasion of Czechoslovakia. The most conspicuous action taken at that time was the reintroduction of the Patriotic Guards, in August 1968. This militia force of 900,000, which can potentially be expanded to include 6 million members, was formed in order to provide a mass defense in case of Soviet invasion through "people's war." The Patriotic Guard is, however, responsible to the RCP Central Committee, and provides the Party leaders with an armed force that can counterbalance the formal military. Similarly, formation of the Defense Council, which became responsible for all matters of national defense and security in 1969, also increased political control over the regular armed forces. The Defense Council is a joint party/state body headed by Ceausescu, and is in turn jointly responsible to the RCP Central Committee, and to the Grand National Assembly, or when that body is not in session (which it is usually not) to the Council of State (Coman et al. 1982: 196-97).

After 1969 statements by Party and military leaders alike glorifying the army as defender of the nation became commonplace in the Romanian media. Past military leaders (ultimately including even the wartime dictator Antonescu) were rehabilitated and turned into symbols of the heroic national struggle for independence. Ceausescu eased the prevailing ideological restrictions to such an extent that Ivan Volgyes, among others, was led to conclude that the label of socialist partiotism is hardly sufficient to conceal the reality of chauvinism, irredentism, and anti-Russian and anti-Magyar sentiment that prevailed within the prerevolutionary military (Volgyes 1982: 54). Nothing of a similar intensity has appeared elsewhere in Eastern Europe, nor for that matter in socialist Romania prior to the advent of Ceausescu. As a more concrete indication of the sincerity of this more positive attitude toward nationalist values a number of officers purged during the Stalinist period were rehabilitated at the time of the Tenth Congress.

A second development of the Tenth Party Congress was the announcement of a new defense doctrine, War of the Entire People, built around the formation of the Patriotic Guard. According to the new policy Romania's entire military potential is directed toward the defense of the nation's territory. The professional military comprises a first line of defense, which would hold off invaders while the population mobilizes. The massive new paramilitary force, on the other hand, would provide the backbone of a guerrilla struggle of the entire population against any invading army.

Announcement of this doctrinal and organizational shift in the late 1960s was clearly a mixed blessing as far as career soldiers were concerned. On the one hand, the return to national values and implicit message that Romania intended to resist Soviet aggression should that be required is very much in keeping with the traditional military ethos. On the other hand, its implication that the Patriotic

Guards units were to be ascribed with significant importance was undoubtedly less than entirely welcome to the regular army. As long as they remain organizationally independent the Patriotic Guards represent an obvious competitor to the regular forces of Ministry of Defense for prestige and resources. Not only do they vie with the Ministry for limited defense funds, but to the extent that popular war becomes the primary deterrent to external aggression, arguments in favor of heavy state spending on sophisticated weaponry for the regular army are weakened.

Furthermore, while a return to traditional national military values might be spiritually fulfilling, it clearly imposed an immediate material cost. Detachment from the Warsaw Pact necessarily reduced Romania's access to Soviet weaponry. To a certain extent the decline in the technical sophistication of Romania's armaments in comparison with those available to its neighbors could be rationalized as being compatible with the country's new defense doctrine. Part of the shortfall was also offset by alternative procurement. Romania embarked upon a determined effort to develop the domestic capability needed to produce its own arms. Alexiev (1977) suggests that research and development allocations for military industry increased by more than fivefold between 1965 and 1970. Items beyond the capacity of domestic industry were procured by diversifying the country's sources of supply to include non-WTO arms producers.[3]

These efforts to make the military/security apparatus a secure base of support for the regime were not entirely successful, as evidenced by the events of 1971. Sometime during the fall of that year, General Ion Serb, Commander of the Bucharest garrison was arrested, and, in all probability, executed (*Die Presse* November 17, 1971; *The New York Times* February 15, 1972; *The Washington Post* February 15, 1972). Serb, who had served as Chief of the General Directorate of the Ministry of Interior Troops, and as Deputy Secretary of Interior, is known to have had close ties with the Soviet Union. The answers to questions concerning exactly what actions lay behind Serb's downfall, and the extent to which disaffection was a widespread phenomenon, remain obscure. On the strength of partial evidence analysts have concluded that General Serb was involved in passing secret information to the Soviet Union (Volgyes 1982: 52); or that the Bucharest garrison commander may have been implicated in a more widespread plot to carry out a coup d'état against Ceausescu (King 1972).

Whether a coup attempt or pro-Soviet espionage, the "Serb affair" generated a sharp reaction by the Ceausescu. In its wake a new Law on the Protection of State Secrets was passed (*Scinteia* December 18, 1971), and the military/security establishment was severely shaken up. Under arrangements announced in early 1972 the Ministry of Interior became directly responsible to the RCP Central Committee in so far as its work concerned security matters. Leadership of the Ministry was shifted from Council of Ministers to joint party state responsibility (*Buletinul Oficial* no. 39, April 19, 1972). In November 1972 the Ministry of the Armed Forces was renamed the Ministry of National Defense and reorganized as well (*Buletinul Oficial*, nos. 115, 130, 1972). The new Law on National Defense made the military responsible for implementing party and state policy rather than simply state policy. It also increased the already significant powers of the Defense Council. The 1972 law placed greater emphasis on the politico-educative role of the military, and formalized the role of the Patriotic Guards, reaffirming the independent status of these units, and charging the Ministry of National Defense with supporting their efforts.

While there is little evidence to support speculation in the Western press that a major purge and numerous executions took place in the wake of Serb's removal, the reorganization outlined above was matched by a second round of personnel changes. At the very top of the system, for example, Vasile Palitinet was removed as RCP Secretary in charge of military and security affairs because of serious irregularities in those fields, and was replaced by Ion Dinca. In April 1972 Cornel Onescu was replaced as Minister of Interior by Ion Stanescu, only to have Stanescu removed in turn and replaced by Ceausescu confederate Emil Bobu less than a year later, in March 1973. Concurrent with these dismissals at the top were what appear to be an unusual number of high level promotions. On December 28, 1972, 25 colonels in the Defense and Interior Ministries were promoted to the rank of Major General (*Agerpres* December 28, 1972). Ion Coman was promoted to Colonel General, Ion Ionita to full General, while Ion Dinca was made a full Member of the RCP Central Committee and Chairman of the GNA Committee on National Defense. It thus appears clear that Serb's actions were sufficiently serious to cause a major restructuring of the military/security establishment. Possible opponents were removed, while supporters of the General Secretary were rewarded and a new "class" of lower level officers who would be dependent on Ceausescu's continued patronage was promoted into positions of increased importance.

Termination of the Serb affair, however, did not inaugurate a new era of stability. Rather, since the mid-1970s the Ministries of Defense and Interior have been subjected to the same policy of periodic upheaval that characterizes other party and state institutions. In the Ministry of Interior for example, Emil Bobu lasted only until March 1975, at which point he was replaced by Teodor Coman (whose brother Ion, a member of the Ceausesecu inner circle, served as Minister of Defense from 1976 to 1980). Coman lasted only three years before being replaced by George Homostean. In the same year Tudor Postelnicu was named to the post of Minister-Secretary of State with responsibility for state security. These new appointees each had previous careers as high level members of the RCP apparat. Homostean had served previously as First Secretary of Sebes, and of Alba Judets; Postelnicu held the top Party post in Olt, and then in Buzau Judets. Both have remained in place up to the present [late 1987], and their appointments seem to have resolved the problem of ensuring the Party elite's control over the security apparat.

No equally satisfactory conclusion was reached in the Ministry of National Defense, which continues to be plagued by problems of civil-military friction, and generates recurrent rumors of planned or attempted coups against Ceausescu.

In 1976 Ion Ionita was replaced as Minister of Defense by Ion Coman. Coman lasted until 1980, at which point he was replaced by Constantine Olteanu, whose previous career was in the Central Committee's section for military and security affairs. Olteanu's tenure was marked by increased tension inside the ministry, which has been widely attributed to resentment over the degree of Party domination which his presence symbolized.

This revolving door policy was not limited to top posts. While little purpose would be served by recounting replacements in detail, it is relevant to note that personnel changes throughout to upper levels of both of the Ministries in question were widespread and systematic. One can hypothesize with some degree of confidence that, at least in the case of the armed forces, this external intervention into functioning of the professional hierarchy is the cause of some resentment. Nor is political interference with promotion the only factor acting to undermine army morale since the 1970s. The security services' penetration of the military is reputed to be more thorough in Romania than in any other Warsaw Pact country except the German Democratic Republic, and the prestige and remuneration of Romania's professional officers compares unfavorably with those of their counterparts elsewhere.[4]

Furthermore, employment of Romania's armed forces in civilian labor projects increased continually during the 1970s. While the use of the army in agriculture is an established practice dating back to prerevolutionary times, its increase under Ceausescu cannot be ignored. Development of the national economy and participation in the building of socialism has, in fact, been defined as an integral part of the military mission (Ceausescu, 1970, 4: 595). In addition to their highly publicized work on the Danube-Black Sea canal, the military has participated in the construction of 250 major industrial projects, the preparation of 663,000 hectares for irrigation, and the repair and reconstruction of 3,300 km of railroad lines (Stanculescu and Anghel 1984:182–83). While this activity meets with continual and positive official reference in Romania, outside observers question its impact on military training and preparedness, and see it as a probable source of civil military friction.

The relationship that developed between Ceausescu and the military/security establishment during the 1970s is characteristic of the RCP leader's mode of behavior in dealing with all politically important institutions. While renationalization of the armed forces provided him with substantial initial advantages in seeking military support, Ceausescu was not willing to base the safety of his regime on an assumption that he could hold the loyalty of the military. Rather, he has employed the same manipulative and coercive tactics that characterize his relations with other institutions. Although the army was highly praised as a national force, its autonomy was undermined, and its privileges reduced. Thus its leaders no doubt have had ample reason to resent the behavior of the RCP leadership over the past decade and a half. Like others, however, they have been given little opportunity to transform that resentment into positive action.

FORMING THE SOCIAL BASE OF NATIONAL COMMUNISM

The transformation of the RCP into a mass organization but one with a small, highly insulated leadership that dominates rather than directs other institutions was an inherent counterpart of Ceausescu's broader socioeconomic strategy. It was the political manifestation of a more general policy designed to resist accommodation with the new social forces generated by the socialist construction and suppress the interests of the growing intelligentsia. As a mode of institutional organization, however, it deprived the RCP chiefs of the benefits that purely vanguard parties provided to leaders in other state-socialist countries in their efforts to direct social life. Elsewhere the Party served to link strategic elites to the political leadership through shared interests, and enabled the leadership to call on reliable agents within nonparty institutions to oversee execution of its decisions. But exercising the strict control over cadres that was required to rule by this method clearly became increasingly problematic for the RCP when membership levels mushroomed, and when the leadership committed itself to a course that was generally antagonistic to the interests of mid-level elites. Romanian political leaders were consequently induced to seek an alternative social base and channels of implementation more congruent with their unique policy orientation. Discussion now turns to these broader questions of the interaction between the state and particular sectors of the society, the deterioration of relations between the Ceausescu regime and the extended intelligentsia, and the search for alternative means of exercising political control.

Following consolidation of the new leadership, Ceausescu's antipathy toward the intelligentsia and its values became increasingly apparent. The RCP's earlier tactic of making limited appeals to technical and cultural elites on the basis of their specific interests was virtually abandoned. The beginning of this shift was first presaged by transformation of the 1967 economic reform into an attack on mid-level managers in late 1969. At that time the number of personnel in the Central Ministries was reduced by 35 percent (Granick 1975: 37) amid growing high level criticism of bureaucratic foot dragging and outright resistance to Party policies. Not long after this preliminary sally Ceausescu was to enter into an all-out assault against the privileged class and its values.

The anti-intelligentsia campaign of the early 1970s, dubbed the "little cultural revolution," was initiated in a speech presented to the RCP Central Committee in July 1971. In his address Ceausescu accused members of the intelligentsia of exhibiting a bourgeois mentality, and chided the Party for a lack of ideological commitment that had allowed such negative phenomena to emerge (*Scinteia* July 13, 1971). Once signaled by the top leader this theme was picked up by the mass media and lower level party and mass organizations. Its targets were members of the technical and cultural elite who were perceived either as a threat, or at least as a growing obstacle to the central leadership's control over lower level affairs (Chirot 1978b: 495; Jowitt 1974a). Those singled out for attention were accused of formalism, of attempting to resist Party policy, and of succumbing to an "intellectualist attitude" (Ceausescu 1983: 157; *Scinteia* November 4, 1971).[5]

Efforts to curb the influence of the privileged class were not limited to symbolic attacks through the media and in mass meetings. Thousands of technical and managerial professionals were dismissed from their positions in research and administration, and transferred into more directly "productive" occupations. This wave of dismissals, while significant, probably did not suffice to alter the political situation in and of itself. Coming in conjunction with the increasingly harsh ideological line, however, it was certainly sufficiently alarming to affect nonpolitical elites' perception of the nature of their relationship with the Romanian party-state, and consequently served as an effective mechanism of reasserting Ceausescu's dominant position.

The cultural establishment, meanwhile, also found itself under attack. Writers and artists were criticized for their failure to produce works which promoted socialist construction and were urged by the Party leader to change their attitudes and to "place all creative capacities . . . at the service of the people" (Fischer 1984: 31). In a statement typical of the period Ceausescu's report to the 1972 RCP Conference demanded that "Beginning with elementary schools, the decisive factor in education, and ending with the modern means of communication all [channels of socialization] must be subordinated to the fulfillment of the obligations of the November Central Committee plenum. . . . It is understood that all ideological educational activities must proceed permanently under the leadership of the organs and organizations of the Party" (Ceausescu 1972: 83). The Romanian media was subsequently reorganized to bring it under tighter political control (Jowitt 1974a: 136), and the editor of the country's most prestigious literary review resigned his post in protest against increasing pressure to conform to the leadership's ideological line. Within the Writers Union substantial resistance was initially expressed against the new wave of dogmatism. Confronted with the Party's firm commitment to have its way, however, this opposition proved futile. Moderates were purged from the Union's leadership, and the delegates to its Congress in May 1972 fell into line with the RCP position on cultural policy (Gilberg 1975a: 81).

Members of the intelligentsia and their supporters were downgraded within the ranks of the RCP as well. During the summer of 1971 central and local Party leaders "voluntarily" submitted to self-criticism of their activity in the ideological field. Those who resisted the direction of Ceausescu's policy were demoted or removed entirely from positions of power. The Party's previously numerous statements concerning the necessity of recruiting skilled professionals were displaced by a renewed worker/peasant orientation. Intelligentsia membership in the Party, which was reported to be between 22 and 23 percent at the height of the transition policy of social detente in the late 1960s, went into decline, falling to 19 percent in December 1972, and finally to a low of 16.5 percent in 1976 (Shafir 1985: 89; Fischer 1979: 10).[6]

Actions such as these palpably indicated Ceausescu's intention to restrict the influence of nonparty elites, and to resist the dissemination of attitudes and values divergent from those promoted by the RCP. This suppression of any open expression of privileged class interests, reminiscent of Stalin's much more violent campaign against analogous elements of Soviet society during the 1930s, was an inevitable correlate of the economic remobilization that was already well underway by 1971. Conciliation of the intelligentsia was simply not compatible with a Stalinist economic course. Repudiation of accommodation with members of the professional/managerial strata, however, impelled the political elite to seek alternative means of ensuring that its policies would be implemented. Having intentionally alienated large numbers of mid-level elites, the regime intensified efforts to establish more direct links with the other sectors of the population. Not surprisingly it focused primarily on urban workers, whose numbers continued to grow rapidly through the early 1970s. It is within this context that one can best understand the emergence of populism as a fundamental element of Romanian national communism.

The peasant/worker population in the cities toward which the Party directed its main efforts in the early 1970s was relatively undifferentiated and incoherent. Economic remobilization created a tremendous upsurge in rural/urban migration (Sandu 1985: 118–19). Agricultural workers recruited into the industrialization process flooded into the cities during the early 1970s forcing the already heavily peasantized working class to absorb a new wave of young people from the villages. The population of the Moldavian capital, Iasi, for example, was of over two-thirds rural origin by the second half of the decade (Floares 1978: 127). According to Cole (1981: 78) the analogous figure for the country's seven largest cities was approximately 60 percent, and as much as one-fourth of the entire urban work force retained residences in the villages. This influx, combined with upward mobility into professional occupations, caused a continual dilution of the ranks of the working class and retarded workers from developing a strong sense of solidarity, at least until quite recently.

The Party's program to mobilize urban workers in its support was epitomized by the inauguration of the system of "Working Peoples Councils" (*Consiliilor Oameniilor Muncii*, or COMs) in late 1971. The COMs served as executive committees of General Assemblies of Working People, which included all employees in each workplace. Originally established at the enterprise, *judgets*, and national levels, the COMs were clearly intended to be likened to the Yugoslav workers' councils, and were presented to the population as a vehicle of direct workers' input into economic decision making. The reality of their influence was somewhat different. According to Granick's estimation in the early 1970s (since corroborated by others), "these collective organs do not exercise any serious restraint on the decision making powers of the head of the unit concerned. . . . It is the individual head of the unit who is still held individually responsible for the unit's performance" (Granick 1975: 112).

While they clearly failed to increase workers' control over the economy, the COMs did play an important role in Ceausescu's political strategy. First, they augmented existing organizational channels of mass mobilization. Dominated at the top by appointive members, and thus responsive to Party concerns, the COMs were apparently viewed as a promising addition to the trade union system through which workers could be enticed into participation that would advance the RCP's goals by acting as a political check on managerial autonomy. Second, in addition to their political/administrative function, which was fairly limited in the early years of their existence, the COMs became a key legitimating symbol in the Party's renewed ideological emphasis on mass participation. Since its inception the COM system has been lauded in the Romanian mass media as the concrete organizational expression of "workers' self-management" in Romania, and as a "new superior form of leadership by those who work through their direct participation in the elaboration of decisions and their implementation" (Moldovan 1982: 125).

Similar "participatory" innovations were introduced in other areas as well. Beginning with decisions made at the November 1971 Plenum of the RCP Central Committee, reforms to promote mass democracy, at least in a formal sense, were introduced into the legislative process (S. Popescu 1983: 164). The significance of democratic practices in the Grand National Assembly was once again reemphasized for the population through a series of changes culminating in the introduction of multicandidate elections to some of its seats in 1975. Selection of candidates, however, remained firmly in the hands of the RCP, which controlled the nomination process through its domination of the Socialist Unity Front (SUF) (Fischer 1977: 230-33). A similar method of selecting multiple candidates through nomination by mass organizations was introduced to the Peoples Councils on the local level as well.

The creation in the 1970s of Councils of Workers' Control Over Social and Economic Activities in December 1972 represented a third institutional modification typical of this aspect of the regime's political strategy (S. Popescu 1983: 167). Staffed by workers and specialists chosen for their technical qualifications (and presumably their high levels of political consciousness) the Workers' Control Councils' express function was the exercise of direct workers' supervision over commerce and production to ensure fulfillment of the development plan. In practice they were under the immediate control of superior Party bodies, to which they were responsible. They thus served as a supplementary and powerful mechanism through which upper levels of the Party leadership could mobilize "public activists" to review the behavior of enterprise administrators; be they Party, managerial, or trade union cadres (Gilberg 1975a: 63).

The preceding examples are but the most prominent of the organizational measures taken to mobilize the Romanian population within controlled channels. An entire array of specialized mass organizations, including the Trade Unions, Communist Youth and Students Associations, Women's Cooperatives, and Creative Artists Unions have been employed to serve this purpose as well. Party leaders' intention in promoting these organizations appears to have been the creation of a network of vertical affiliations which would enhance feelings of "organic" unity among Romanians and act to counterbalance class or group distinctions. Among the functions attributed to the so-called "public and mass organizations" (*organizatii obstesti si de masa*) by Party theorists were mobilization for socialist construction; integration along the lines laid down by the program of the RCP; education in socialist values following the ideological leadership of the RCP; public control; support of the Party's foreign policy, and unmediated participation in the resolution of the everyday problems of life of working people" (Hagan 1985: 191-92).

In reality there is almost no disagreement among those familiar with the subject as to the extremely limited nature of substantive political participation in Romania. In virtually all of the formal associations alluded to above, decision making is constantly supervised and tightly controlled by Party cadre. Attendance at meetings and the recurrent demonstrations staged by the RCP is mandatory, at least if one wishes to avoid negative interactions with those in positions of authority. Yet as a consequence of the near total stifling of rank and file initiative, participation tends to be lackadaisical at best, and in turn elicits nearly continual complaints about "formalism," by the Party leadership. Shortcomings in participation by workers in their representative councils, for example, have been repeatedly commented upon in the Romanian sociological literature (Petrescu 1977; Botezatu 1984; Sarbu 1978). While more information is available concerning workers' associations than other mass organizations, there is good reason to believe on the basis of personal observation and informal discussions with Romanian sociologists familiar with the subject that the pattern of rank and file alienation is generalizable to other institutions, not excluding the RCP itself. The situation is serious enough for Gilberg (1975b: 190) to conclude that "The most problematic development for the current regime is . . . mass withdrawal from any field which can be defined as 'political.'"

That workers meet the RCP elite's mobilization efforts with passive hostility and skepticism is not at all surprising, given the cultural traditions of the Romanian population and the nature of the Party's appeal. Neither is the current leaders' determination to maintain an increasingly tattered facade of popular participation and support out of character with the behavior of their prerevolutionary counterparts. It is, as Shafir (1985: 58) points out, consistent with the "dissimulative traditions" of the old elite. After all, prewar politicians of both parties legitimated their rule for decades on the basis of elections that were widely known to be unrepresentative in the extreme. Nor was this the only such historically atavistic practice that reappeared in Ceausescu's political repertoire. As the RCP economic strategy became increasingly burdensome during the 1970s more and more elements of traditional Romanian political practice would be integrated into the framework of the Leninist party-state.

THE ECONOMIC CONTEXT OF NATIONALIST COMMUNISM

Freed from the necessity of compromise that characterized the late 1960s transition period, Ceausescu and his supporters committed Romania fully to a renewal of extensive development beginning with the 1971-1975 Fifth Five-Year Plan. Even after the Fifth Plan got underway, a series of reevaluations occurred during which nearly every major economic indicator was increased. The projection for national income was stepped up from an original 7.7-8.5 percent range to a planned 11-12 percent per annum. Estimated agricultural output was increased to 6.4-8.3 percent from an originally intended 5.1-5.6 percent; and annual industrial targets rose to 11.1-12.0 percent from an 8.5-9.5 percent preliminary range, committing the country to a hike in production of 55-60 percent for the entire five-year period (Ceausescu 1972: 38-39; Tsantis and Pepper 1979: 90). Increases in consumption, while significant, were held at the original plan levels according to which real wages would rise by 20 percent in the course of the plan period. In a final burst of enthusiasm at the RCP National Conference in July 1972 Party leaders called for the fulfillment of the entire plan in four and one-half years (Ceausescu 1972: 12). With these 1972 changes in place Romanian growth rates were approximately double those of other East European countries and the accumulation rate rose to between 32 and 34 percent, by far the highest within the CMEA (Alton 1977: 214; Jackson 1977: 897).

Planners' intentions during the 1970s are obvious from the structure of investment in the national economy during the Fifth and Sixth Five-Year Plans. In line with Ceausescu's demand at the 1972 National Party Congress that Romania be transformed into an industrially developed state as rapidly as feasible, both plan periods called for high investment growth rates and continued concentration on the expansion of basic industries (*Anuarul Statistic* 1980: 400-1). Metallurgy, machine building, power, and chemicals were slated to lead the new growth drive (Maurer 1969). By keeping average annual investment growth rates at above 11 percent for both the Fifth and Sixth Plan periods Romania's economy became the most consistently investment-intensive within the CMEA (Jackson 1981b: 260). During the Fifth Plan, 83.3 percent of total investment was allocated to the productive sector. Of this amount, 50.3 percent was absorbed by industry (42.1 percent to group A and 8.4 percent to group B), while 14.1 percent went to agriculture (Tsantis and Pepper 1979: 97-98). Iron and steel, machine building, and chemicals industry, which accounted for 28 percent of national investment in 1960, were absorbing 46 percent by 1975 (Tsantis and Pepper 1979: 201).

During the course of the Sixth Plan concentration on industry intensified, with its share of investment rising to over 58 percent of total allocations (Jackson 1977: 914). As the decade progressed increasing attention was paid to developing more technically complex production processes and diversifying production on the foundation of existing basic industry, but in general light industry and trade, both continued to suffer from lower than average investment. In order to compensate for the transfer of labor into other sectors, the growth of investment in agriculture was considerable in both periods, and during the Sixth Plan continued at above targeted levels despite difficulties experienced elsewhere.

The implications of this level and distribution of investment are quite clear. The Romanian pattern in the 1970s strongly resembled the wave of "forced industrialization" that swept Eastern Europe in the early 1950s, and the Soviet Union several decades before. The pace of industrialization envisioned by Party leaders demanded that both the flow of labor from agriculture into the urban work force and the rate of capital formation be increased, despite the fact that its social transformation had now been underway for nearly 25 years, and the country's supply of surplus labor was rapidly dwindling. The RCP's development strategy required an intensive effort on the part of the entire population, and according to Jackson (1981a: 266), inaugurated the period of Romania's greatest structural change. It also required that central planners retain a tight grip on resource allocation and utilization. The growth of consumption had to be kept under control, and the economic surplus generated had to be directed to priority sectors of the economy. Once available, investments then had to be tightly supervised if plan goals were to be successfully met.

Administrative measures designed to contend with the latter problem were undertaken beginning in 1973 as part of the previously mentioned program of combining party and state institutions. A "Unitary National Socioeconomic Plan" was introduced by the regime in place of the traditional state plan. In conformity with the blending tactics employed elsewhere, the new economic blueprint was formulated and overseen by joint party/state leaders, through the Supreme Council for Social Economic Development, rather than in the Council of Ministries as had been the case in the past (Ceausescu 1972: 55-58; Gilberg 1975a: 164; Smith 1980: 41). Simultaneously, intensified use was made of RCP controlled mass organizations for the purpose of supervising the work of enterprise managers "from below."

Nearly all changes in economic organization introduced during the early 1970s promoted increased centralization. The efforts of the previous years were attacked by Ceausescu for failing to resolve the problem of efficient use of professional personnel (Ceausescu 1972: 54-55), and the number of industrial *Centrale* was reduced from 207 to 102. Several of the remaining units were increased in size, becoming nationwide administrative units analogous to general directorates of the ministries, while others were merged with the leading enterprises in particular industries. As part of the new reorganization overall administrative staff was significantly reduced, and the planning autonomy of subordinate economic units limited (Granick 1975: 40; Smith 1980: 42-43). Finally, the Ministry of Technical and Material Supply was given increased oversight authority with respect to capital utilization, and central planners resumed control over investment. The remains of the decentralizing reforms of 1967 and 1969 were thus effectively buried, and political control over the direction of the economy was reinforced. By 1974 political leaders could be satisfied that Romania had an intensely centralized economic system, compatible with the development strategy that they intended it to implement.

Through most of the 1970s Romanian economic performance was quite impressive, and was particularly so in the earlier years of the decade. Even if the accelerated targets announced in 1972 were not achieved, most of the already ambitious original Fifth Five-Year Plan indicators were surpassed. National income during the plan period grew by 11.3 percent and gross industrial production by 12.9 percent per annum. Priority sectors within industry far outperformed their goals: engineering and metal-working increased at an average 18.1 percent annual rate, and chemical production by nearly 16.0 percent (Tsantis and Pepper 1979: 93-95). On the other hand, and not surprisingly given the leadership's priorities, light industry, with the exception of textiles and clothing (which were increasingly important as a source of foreign exchange), continued to lag behind the rest of the economy throughout the Fifth Plan period.

The most evident problem area at the end of the Fifth Plan period was agriculture which, although growing substantially faster than in the preceding decade, underfulfilled its production targets by more than 10 percent, and exhibited an increasing difficulty in meeting target indicators as the plan progressed. Strain was also evident in the fact that consumer oriented goals had to be sacrificed in the struggle to achieve results in priority areas. Neither real wages nor consumption met their planned rates of increase, and badly needed housing construction fell short of its targets as well. On the other side of the coin, goals for accumulation and investment in industry were overfulfilled, as was the target for bringing new workers into the labor force (Tsantis and Pepper 1979: 98).

Beginning in 1976 major indicators, with the exception of labor productivity and investment, were all marginally eased in response to difficulties encountered in the Fifth Plan (Jackson 1977: 897-98). Otherwise the 1976-1980 Sixth Five-Year Plan can be regarded as a continuation of the established policy. Halfway into the Sixth Plan, however, the RCP's renewed industrialization drive bogged down, and in its final years signs of real crisis began to appear. For the plan period as a whole, Net Material Product growth rates declined to 7.3 percent, as opposed to a target rate of 11 percent, despite the fact that the accumulation rate was maintained at the 32-33 percent level, ultimately equaling the total investment of the preceding three periods combined (Ceausescu 1979: 10).

In addition to international factors (discussed in detail in Chapter 7) and unforseen accidents, such as the 1977 earthquake, purely structural causes within the domestic environment responsible for the decline in growth rates are not difficult to identify. Significant improvements in agriculture output were an essential element in the success of the early part of the industrialization drive. These resulted in part from wage and social reforms that benefited peasants in the early 1970s, and from continually increased capital investment intended to compensate for the diversion of labor. Regardless of the general improvement of conditions in rural Romania, however, industry continued to attract better qualified workers, and the quality of agricultural labor consequently suffered in comparison to that found in factories. Furthermore, planners' preoccupation with industry meant that resource utilization was far less than optimal in the agricultural sector (Jackson 1981b: 292-95). Thus despite a very good year in 1976, agriculture became the site of growing problems during the later years of the decade, and failed to meet most of its production goals for the Sixth Plan (Radio Free Europe, Romania/Situation Report 7, February 19, 1981). The sluggishness of agricultural growth in turn had a negative ripple effect on growth in other areas of the economy throughout the plan period.

Related to the evolution of the agricultural economy, problems also emerged in the recruitment of new workers into industrial occupations, which constituted an essential element of the RCP's remobilization effort. During the 1970s, the proportion of the population employed in agriculture declined from 49.1 to 30.7 percent, while the share of industrial workers increased from 23.0 to 34.7 percent of the total labor force (*Anuarul Statistic* 1980: 113-12). At 11 percent per annum, the rate of net migration from the villages between 1971 and 1978 was nearly twice the annual rate of the preceding two decades, and significantly higher than it had been even during the initial collectivization drive (Sandu 1985: 119). This massive shift in employment accounted for a significant part of the increase in Romanian labor productivity, due to the fact that the ratio of national income produced per employee in industry was several times that found in agriculture. As a consequence, overall increases in productivity more than fulfilled expectations during the Fifth Plan, despite the fact that productivity growth fell below plan levels in either sector taken separately (Jackson 1977: 932-36).

By the late 1970s continued reliance on brute transfer of labor from agriculture was no longer an option. Despite the fact that the absolute number of those engaged in agriculture was still relatively large (approximately 35 percent), the proportion of those remaining who were easily employable in industry was in fact quite limited (Jackson 1981b: 281-82). Consequently, in the second half of the decade targets for the introduction of new workers into industry were not met, and the rate of increase in industrial employment declined by nearly half from that of the preceding five-year period (*Anuarul Statistic* 1980: 112-13). The approaching limit on rural/urban transfer was thus clearly beginning to impact upon industrial growth.

Other factors also hindered efforts to improve labor productivity. One obvious cause of concern was the inability of planners to utilize the masses of new workers that they had already brought into the economic system effectively, because of shortcomings in industrial organization. Second, by the end of the decade signs appeared indicating that long-term restriction on consumer goods production was beginning to reduce the effectiveness of labor incentives. Despite remarkable increases in per capita production, per capita consumption and the availability of services remained quite low in comparison to other state-socialist regimes in the region. During the Sixth Plan sales turnover in the services sector increased by only approximately 29 percent instead of its 60-68 percent target range, while retail trade, housing, and real income all failed to achieve their objectives (Radio Free Europe, Romania/Situation Report 3, February 19, 1981: 9, 19). The combined impact of these factors was well illustrated by the fact that the Sixth Plan which, in its revised edition, called for increases of 9.2 percent in labor productivity failed to meet its goals, achieving only a 7.2 percent increase.

Simultaneous with the appearance of growing labor constraints, both industrial output and capital productivity growth rates dropped off as well. While his report to the RCP Central Committee in late 1977 on fulfillment of the Party's goals during the first part of the plan painted a generally rosy picture of the economy, Ceausescu himself was already sounding a note of warning, calling attention to shortcomings in the raw material sector, labor organization, and the growing stock of uncompleted investment projects (Ceausescu 1982: 372-78). Jackson (1981a: 275) attributes the latter problem in part to the same factors that led to the sharp production decline in the 1964-1965 period: that is, planners had overextended themselves beyond their organizational capacities and lost control of the flow of investment. Indeed, the available data indicated that by the final years of the plan the proportion of unfinished construction had risen to between 21 and 29 percent of annual investment (Jackson 1981b: 267). Furthermore, investment plans in industry began to go unfulfilled for the first time since renewal of the economic drive.

A final important constraint was imposed by the increasing difficulty of obtaining the raw materials required to fuel extensive development. After decades of uninterrupted growth Romanian oil production peaked in 1977 and began to slip thereafter (CIA 1982: 121). Coal, electricity, and natural gas all failed to meet their targets in the late 1970s as well (Tuitz 1981: 43). In an economy geared almost exclusively to heavy industrial development these shortfalls were disastrous. Romania's growing steel industry, particularly the massive Galati and Carlarasi steel complexes, required huge amounts of imported iron and coking coal, as well energy, which was equally true of the chemical industry that became one of the keystones of economic development after 1970.

In order to feed an industrialization process based on such projects energy consumption was increased by an annual average of 6.2 percent during the first half of the 1970s. Consequently, the energy crises of the late 1970s proved particularly damaging. While some measures were taken to restrain further growth in consumption, planners still called for 6.8 percent annual increases for the Sixth Plan period, indicating that they had failed to comprehend the seriousness of their situation. In 1976, however, the full force of the energy crisis struck the economy, and consumption increases dropped to a 3.1 percent annual rate. As Jackson (1981b: 285) points out, the impact of this decline was illustrated by the fact that the three most disrupted sectors of the Romanian economy in the late 1970s, chemicals, fuels, and metallurgy, were also the three most energy intensive.

Bucharest began to take remedial steps to meet the threat of economic collapse beginning in 1978. In March of that year a reform initiative, the New

Economic-Financial Mechanism (NEFM) was introduced. This proved to be merely the first in a long series of efforts to improve management and economic planning which continue up to the present. The core of the 1978 reform program consisted of innovations in two areas. First, each enterprise was to be made more responsible than previously for its own planning and internal accounting, and was (at least in theory) allowed to establish contracts with suppliers of its choice. Second, an attempt was made to link worker and management incentives to output and production costs through an improved system of bonuses that would rise and fall with the enterprises' net profit indicators (Traistaru 1983: 103; Ceterchi, Florea, and Cioba 1981). Funding for the bonuses was to be provided by the 37 percent share of above plan profits that could, under 1979 guidelines, be retained by each enterprise (Smith 1980: 48-49). Finally, in addition to these financial and administrative measures (*Autogestiune*), the system of Workers' Councils was marginally modified and given a new importance. As a part of the New Economic-Financial Mechanism, Party leaders once again attempted to utilize the COMs as a means of overcoming workers' apathy and increasing their identification with the goals of enterprise management (*Autoconducere*). Once again however, they failed to increase workers' real control over conditions in their enterprises (Nelson 1981).

Signs of economic readjustment were also evident in the preparation of the 1981-1985 Five-Year Plan. Target indicators for the new plan proposed in 1979 called for a growth pace significantly below those of previous years, even before final figures on the Sixth Plan became available (Ceausescu 1979: 25; Smith 1980: 54). Thus industrial production for the new plan period was projected at an annual rate of 8-9 percent, and investment growth was intended to slow down to between 5.4 and 6.2 percent. When they did become available, the 1979 results proved as disappointing as those of the previous two years. Production plans were underfulfilled for nearly every industrial commodity, and income, investment, and labor productivity all fell behind their goals as well (Tuitz 1981: Radio Free Europe Romania/Situation Report 3, March 18, 1980). In the wake of these results final targets for the new plan were reduced to even lower levels (*Scinteia* July 2, 1981). Social Product, for example, was slated to increase by 6.1 percent per annum, and industrial growth was projected at 7.6 percent as opposed to the 10.2-11 percent called for in the preceding period. Similarly, the rate of investment growth was reduced to less than half that of the levels called for in the Sixth plan; 5.2 percent instead of 11 percent.

CONCLUSION

By the early 1970s Nicolae Ceausescu was firmly established at the helm of the RCP leadership, and the general orientation of his policies was becoming clear. Other state-socialist regimes moderated their economic goals after an early period of intense transformation, accepting the necessity of industrial deceleration and at least limited reform. They entered into a new stage of development founded on party elites' implicit acceptance of a new privileged class as an inevitable fact of life in the postrevolutionary social structure. The RCP, however, pressed forward on its own particular course, which precluded the political strategy of state/society accommodation pursued by other East European countries, even had leaders in Bucharest desired to follow suit. Previous efforts to gain intelligentsia support were abandoned in favor of a populist strategy. The Ceausescu faction established a remarkable degree of political control, even in comparison to other leaders in Eastern Europe. Political institutions were reorganized, and those forces within the society favoring accommodation were effectively excluded from access to power.

Concurrently, efforts directed toward achieving extensive development were redoubled. The "campaign" style and centralization of planning efforts evident in the economic remobilization were characteristic of the Stalinist phase in other state-socialist countries, and comprised the economic correlate of the RCP's rejection of political accommodation. The transfer of labor from agriculture to industry reached new heights, investment rates soared, and massive projects typical of Stalin's heyday began to rise from the ground. It may well be as Jackson (1981a: 266) suggests, that 1971–1978 were "Romania's best years as far as economic performance is concerned." It is no less true, however, that if this were the case, success was bought at the expense of squandering the country's resources and creating tremendous difficulties in succeeding years. Rather than seeking alternatives to an already extremely centralized economic model, the Ceausescu regime relied on "commandism" and mobilizational tactics to stimulate growth. By the close of the decade the pool of unexploited resources necessary for extensive development had been all but entirely consumed, and no groundwork was laid for shifting to an intensive development model. Neither "Self-Management" and "Self-Financing" (*Autoconducere si Autogestiune*), pronounced to be ground-breaking revolutionary contributions of the Romanian New Economic–Financial Mechanism by the RCP, nor obvious efforts to pull in the reins on breakneck industrialization could compensate for the dislocation caused by the previous years of economic upheaval. As its economic program faltered, the political leadership would turn to increasingly desperate measures to stave off imminent collapse.

facing political leaders was that of how to deal with the growing "underdevelopment" of the countryside. Despite remedial efforts by the state, remuneration for agricultural labor remained significantly below that for industrial work, and the gulf between urban and rural standards of living continued to be more substantial than was officially recognized.[1] According to a random survey of families in 25 rural communes in Iasi *judets* in the mid-1970s, for example, 63.3 percent of households were without gas and 33.5 percent without running water, while only 3.9 percent had refrigerators and 3.0 percent had washing machines (Floares 1977: 104). Entertainment and service outlets also continued to be lacking in rural Romania, with the consequence that the attraction of urban employment proved high, even for those who were otherwise well paid (Sandu 1984, 1985; Cole 1981).

Differentials in labor productivity were magnified by the selectivity of migration from rural to urban localities. Those with the highest probability of abandoning agriculture were young people and adult males who could most easily find employment in industrial settings. Hence the population left behind in the villages became increasingly older and increasingly feminine (Miftode 1984: 77, 99). The preponderance of female labor in the total rural work force was officially reported to be 14 percent in 1979, however, feminization of agricultural labor is clearly more substantial in the cooperatives, and in all probability is a greater problem on state farms than implied by the official figures. Although nationwide data is not available, local studies indicated that the ratio of females to males in the active population on the agricultural cooperatives ranged around 2:1, and was much higher in some cases (Fulea and Tamas 1982: 139–43; Floares 1977). Furthermore, those active adult males who remained in agriculture appeared to be those least able to meet the minimum demands of urban employment; that is, they were the least intellectually proficient and economically productive of the group (personal interviews, 1983 and 1985). Despite the RCP's continued efforts to promote social development in the countryside, educated individuals tenaciously resisted relocation from the cities. Intellectuals ultimately assigned to villages tend to be those least able to compete effectively for more valued positions, and to perceive themselves as forced exiles from the cities. In a study carried out in Ialomita *judets* during the late 1970s one-third of those in intellectual occupations commuted from nearby cities instead of changing their residences to the villages (Glodeanu 1979). The same survey indicated very clearly that such personnel were at best marginally integrated into rural life.

In part, economic conditions in the villages were ameliorated by the growing practice of commuting, by workers, from rural dwellings to urban industrial workplaces (*navetism*) (Miftode 1984: 159; Sandu 1985: 94, 131).[2] A number of Western scholars have come to the conclusion that *navetism*, along with efforts to decentralize geographically, has had a politically stabilizing effect on the country (Chirot 1978b; Cole 1981; Shafir 1985). It does seem clear, as those observers suggest, that through the links created by commuters (*navetisti*) and their home villages, closer ties have been maintained between rural and urban populations in Romania than elsewhere in Eastern Europe. A widespread practice has arisen in which dual-status families send one member to work in an urban setting, while at least one member works on the village cooperative farm, and thereby gains the privilege of retaining a private plot for the use of the family as a whole (Cole 1981; Miftode 1985: 159). Even when family members migrated to the city, close and mutually advantageous economic ties were normally maintained with the villages (Cole 1981: 90-91). Materially speaking, these practices substantially benefited the village communities in an absolute sense. On the other hand, however, the interpenetration of urban and rural modes of life appears to have added to the dissatisfaction of rural dwellers, who became all too aware of the limitations of their current situation.

The negative consequences of these conditions are manifest. As a result of the constant draining off of effective personnel and the continuation of poor living conditions, labor relations in agriculture remains quite low, and in general the Party's penetration of rural Romania is significantly less effective than in the cities.[3] Consequently informal corruption and passive subversion of the regime's economic goals represented ongoing problems in the villages throughout Ceausescu's remobilization effort. The intensity of the peasantry's (especially Cooperativists') dissatisfaction is evident in the nearly universal desire of young people to enter occupations that would take them out of the rural setting, and in parents' hopes that their children would succeed in escaping their home villages, despite very strong sentiment in favor of maintaining family unity (Nydon 1984; Ratner 1980; personal interviews carried out in 1983).

While the standard amenities of life were certainly more available to urban workers than their rural counterparts, discontent nonetheless appeared in the cities and factories as well. The standard of living in Romania has undergone a steady if slow increase, at least up to 1980 (Jackson 1981b: 256-57). But Romanian workers' expectations about their standard of living have been increasingly left unmatched by the regime's performance, and as a consequence developed into a growing source of discontent. This effect was exacerbated by the fact that the RCP (unsurprisingly) responded to its economic difficulties in part by the diversion of resources originally dedicated to increasing the workers' real income into the producer goods sector. Hence imbalances in favor of production were intensified rather than reduced (Tuitz 1981: 44-45). While remuneration continued to be the most influential determinant of worker morale (Chelcea 1979), it was far from being the only one. Both the level of consumption of most goods, and the performance and sufficiency of the retail network were substantially below those of neighboring Hungary and Bulgaria in the late 1970s, not to speak of the more developed East European states. The growing strain on urban housing was indicated by the fact that the number of young workers housed in hostels, for example, was ten times greater in 1978 than in 1968 (Mihut 1985: 133).

Conditions in the workplace remained poor through the second half of the decade as well. Due to the growing labor shortage RCP pledges to reduce the work week to 44 hours were continually delayed, while the number of hours

devoted to unpaid "patriotic work" was steadily raised. An increasingly problematic source of dissatisfaction, especially among younger workers, was the
slowness of the promotion process. Long periods of stagnation for individuals in
the lower ranks of the industrial hierarchy were an almost inevitable outcome of
the slowing down of economic transformation. By the late 1970s, the rapid
social mobility of earlier revolutionary decades was less evident than ever. The
rate of self-reproduction in the working class rose to between 35 and 40 percent
(Traistaru and Traistaru 1979: 212), and exit from the working class into the
ranks of the intelligentsia became progressively more difficult to achieve (see
below). Consequently, there were simply less positions becoming available at the
upper levels of the industrial work force to be filled by newcomers from lower
occupational categories. In a 1978 study of enterprises in three *judets*, the large
majority of younger workers in lower work categories declared themselves to be
dissatisfied with the promotion processes. Sixty-eight percent of those surveyed
declared that the regulations concerning promotion were not being obeyed by
their superiors (Dragut 1978). The impact on morale created by these conditions
was indicated by the fact that newcomers from the peasantry exhibited a better
work attitude, and were substantially less likely to change places of employment
than second generation members of the working class (Basiliade 1982: 122–23;
Mihut 1985: 116–17; Zamfir et al. 1984: 116).

Nor did workers respond positively to the RCP's "participatory" initiatives in
the factories. According to Nelson (1981: 181), mid-1970s survey data indicated
that only approximately one-third of workers actually made proposals to their
enterprise Workers' Councils, and that even among these only 40 percent thought
that their efforts to influence policy would be successful. More recent data cor-
roborates this finding. In a survey of over 2,500 young workers at 18 enterprises
across the country, only 13 percent of respondents felt that they could have a
major impact on decisions in their enterprise Workers' Councils, while 43 percent of those questioned felt that they had no influence at all. Fifty-three percent of the entire sample had never participated in Workers' Assemblies beyond
the level of mere attendance (Basiliade et al. 1982: 64–65).

The source of workers' alienation from institutions that theoretically represent them is not difficult to identify. Available evidence strongly suggests that
the COMs are dominated by the same functionaries who control the union,
management, and party hierarchies (Sarbu 1978). The agendas of enterprise
Workers' Council meetings are set by their presidents (that is, the enterprise
party secretaries), and are generally unknown to workers beforehand. COM sessions are dominated by enterprise management and representatives of the central
or other higher bodies. Discussion in them is highly circumscribed by the requirement that the COMs must abide by production plans that are formulated at
higher levels and then sent down to the enterprise for approval. Consequently,
workers' participation has generally been limited to requests for clarification of
target indicators, and suggestions as to how to better fulfill production plans
established by the Central Ministries. Those workers who do have a high rate

of participation in the COMs tend to be those who also hold responsible positions in the Party, the UTC, or the unions (Basiliade et al. 1982: 68). As Nelson points out in a summary of his research on the subject, members of Workers' Councils are not primarily workers, they are not noted for consulting with enterprise employees, workers' participation in sessions organized by them is perfunctory, and workers generally do not appeal to them to correct inefficiencies (Nelson 1980: 551). The depth of the gulf between Romanian Workers' Councils and the enterprise rank and file is amply illustrated by the fact that "in the great majority of cases [worker representatives] are not even known, often even to their own work-mates" (Sarbu 1978: 484).

Taken as a whole such information suggests that by the late 1970s Romanian workers were far from satisfied with their lot. Except for rare outbreaks such as the Jiu valley strike in 1977, however, their reaction has been limited to passive hostility rather than active opposition (Nelson 1981; Shafir 1985). Numerous analysts, beginning with Kenneth Jowitt (1974b), have suggested that Romanian workers' response has been characteristic of a "peasant" political culture, which is hardly surprising since a very large proportion of the Romanian industrial work force is, after all, in its first generation away from the rural environment.[4] It must also be remembered, however, that despite their very real complaints, at least until the economic collapse of the early 1980s, urban workers perceived many of their basic interests as being fulfilled (Zamfir 1984: 158-78).[5]

Relative satisfaction on the part of the workers appears especially clear when their attitudes are compared with those of the intelligentsia. To paraphrase Daniel Chirot (1978b: 466), what was satisfying for the working class was somewhat less than so for the middle class, and was particularly unacceptable to the intelligentsia. In essence, decision makers obtained much of the wherewithal needed to meet the minimum requirements of workers during a decade of intense industrialization by restricting consumption at the upper levels of the occupational hierarchy. Rather than developing a service sector geared to appeasing the increasingly sophisticated demands of the privileged class, the political elite concentrated available resources on providing basic requirements to the mass population. From the 1960s to the 1970s, the ratio between the highest and lowest wage earners was reduced to 1:4.5 (Jackson 1981b: 293). The base differential (1:4.2) was even lower by late 1983, but with the inclusion of supplementary "leadership pay" the difference between the highest and lowest paid individuals remained approximately static in the early 1980s (Raboaca 1984: 88-91).

Perhaps even more significant, if one considers the differences within pay scales, it is clear that foremen and workers in the upper level of their remuneration categories have greater potential earnings than their lower level white collar colleagues. The discontent created among mid-level personnel in industry by their present levels of remuneration is clearly evident in data gathered by Chelcea (1979: 97), indicating enterprise technicians, managers, and engineers to be less satisfied with their earnings than production workers, team leaders, and foremen.

This finding is corroborated by a large-scale survey undertaken during the early 1980s, which shows intellectuals (members of both the cultural and technical intelligentsia) answering in significantly greater numbers than workers that they are dissatisfied with the level of their incomes (Zamfir 1984: 158-79).

Nor is remuneration the only area of professionals' concern with conditions in the workplace. Engineers and managers also appear to be less satisfied than production workers with regard to their possibilities for future promotion and are, along with lowest level manual workers, least satisfied with the actual content of their day to day work (Chelcea 1979). The question of remuneration aside, the most general source of white collar discontent has been the structure of decision making in the Romanian economy. Efforts by the political elite to restrict the influence of managers through recentralization on the one hand and reliance on mass organs to enforce Party priorities on the other have, as Granick concluded in his study of Romanian enterprise, created a situation in which "the functions of their top managers were much more comparable with those exercised by foremen and junior managers in Western capitalist firms than with the functions exercised by top or even middle management in . . . Western companies" (Granick 1975: 127). The current relevance of this view is substantiated by Vasilescu's mid-1980s study of a Brasov industrial enterprise, which led the author to conclude that "a large proportion of engineers and sub-engineers are enrolled in posts which do not require substantial intellectual capacity, resolving problems which do not allow them to rise to the true professional role that they would like to play" (Vasilescu 1985: 15).

The impact of Ceausescu's sociopolitical strategy on the day-to-day existence of members of the Romanian intelligentsia was strikingly indicated by Zamfir (1984). Intellectuals among the nearly 2,000 respondents in the study coordinated by Zamfir exhibited distinct characteristics on a variety of indicators. The effect of compressing consumption, for example, was evident. Intellectuals' individual incomes were on average only one-third higher than those of workers.[6] The narrow margin of income differential separating workers from the intelligentsia conformed with what one would expect on the basis of the RCP's development strategy. The intellectuals' perception of their material situation, however, was more remarkable. Table 6.1 clearly indicates the sharp distinction between the various social categories with respect to their actual income levels in relation to their perception of the *adequacy* of their respective incomes. The effect of "rising expectations" upon those occupying the upper ranks in the occupational hierarchy is striking.

Other aspects of the Zamfir study demonstrated the intelligentsia's "marginalized" status in the present order of things as well. As part of their analysis the Romanian researchers created synthetic indicators designed to measure the degree of satisfaction with life, perceived quality of life, perception of the future, and social integration versus alienation. Across this entire spectrum intellectuals showed the lowest levels of satisfaction, at statistically significant levels (Table 6.2).

Table 6.1
Average monthly family income, and perceived rapport between estimated income and required income (Zamfir et al. 1984: 86).

	Average income in Lei	Estimate of income/ Need (scale 1-7)
Worker	3,590	3.97
Service Worker	4,110	4.12
Mid-Level Worker	4,520	3.82
Intellectual	5,470	3.62

Table 6.2
The difference between socioprofessional categories with respect to global indicators of the quality of life, scale of 1-7; 1,804 respondents (Zamfir et al. 1984: 122).

	Intellectuals	Workers	Mid-level Workers	Social Workers
Perceived Quality of Life	4.49	4.67	4.70	4.98
		p<.001		p<.01
Satisfaction with Life	4.13	4.25	4.25	4.45
		p<.05		p<.05
Perception of the Future	2.87	3.11	3.11	3.30
		p<.001		p<.05
Integration /Alienation	3.16	3.29	3.32	3.46
		p<.05		p<.05

Intellectual respondents scored most markedly below average on the researchers' indicators of social integration. They exhibited a greater degree of pessimism concerning social progress and lower confidence in the individuals' ability to control events. They also tended more than members of any of the other category to view other people as self-interested and unwilling to support another person in cases of unfairness or injustice (Zamfir 1984: 97–98). This rather bleak outlook on society was matched by an attitude of withdrawal into private lives, which are as far as possible insulated from the vagaries of the politically charged public realm. Members of the intelligentsia rated the importance of participation in the activities of public organizations lower than any other group, and instead focused their aspirations more than the others on family, friends, and personal pursuits (Zamfir 1984: 150, 158–78).

A final aspect of the evolution of Romania's social structure that deserves detailed attention is the progressive decline in social mobility that took place during the 1970s. Evidence of this trend, the effect of which has already been mentioned above in regard to the working class, is available from a variety of sources (Petre and Stefanescu 1985; Marginean 1985; personal interviews carried out in Romania during 1985). Work carried out by the Bucharest Center for Sociological Research from 1982–1985 suggests that self-reproduction within the working class has reached 87 percent in recent years. The rate of total intergenerational mobility of young people (18–29 years of age) was 24.6 percent less than that of those between the ages of 33 and 44, and 28.6 percent less than that of those between 45 and 60 (Petre and Stefanescu 1985: 248). According to most sources, the category exhibiting the greatest degree of social self-reproduction during the 1970s was the intelligentsia (personal interviews; Traistaru and Traistaru 1979: 248). There is, however, some reason to question whether this trend still continues at present.[7] If it in fact does not, its attenuation may well reflect active measures taken by the regime to "stimulate" members of the intelligentsia to increase their "circulatory" mobility in order to counteract self-reproduction (Marginean 1979).

Despite Ceausescu's ideological assault on the "privileged class," and the obvious slowdown of movement between social categories, the aspiration for mobility into intellectual occupations remained high among young Romanians throughout the remobilization period. Suteu and Ozunu (1977: 15, 23) indicate that the very large majority of students planned on entering higher education, while virtually none evinced a strong desire to become workers.[8] But as the 1970s drew to a close opportunities to enter intellectual professions became increasingly rare as a consequence of the RCP's efforts to check growth in nonproductive employment. Beginning in the early 1970s educational institutions were reorganized to channel more of the population into productive labor (Ratner 1980: 39–43). The impact of the regime's reorientation on higher education was dramatic. The number of students enrolled in technical areas increased from 53,595 to 124,000 between 1970/1971 and 1980/1981 (*Anuarul Statistic* 1982: 291-92); as a consequence of which the country now enjoys a surfeit of low paid and low prestige engineers and subengineers.

Meanwhile the success of intellectuals in gaining admission to higher education for their children has, if anything, become greater, with the result that by the end of the 1970s they occupied between 45 and 50 percent of places in universities (Mihut 1984: 188; Traistaru and Traistaru 1979: 248-50; see Zaslavsky 1982: 72-76 for a discussion of similar conditions in the Soviet Union). Mitchell Ratner's analysis of data gathered in Cluj *judets* suggests that the probability of an intellectual's child entering the university is above 70 percent, while one belonging to a worker or peasant family now has approximately a 10 percent chance (Ratner 1981: 141). Furthermore, it appears that the intelligentsia has tightened its grip on the more prestigious university faculties, and on the mathematics and physics high schools that lead most directly into higher education, leaving the less sought after technical and agricultural fields to others (Ratner 1980; Traistaru and Traistaru 1979: 248-50).

The dual impact of this trend in mobility is obvious. First, under previous conditions potential pressure from within the working class to increase consumption was partially absorbed by upward mobility or, failing that, at least a high probability of upward mobility for one's children. As this became less and less a realistic alternative the salience of current material conditions naturally increased, and with it the potential for working class unrest grew as well. Second, higher levels of social reproduction almost necessarily increased the likelihood of class formation. The beginnings of a differential social consciousness are already obvious among the intellectuals, who exhibit attitudes and interests quite different from those of other sectors of the society. Despite the retarding effect of previously rapid mobility rates and inundation of the proletariat by emigrants from the countryside throughout most of the postrevolutionary period, a number of analysts have noted the appearance of increasing class consciousness and dissatisfaction among workers as well.

The combined effects of the Party elite's efforts to resist political accommodation with the growing numbers of highly trained managerial, technical, and cultural personnel, as well as the direct economic impact of remobilization, thus brought Romania to a state of increasing social disruption. The community infrastructure of the villages that served for centuries as a stable foundation of society was altered beyond redemption, while the working class, a reliable base of support for the Communist Party during the revolutionary transition of the 1950s, was transformed into a source of growing discontent. Finally, the intelligentsia, marginalized in the cause of Ceausescu's revolutionary renaissance, had been alienated from the RCP and its goals, and was lost as a reliable agent of the Party's social/economic policies.

REGIME ADAPTATION AND NATIONALIST COMMUNISM

Erosion of the marginal support enjoyed by the RCP during the earlier transition period caused the Ceausescu leadership to turn to ever more extreme organizational and ideological measures in its quest to retain control of the political system. Among the most obvious institutional innovations in recent years has been the RCP General Secretary's increasing reliance on members of his own extended family to secure his grip on key components of the state. Nepotism within the RCP first began to be widely commented on following the appointment of Ceausescu's wife Elena to the Party Central Committee in July 1972, and then to its Executive Committee in June 1973. The presence of Elena Ceausescu (*née* Petrescu) in these bodies was far from being merely symbolic, and as the years passed her personal authority has continued to grow. By 1977 she had been appointed to the Permanent Buro of the Political Executive Committee, and was considered by many to be the second most powerful figure in the political hierarchy. Since 1979 she has also served as a First Deputy Prime Minister and as head of the National Council on Science and Technology, where she exercises considerable influence over research and technology policy. Most significantly, she currently heads the RCP Central Committee Commission on Cadres.

A second member of the General Secretary's immediate family, his son Nicu, enjoyed an even more startling rise to prominence. Born in 1951, Nicu Ceausescu became politically active soon after his mother, upon his "election" as Vice Chairman of the National Students' Association in 1973 (Radio Free Europe, Romania/Situation Report 1, January 7, 1984). In 1974 he became a member of the Council of the Socialist Unity Front, and was elected in 1975 to the Central Committee of the Romanian Communist Youth League, the *Uniunea Tineretului Communist* (UTC). Soon afterward the younger Ceausescu was made a UTC Central Committee Secretary and a member of its Buro. He was named a candidate member of the RCP Central Committee in 1979, and a full member in 1982. In 1980 he became a deputy in the National Parliament, the Grand National Assembly. December 1983 saw him made First Secretary of the UTC, and thus automatically a Minister in the government as well. Finally, Nicu Ceausescu joined his parents at the summit of the RCP hierarchy, on being made an alternate member of the Party's Political Executive Committee, in late 1984.

The close collaboration in power that developed between Nicolae and Elena Ceausescu during the past decade, and their obvious attempt to elevate their universally unpopular son Nicu to the status of "heir apparent," by no means give a full picture of the importance of family relations within the upper stratum of the Romanian political elite. The leadership of party and state institutions alike is rife with members of the Ceausescu and Petrescu extended families. Some accounts suggest that as many as two dozen members of the two clans are to be found in top political positions. Even a cursory review reveals that their presence in commanding posts is remarkably pervasive.

According to Vladimir Tismaneanu (1985: 65), just among Nicolae Ceausescu's siblings, "one brother, Nicolae A., is Secretary of the Political Council of the Ministry of Interior; another, Ion, is Vice Chairman of the State Planning Committee, Secretary of the National Council for Agriculture, Food Industry, Sylviculture, and Water, and a member of the Central Auditing Committee; Marin . . . holds a post in foreign trade; Florea is a member of the staff of Scinteia." Another brother, Ilie, is a General, a Deputy Minister of Defense, and a member of the Higher Political Council of the Romanian Army. Of the brothers-in-law, Ilie Verdet, Corneliu Burtica, and Manea Manescu have all played key roles in central party and governmental bodies and have been prominent members of the Ceausescu inner circle during recent years. Brother-in-law Vasile Barbalescu serves as Olt *Judets* RCP First Secretary. Elena's brother, Gheorghe Petrescu is Deputy Chairman of the National Trade Union, holds membership on the Council of State, the Party Central Committee, and the Supreme Council for Social and Economic Development, and is a Deputy Prime Minister.

While nepotism is far from unknown among the rulers of other state-socialist countries, such extensive penetration of the formal institutions of power by close relatives of a party leader has appeared only in Romania. Its existence is important in itself as an explanation of how Ceausescu has managed to retain power through an extended period of extreme economic difficulty. However, it is also indicative of a much more widespread breakdown of formal institutional norms that is becoming a fundamental characteristic of the contemporary Romanian political organization. Reflecting on the experience of Leninist regimes in general, Jowitt (1978: 70) has termed this development party "familialization," which he defines as "the routinization of a charismatic organization in a traditional direction."

That this phenomenon should be more pronounced in Romania than elsewhere in Eastern Europe is hardly coincidental. Utilization of formal governmental institutions as a means to pursue private ends, implicit toleration of corruption, and transaction of business on the basis of relations rather than rationally established procedures were all standard in the Ottoman bureaucracy that ruled Romania for centuries. As previously indicated, the practices of traditional "bureaucratic despotism" were by all accounts continued up to the very end of the interwar period under the indigenous political elite that came to power following the Turkish decline. An equally mercenary attitude toward public office has become evident in the current political environment.

Examples of such "traditionalist" behavior within the Romanian political elite are too numerous and too well known to warrant recounting here.[9] Suffice it to comment that the exploitation of official positions by individuals in pursuit of their own interests and those of their relations has become the norm, rather than a deviation from the norm in any meaningful sense. Aside from the pervasive practice of virtually open bribery, and an extortion of the public that is truly corrupt by nearly any standard, bureaucrats at all levels routinely rely on personal relations to promote their careers and to insulate themselves from the

deleterious effects of decisions taken outside of their own administrative domains. A network of informal relations, in which the General Secretary's relatives
merely represent the tip of the iceberg, permeates the entire formal Romanian
institutional system.

If Romania had remained more firmly under the influence of the Soviet
Union it is likely that familialization would have been at least held in check; but
the RCP's independent course effectively released the country's political elite
from whatever constraints would otherwise have been imposed by Moscow, and
at the same time denied them access to any aid that might have been forthcoming
from that source to combat the decline of "Leninist party norms." Just as important, with the purge of suspected "Muscovites" the Dej faction and the succeeding Ceausescu leadership were increasingly drawn from those elements of
the Romanian Communist Party that were most deeply imbued with traditional
Romanian culture and least influenced by Leninist political culture. Left to their
own devices it is not surprising that members of the national communist faction
should rely heavily upon the techniques of rule with which they were most
familiar.

It is not remarkable, either, that in what was until very recently a predominantly peasant culture, members of Romania's agricultural and industrial laboring
classes readily adapted to a resumption of prerevolutionary patterns of interaction
with the political elite. In accord with this tradition, the state itself continues to
be generally perceived as a hostile force that must be tolerated more than supported. The intentions of its local agents, unless they happen to be family
members, are necessarily suspect. Cole (1985: 85) correctly points out that in
contemporary Romania as in the past informal relations are essential in establishing links between the population and representatives of the state:

The consumer of services, the worker or citizen, faces a system which claims to
make its decisions on rational impersonal grounds. Yet, the individual knows
that an edge can be gained if he or she can approach the office holder on a personal basis. Such relations may already exist for the consumer, on the basis of
such non-corporate relations as kinship. . . . At the same time, individuals who
must approach the administrative system on an impersonal basis are inevitably at
a disadvantage. (Cole 1981: 85)

Through the early 1970s the predominance of traditional over rational/insti-
tutional ethics and practices (that is, the growth of corruption) was particularly
evident in the service and consumer sectors where the bureaucracy most often
interfaces with the society (Jowitt 1974b: 1184). In the wake of remobilization,
however, this situation has changed significantly. Political exclusion of the managerial class seriously undermined the state's ability to administer the planned
economy on a strictly technical/rational basis. It also disrupted links between
the political elite and the general population. Formation by the RCP of the alternative formal channels of mass participation discussed above met with limited

success at best as a substitute vehicle for mobilizing popular support. The Party's failure to provide suitable institutional means to meet these needs left a serious social and organizational gap, and this was filled by resort to informal relations. Consequently, and no doubt initially more by chance than design, "traditional" practices emerged as an important alternative method of resource allocation, and as a channel of elite/mass communication. The dramatic resurgence of familialization under Ceausescu in the 1970s was thus not merely the result of political maneuvering internal to the regime. Rather, it is a systemic phenomenon, inherently linked to the Party elite's rejection of accommodation with the "extended intelligentsia," and it now constitutes an integral part of the general political economy.

THE SEARCH FOR IDEOLOGICAL HEGEMONY IN THE 1970s

Political changes that occurred in Romania under Ceausescu's leadership, the concentration of power, increasing reliance on mass organs to enforce policy decisions, and familialization, were matched by transformation in the ideological sphere. In essence, having altered the structural base of its support, the RCP was impelled to seek a compatible source of regime legitimation. The increasingly xenophobic tenor of contemporary Romanian ideology and the growth of Ceausescu's personality cult are best understood as the most immediately visible products of this search. As an alternative to the consumer based legitimacy common in the rest of Eastern Europe, the RCP attempted to establish its ideological hegemony through cultivation of a "siege mentality," which justifies continued material sacrifices and strict political discipline as requisites of national survival. Thus as economic dissatisfaction has increased, numerous books and articles began to appear emphasizing the necessity of industrial development for the defense of the country.[10] According to one of a series of nearly identical Ceausescu statements on the subject:

The Romanian people know through their own experience, through their long history as a nation, that real independence can only be assured to the degree that it is established on the base of a powerful modern economy which permits it to collaborate in complete equality with other countries and people. (Ceausescu 1980: 121-29)

Lending credibility to this argument, however, demands that the environment be inhabited by "enemies" of the Romanian people, and this requirement has conditioned all other aspects of the regime's ideological development. In light of the country's history the obvious targets of opportunity in the RCP's campaign to mobilize Romanians against external threats to their independence are Hungary and the Soviet Union. Naturally, given the objective reality of Soviet regional hegemony, the Ceausescu regime's postures vis-à-vis the U.S.S.R. cannot be entirely straightforward. In the Byzantine realm of "crypto-politics," however, Bucharest constantly tests the limits of Soviet tolerance.

Discord, which has every appearance of having been purposely incited by Ceausescu, has punctuated Soviet/Romanian dialogue at crucial points during the course of the RCP's drive for domestic legitimation. One key point of contention is the debate over the status of Bessarabia. While its current status is never directly raised, the formerly Moldavian territory is continually alluded to obliquely in a dialogue that stretches back at least as far as the 1865 publication of Marx's *Notes on the Romanians* in Bucharest. The significance of the piece resides in the fact that in it Marx attacked the Russian annexation of Bessarabia as imperialistic, thus upholding the Romanian position on the rightful affiliation of the territory (Shafir 1985: 50). "Semi-official" Romanian/Soviet polemics over Bessarabia (and other issues) is carried on in the journals of literature and historiography. In this case debate spilled over into other disciplines as well, with anthropologists and linguists on each side seeking to establish a "natural" claim to the region.

In recent years Soviet occupation of Bessarabia has also been addressed more directly by Party leaders on occasion. Ceausescu, for example, pronounced the decisions of 1918, which awarded Bessarabia to the Romanians, to be "the result of a decisive struggle by the large masses of the people, an act of profound national justice, the realization of a legal harmony between objective reality and the inalienable rights of the people on one side, and the national framework that was acutely required by these realities" (quoted in Coman et al. 1982: 39). Similarly, according to the Soviet view the prerevolutionary government of Romania was an imperialist regime that illegally occupied foreign territory and participated in collective aggression, for example, the First World War and occupation of Bessarabia. The RCP, on the other hand, now argues that the previous regime was "bourgeois/landowner," but views it as the victim of imperialist domination and therefore incapable of simultaneously being imperialist itself. Controversy has also arisen over Romanian literary efforts to rehabilitate Marshal Ion Antonescu, and to present a more negative interpretation of Soviet postwar involvement in Romania (Maier 1983). In the most recent and heated of these exchanges, *Literaturnaya Gazeta* writers accused the author of one of a seemingly endless stream of novels concerning the war and socialist construction (who in this case also happened to be a member of the RCP Political Executive Committee: Dumitru Popescu) of deviationism, anti-Soviet slander, and misrepresenting the nature of the Second World War.

Perhaps the most politically charged focus of historical contention, however, has been the debate over Romania's change of course at the conclusion of the Second World War. The remarkably plastic events of August 23, 1944, have undergone over 40 years of constant reinterpretation in light of changing political conditions; but the RCP's most recent version of events is clearly the boldest yet. In their earliest statements, postwar Romanian leaders considered their country to have been liberated by the armed forces of the Soviet Union. In his initial years as Party General Secretary, Nicolae Ceausescu distanced himself from this scenario, suggesting instead that the Romanian and Soviet armies had struggled together to free the country. As of late 1984, however, he had pronounced that what in fact took place was a revolutionary upheaval by the Romanian people, acting under the inspiration and guidance of the RCP, and that German forces had been effectively overthrown before the Red Army entered the scene. According to a recent and authoritative Romanian work dedicated to the subject:

The victory of the Romanian Revolution of August 1944 precipitated events and compressed the progress of the war, bringing the United Nations' victory closer in three major domains in the framework of the war in Europe—military, economic, and political.
   The most significant occurrences were evidenced in the military domain. This fact is entirely explicable, since the Romanian revolution constituted the decisive factor in disengaging the German military system from South-eastern Europe, by "opening" the gates of Fosani. (Olteanu, Ceausescu, Tuca, and Mocanu 1984: 220)

Thus, according to this most recent reinterpretation, Romania should be remembered not as a country that collaborated with Nazism and suffered defeat, but on the contrary, as a subject nation that liberated itself from hostile occupiers. Far from sharing the guilt for the Fascist period, Romania should be honored as having made a considerable contribution to the defeat of Hitler.
   The Ceausescu regime's recurrent confrontation with Hungary has been much more defined, if no less acerbic. In essence, it centers on the status of Transylvania and treatment of the Hungarian national minority residing there. Noticeably less care has been taken to disguise public reference to the Transylvanian question than is the case with issues directly concerning the Soviet Union. Thus Ceausescu has publicly expressed dismay at the fact that for centuries the Romanian majority (two-thirds by his figures) were "merely tolerated on their own soil" (Ceausescu 1983: 428–50). Other champions of the Romanian position have endeavored to establish that: a) Romanians have always inhabited Transylvania and have an absolute moral right to the territory; b) later-arriving Hungarians invaded the region, then suppressed and unjustly exploited its Romanian inhabitants; c) there is therefore a clear historic identity between the Romanian national cause and the cause of the exploited urban and rural proletariat in Transylvania, and finally; d) Hungarians have never accepted the Romanian interpretation of Transylvania's history, and have never given up the idea of regaining the lost territory (Maier 1985a).
   The impact of intensified hostility toward neighboring states is also evident in increasingly acute minority problems inside Romania in recent years. Under present circumstances acceptance as a fully committed communist requires whole-hearted identification with the RCP's position on the historic role of the *Romanian Nation* in all of the territory of contemporary Romania. This demand is clearly problematic for members of the Hungarian community, and for other less numerous ethnic groups as well.[11] Since the close of the 1960s transition

period, increased pressure has been brought to bear on Germans and Hungarians (particularly the latter) to assimilate into the majority population. Linguistic and cultural rights have been undermined, and efforts have been made to break up the minority communities by introducing Romanians into their regions, and channeling minority migration into predominantly Romanian areas (Fischer-Galati 1985; Gilberg 1981; *Witness to Cultural Genocide* 1980).

Nor was resurgence of ethnic hostility restricted to the German and Hungarian minorities. Recent years have also seen a resurgence of anti-Semitism in Romania, despite the fact that the Jewish population of the country has dwindled to an extremely low level; approximately 40,000 in 1982 according to Fischer-Galati (1985: 193). Expression of anti-Jewish sentiments in the official press has taken the form either of criticism of Zionists, or, as shown by Shafir (1983), has appeared in slightly more veiled form in contemporary literature and in the rehabilitation of works by anti-Semitic authors of the prerevolutionary period. Thus figures ranging from the extreme nationalists Mihai Eminescu and Nicolae Iorga, to the openly Fascist poet Octavian Goga, have found their ways back into the national literature (Chirot 1978b; Shafir 1983).

Nor are anti-Semitism and other expressions of national chauvinism limited to the official press. Anti-Hungarian and anti-Jewish views that go beyond publicly permissible bounds can also be found in nonofficial literature circulating among right-wing extremists; in all probability with the collusion of the political leadership.[12] The receptivity of much of the Romanian population to these attitudes appears to remain high; and the RCP has done little to discourage them even within its own ranks. In unofficial conversations RCP members at nearly all levels express xenophobic attitudes with a freedom that would hardly be the case if they were unacceptable to those in the Party with greater authority than themselves. In addition to the omnipresent Soviet threat, the primary themes of these neonationalists are the injustices suffered by the Romanians during the interwar period, when minorities "ran everything"; the past cruelty of the Hungarians and their present untrustworthiness as defenders of Romanian sovereignty; the current danger of Hungarian revanchism; and the fault of elements "alien" to the Romanian people for the excesses of the Stalinist period.

The parallel between current efforts to court popular support on the basis of ethnic identity and the program of the prerevolutionary right, both conservative and fascist, is apparent. The cultivation of a growing leadership cult is another such recurring phenomenon. Mary Ellen Fischer attributes the full blooming of the Ceausescu cult during the 1970s to a combination of two factors. First, the regime's failure to follow through in fulfilling expectations that it created during the 1965-1969 transition period (in the terms employed above, failure to pursue a promised strategy of social accommodation) caused a high level of social discontent. The General Secretary felt that this could be overcome by establishing a direct relationship between himself and the population of the sort which had been so successful at the time of the Czechoslovak crisis. Second, Ceausescu is unfortunately lacking in any degree of individual magnetism that might have enabled him to make such a personal appeal effective, or to exercise real charismatic leadership. His speaking style is pontifical and unimaginative, and he unfortunately suffers from a conspicuous lack of inspiration. Therefore:

Once the gap between his own priorities and the expectations of the masses became clear to him—and a variety of indicators such as absenteeism or low productivity would have revealed the lack of support—the cult began. Ceausescu and his colleagues had to create an idol to be obeyed, an image which would mobilize the popular support which regime goals and Ceausescu's personality could not produce, Ceausescu could not lead the masses, and so had to fool them. (Fischer 1981: 126–27)

Idolization of the Party leader manifests itself in diverse ways, and has grown consistently more pronounced over time. Since the beginning of the 1970s Ceausescu has been credited with being either the initiator of or the inspiration for virtually all positive developments in political and economic life. In March 1974 the office of President of the Republic was established largely so that it could be added to his list of positions (he was already President of the State Council). From their earliest years school children learn their lessons by rote memorization of songs and poems in praising the "party, the leader, and the nation." Poetic tributes to Ceausescu as "founder of a new era of the nation" commonly appear in newspapers and magazines (including the Romanian Communist Party's own) in which the General Secretary takes on godlike qualities.

Ceausescu has also been continually praised as a political theorist of genius, who has made important contributions to the development of Marxism-Leninism. According to one recent Romanian work on the theory and practice of socialism, "the first place in the contemporary epoch is held by the noteworthy, internationally prestigious personality of comrade Nicolae Ceausescu, with a decisive contribution to the definition of scientific socialism as a science of world transformation, and as an instrument for the construction of socialist and communist society" (Hagan 1985: 20). In 1973 a massive tome, *Omagiu*, was published in his praise. Together with his collected works, which appear at regular intervals in several languages, they now reach into the tens of volumes. Both are virtually omnipresent in Romania, along with both Nicolae and Elena Ceausescu's photographs and portraits. A constant effort is also made to represent the RCP General Secretary to the Romanian population as a statesman of remarkable international repute. Party newspapers publish laudatory telegrams addressed to the President almost daily, along with accounts of his foreign policy accomplishments. According to the daily newspaper of the Bucharest City Committee of the RCP, for example: "The prodigious activities and brilliant initiatives of 'The Hero of Peace,' as President Nicolae Ceausescu is known in the world, constitute a lofty example of devotion and responsibility to his own people, and to all humanity, of belief in the future, in the united force of the struggle of all people to realize their desire for peace, understanding, and prosperity" (*Informatia* July 24, 1984: 8).

In fabricating the cult evident care has been taken to represent Ceausescu as a heroic leader in the national tradition. One particularly noticeable aspect of this propaganda effort is the return of monarchial symbolism to Romania. On his investiture as President in 1974, Ceausescu was presented with a scepter and a sash of office in the national colors; these traditional symbols of power have since recurrently appeared in his official portraits and photographs (D. Ionescu 1985: 14). Both Nicolae and Elena Ceausescu's birthdays are national holidays, which in recent years have been celebrated by a stream of poems, songs, and essays praising their virtually supernatural qualities.[13] The first family has also taken up residence in previous royal palaces, which are now reserved for their exclusive use. Remarkably, several of the recent massive public construction projects in Romania have been presented as "gifts by Ceausescu to the Romanian people."

On the other side of the coin, the President's status as "one of the people" who has risen to the top through his own efforts is equally emphasized. Far from being incompatible with promotion of his image as an omnipotent ruler, his humble origin is transformed into an asset by linking him symbolically with the tradition of popular rebels such as Horea, and Avram Iancu. His parents' home in the village of Scornicesti has been turned into a revolutionary museum, and is the site of virtual pilgrimages (Maier 1984b: 8). His background as a poor peasant and revolutionary hero is incessantly referred to, along with his status as the "most beloved son of the people" who, according to one of his numerous biographies "entered, when only a child, the proletarian milieu, started living among the workers, experiencing the exploitation, the social injustice, the way of living, the preoccupations and aspirations of the working class in Romania" (Maxwell 1983: 25). Romanian mass media perpetually broadcast images of the President personally intervening on the peoples' behalf in the operation of factories, collective farms, and local government to set matters straight when others have failed to fulfill their duties faithfully.

Personality cults of the sort that now surround Ceausescu are complex social phenomena, with multiple and overlapping functions. Their overall effectiveness is thus difficult to evaluate. The cult does serve to preclude any public opposition to the General Secretary, who is by definition infallible, and therefore above all criticism. The last known and only really open political attack on Ceausescu occurred in 1979, when Constantine Parvalescu, the single remaining representative of the old guard in the Party leadership, denounced him on the floor of the 12th RCP Congress. Immediately afterward Parvalescu disappeared from public life never to be heard of again, and to date no repetition of his performance has been attempted. Idolization of the General Secretary also serves to preempt innovation on the part of subordinates, and thereby reinforces Ceausescu's central role in policy formulation. Consequently, in the estimation of Gilberg (1975a: 84–85), "most important decisions in Romania today are responses to Ceausescu's personal initiative. . . . The apparatchiks either wait for an initiative from the general secretary, or attempt to anticipate his wishes."

Whether the cult has been equally successful in "eliciting approval from diverse constituencies: on the one hand, the peasant, the apparatchik and the new class, and on the other, the professional, and the managerial-type party cadre," as Jowitt (1974: 1190–91) suggested it was intended to do in the early 1970s, is much more in doubt. That it has improved the regime's relations with the intelligentsia is at best an unlikely proposition. While many among the nonpolitical elite have gained by the RCP's rule in the past and support its promotion of industrialization as a national goal, the majority of educated Romanians inside the Party and out who are willing to discuss the subject find the personality cult in itself objectionable. In recent years many who otherwise strongly support the RCP and its agenda seem increasingly embarrassed by the grotesqueries indulged in by the General Secretary. The attitude of apparatchiks simply cannot be known, since the topic of the cult will not normally be discussed by them. One can assume, however, that since the cult acts as an effective weapon for the defense of a political order representing their interests more than any other, they are more likely to accept the cult on an instrumental level and to internalize its values.

In the absence of survey data the disposition of those who are the real objectives of the cult, the peasants and workers, must to some degree remain shrouded in uncertainty as well. The regime is obviously able to mobilize massive participation in the demonstrations that it organizes to express support for the leader. It may very well be that mass participation in support of the Party leader is in part a reflection of conformist behavior attributable to peasant political culture rather than any authentic attachment to the RCP General Secretary. There is little doubt, however, that the image projected of Ceausescu as a strong decisive leader, particularly in combination with the renewed nationalist appeal, does exercise a powerful attraction over thousands of minimally educated and socially displaced individuals who currently inhabit the lower levels of the Romanian polity. Stephen Fischer-Galati, for one, suggests that as a result of increased opportunities and the regime's foreign policy "there has been wider popular acceptance, or at least toleration, of the autocracy and the corollary deification of Ceausescu than critics would like to have us believe" (Fischer-Galati 1985: 13).

Along with this "mystification" of the relationship between the leader and the people, "mythification" of the nation's distant past, which was also integral to the world view of Romania's interwar fascists, has also become a conspicuous element of the Ceausescu ideological system. One can visit seemingly endless museums and archaeological exhibits, and read innumerable "scientific" works proving that Romanians striving to defend their independence have uninterruptedly occupied the territory of the modern nation state far back into prehistoric times. Otetea's *History of the Romanian People*, for instance, places the origin of the Romanians at least as far back as 2000 B.C. (Otetea 1970: 30–31). Utilization of a mythic history for political ends is epitomized in a typical Ceausescu statement.

The facts attest that in the contemporary regions of Romania every social order known to humanity has existed in succession in the course of the millennia; that the history of the Romanian people is the history of the development of the forces of relations of production, and of the struggle of social and national liberation, against invaders and foreign domination, for liberty and independence.

From the formation by Burebista of the centralized Dacian state in the first century before our era, from the epoch of the flourishing of the Dacian society of Decebal and then through two millennia of existence, until present days, our people have had to give harsh struggle to constitute and to defend their own existence, their national being. (Ceausescu 1983: 73)

Furthermore, RCP theorists began to argue for a virtual identity in the modern period between history of the communist party and that of the Romanian nation. Thus it is no longer admissible to consider the history of the nation and the history of the Party as "parallel." Rather, according to the RCP Secretary General, "it must be understood that our party is not separate from the nation or the people, that our nation has a single history, that our party was born in the social struggle, in the context of the history of the people: its history is the history of our nation and, the national history is the single history which must reflect the entire development of our people" (quoted in Cartana and Mocanu 1986: 23).

The regime expends an enormous effort in exploring every detail of the national past to produce evidence showing that virtually every aspect of its current policy is an organic extension of Romania's historical legacy. Hence the current heroic leader is the natural expression in modern times of a tradition that is imbued in the life of the people. Historians, poets, novelists, and filmmakers have detailed how past heroes beginning with the legendary Geto-Dacian leaders, stretching through Vlad Tepes and Michael the Brave, to the liberal revolutionaries of 1848, and ending up (unremarkably) with Ceausescu, have always played a decisive role in defending the interests of the Romanian people during times of crisis. Similarly, when the RCP limited its commitment to the Warsaw Alliance and adopted a military policy of "war of the entire people" as the basis of national defense, military historians were quick to produce works showing that poeple's war is a longstanding Romanian tradition that has appeared recurrently in history since the Dacian defense against Trajan (Coman et al. 1982: 11-50).

Neither has Ceausescu been reticent in enlisting the support of another traditional institution favored by the prerevolutionary right, the Romanian Orthodox Church, in his efforts to establish the regime's credentials as a truly legitimate national force. Since as early as 1948, when the state compelled members of the Uniate religion to incorporate with Romanian Orthodoxy, relations between the RCP and the Orthodox Church have been at least cordial. Following Ceausescu's nationalist consolidation they have grown consistently warmer. In 1974 the Church was included as an institutional member of the Socialist Unity Front (Jowitt 1974: 137). Under Patriarch Justin Moisescu, who assumed his post in 1977, the Orthodox hierarchy has been openly supportive of the goals of the

RCP and, in contrast to the role of the Polish Catholic Church, it has refrained from attempts to defend those who resist the regime's political line. Significantly, Orthodox religious services now begin with prayer for the well-being of the Party and state leader.

Popular rituals designed to stimulate public enthusiasm for the nationalist renaissance, which bear much more than a passing resemblance to the Iron Guardists' mystical practices, have reappeared as well. Massive extravaganzas, such as the one organized to celebrate the "2000th anniversary of the formation of the first unitary state" in Romania, bring thousands of participants together in outdoor rallies. Beginning in 1977 the regime has annually organized the "Hymn to Romania" celebration, which is designed to unite members of all social strata on the basis of their common Romanian culture. During the weeks building up to this nationwide event the regime attempts to mobilize the entire population. Activists organize everyone available into amateur groups for the preparation of performances in the "popular" mode to eulogize the leader and the nation.

With the exception of marginal innovations and a great deal of detailed elaboration, little of the current RCP mythos differs greatly from the handiwork of the prewar ultranationalists (compare the preceding examples, for instance, with Walter Kolarz's treatment of "the Daco-Roman Empire," in his *Myths and Realities in Eastern Europe*). Like the reappearance of informal corruption in the economic sphere, the political elite's recourse to those aspects of the pre-revolutionary ideological tradition occurred on an ad hoc basis under the pressure of events. Given the dictatorial character of the RCP leaders' political regime, their pursuit of a base of social support in the relatively new and under-developed working class rather than the intelligentsia, and the direction of their developmental program, it was natural, if unfortunate, that they should draw on the heritage of the radical fascists rather than the liberal democratic political parties.

CONCLUSION

During the course of the 1970s Romania moved decisively away from the other state-socialist countries of Eastern Europe. Both its economic model and its domestic political behavior were perceptibly remolded as part of Ceausescu's remobilization program, and the directions pursued by Bucharest in these spheres were inextricably bound together. Far from accepting the formula of economic decentralization and depoliticization in evidence elsewhere in Eastern Europe, the RCP's leaders made use of their hegemonic position to launch a determined drive to suppress the interests of the extended intelligentsia. As an alternative to elite accommodation they pursued a populist strategy.

But the RCP was not in possession of any new development model, and in recent years the limitations that forced reform elsewhere have plagued Romania as well. Similarly, Ceausescu's political strategy encountered growing difficulties.

Mobilizational techniques without actual participation did not succeed in attaching workers to the RCP's program, and, despite continuing efforts, political leaders have yet to discover an effective alternative to the role played by the privileged class in managing other state-socialist societies.

Rather than seeking avenues of reform when faced with the possibility of economic collapse, the political elite became more coercive, and intensified its efforts to dominate all channels of domestic political activity. In order to do so, it fell back ever more openly on the prerevolutionary political tradition. Consequently various practices common to the presocialist period reappeared and were incorporated into the Romanian political economy. "Corruption" that is an integral element of the system of material and social reproduction, pervasive nepotism, manipulated participation, and the personality cult are all obvious manifestations of this phenomenon. Having rejected political legitimation based on limited state/society accommodation, the Ceausescu regime sought to establish its ideological hegemony on the basis of "traditionalistic" values. Thus the RCP has played down its role as representative of the proletariat in favor of a new identity as the political embodiment of the nation. It cultivated the concept of "organic unity" among the Party, the leader, and the people, and in the process became increasingly xenophobic. In its return to the Balkan authoritarian tradition the communist party elite found the means to retain its grip on power, but it moved no closer to resolving the fundamental contradictions plaguing Romanian society.

7 NATIONAL COMMUNISM, THE INTERNATIONAL CONTEXT, AND ECONOMIC CRISIS

INTRODUCTION

While the nature of the economic ties between East and West and the effect of changes in the international climate on the planned economies are reasonably understood, the relationship between these same factors and East European domestic and international politics has been more problematic.[1] Establishing such links is difficult and controversial, even in the case of countries where access to information concerning the political process has been relatively free. Because of the present dearth of empirical data any analysis of contemporary communist states must necessarily be based on a higher degree of supposition, and is therefore more tentative. Such an analysis is nonetheless essential to understanding the evolution of Romania's domestic political economy.

In many current conceptions of this subject, most notably those deriving from the work of Immanuel Wallerstein, it is argued that national politics are shaped by a country's location within the international division of labor.[2] Proponents of this view often suggest that the communist countries as a group constitute a "semi-periphery," a structural intermediary between the developed core and underdeveloped "periphery" of the world economic system (Wallerstein 1979; Chase-Dunn 1982). National political institutions, according to this argument, are determined by international economic forces. Here, at least in the case of Romania (which has established itself in an intermediary location in the international division of labor), the opposite argument will be advanced. That is, while the two phenomena are intimately related, Romania's role in the world economy was initially an effect, not the cause, of its domestic and international political circumstances. As will be shown, however, once it became firmly committed to entering the world economy Romania's trade links began to exert a powerful influence both on its domestic politics and on the further evolution of its foreign policy orientation. Recent events have accentuated this trend. Faced with a balance of trade crisis beginning in 1980, Bucharest reacted in a manner strikingly similar to that seen in noncommunist developing countries that were subject to analogous economic constraints.

THE BACKGROUND TO AUTARKIC DEVELOPMENT

As discussed at some length above, Romania's prerevolutionary experience with the international economy was far from felicitous. Prior to the imposition of communist rule it was among the most underdeveloped of the European nations.[3] Up to the mid-nineteenth century the country was a direct dependency of its more powerful neighbors, and from then on until the outbreak of World War Two it was effectively transformed into a "semi-colony" of the more advanced West European industrial states. In spite of its fairly extensive natural resource base it failed to achieve industrialization. Its history of international economic subordination had severe repercussions for domestic economic and social development. It also fundamentally shaped the attitudes of the Romanian intelligentsia toward nationality issues in general, and the question of autonomous industrialization in particular. That prewar convictions were carried over into the postrevolutionary generation of leaders became starkly evident in Romania's drive for autarkic development.

By the late 1950s the emergent RCP leadership was already on somewhat uneasy terms with Moscow. Party First Secretary Gheorghiu-Dej outmaneuvered his political rivals, among whom were those individuals that were on the best terms with Moscow during Stalin's reign (that is, Anna Pauker, Vasile Luca, and Teohari Georgescu), as well as liberal elements within the Party that might have constituted an alternative to his rule after Stalin's death (Miron Constantinescu and Lucretiu Patrascanu). In doing so, Dej managed to stabilize a domestic leadership group that was neither reformist nor in line with the ascendant faction in the CPSU, and as a consequence Romania remained committed to rapid heavy industrialization while the Soviet Union and its other allies moved in the direction of moderated growth strategies.[4]

The "national" communists who gained control of the RCP were determined to end their country's relative backwardness as quickly as possible through a program of rapid economic development. Pursuit of this course required that the RCP deviate from its East European neighbors in its international economic relations as well as in its domestic policy. Consistent with the practice in all of Eastern Europe during the Stalinist period, Romania had been closely and intentionally tied to the U.S.S.R. through bilateral trade agreements. By 1958 the Soviet Union, which had played a negligible role in Romanian trade before WWII, accounted for over 50 percent of all foreign exchange; an additional 20 percent went to the rest of the CMEA, and less than 25 percent to the developed West. This arrangement served not only to benefit the U.S.S.R. in a material sense, but also reinforced Soviet hegemony in the region by creating dependence on it as the dominant economic partner in each bilateral relationship.

The decision to pursue a policy of autonomous national economic development caused a fundamental shift in this foreign trade structure. Commercial relations with the West began to shift dramatically in 1959, climbing by 80 percent in that year alone, and continuing to rise throughout the 1960–1965 plan period.[5] By 1965 the Soviet Union's share of total foreign trade had been reduced to 38 percent and that of the West increased to 36 percent (*Anuarul Statistic* 1980: 503). This change occurred in conjunction with the Dej faction's move to insulate itself from Soviet interference, even before its successors moved openly to redirect the country's foreign policy away from that of the other East European countries. The scope and rapidity of this shift clearly illustrates the degree to which Romania's foreign economic behavior was shaped by political considerations at the end of the 1950s.

Initially, economic redirection toward the West was thus intended to aid in establishing a degree of autonomy, both economic and political, from the Soviet Union. Unlike the pattern emerging among the other East Europeans, Bucharest initiated its trade liberalization not as part of a broader reform, but rather in order to maintain its chosen economic model, and more specifically, to do so in the face of Soviet attempts to increase East European integration through a program of supranational planning at the expense of Romanian industrialization.[6] Resistance to Khrushchev's 1962 plan to increase the socialist international division of labor, which would have relegated the Balkan CMEA members to the position of raw material producers for the economically advanced Northern Tier, was primary among the factors culminating in the famed April 1964 "Declaration of Independence" from the Soviet Union (Gill 1975: 98).

CEAUSESCUISM AND THE TURN TO THE WEST

Far from reversing this tide of events, the ascent of Nicolae Ceausescu to leadership of the RCP in 1965 served to reinforce the prevailing trend. Faced with political competition from well established rivals within the political elite, and with severely limited possibilities of obtaining support from Moscow, the new Party leader chose to intensify Romania's independent course. At the RCP's Ninth Congress in July 1965 Ceausescu reaffirmed the country's sovereignty. His foreign policy, clearly designed to strike a resonant chord with the Romanians' traditional nationalism and anti-Russian feelings, was a conspicuous success with the population. Three years after its inception Ceausescu's "heroic" public stand in defense of national autonomy during the 1968 Soviet invasion of Czechoslovakia established him, for the moment at least, as a truly popular leader.

Ceausescu's show of independence in the international sphere, coupled with the promise of reform in the late 1960s, provided him with a badly needed base of personal support among the population during the period of leadership transition, and was an important factor in his successful efforts to establish control over the RCP. As discussed above, however, the ultimate goal of these tactics was far from the general liberalization that his early rhetoric led the population to expect. Within a decade Ceausescu had established himself as the most powerful personal ruler in Eastern Europe, and had strengthened rather than restricted the coercive apparatus of the state. The strain of extreme nationalism that became a pervasive feature of Romanian political life after the mid-1960s was thus closely tied to this maintenance of the Stalinist model. It was also, as Mary Ellen Fischer (1983: i) has pointed out, inherently related to the country's behavior in the international environment.

This complex of related foreign and domestic policies necessarily manifested itself in foreign trade as well. The diversification that began in 1959 continued to gain momentum after Ceausescu's assumption of power. Participation in the world market presented the prospect of substantial advantages for RCP planners. Economically it allowed the Romanians to take advantage of their natural resource base as a source of exchange for Western industrial raw materials and equipment in short supply in the East, while continuing their inter-CMEA trade in "soft" goods that could not find a market in the West. Politically, it provided the Ceausescu faction with an added margin of insulation from the pressure that it experienced as a result of its continuing feud with Moscow.

Disenchantment between the two formal allies increased as Romania became the first Soviet ally to return its ambassador to Albania (in January 1963) despite that country's "excommunication" from the Soviet alliance, and took an independent position with respect to the Sino-Soviet split. Bucharest also became a thorn in the side of Soviet Warsaw Pact policy by reducing compulsory military service, resisting Soviet dominance of the Pact command structure, and refusing to participate in joint military exercises (Gill 1975: 99). This increasingly hostile relationship was quite beneficial in generating domestic support for the Ceausescu regime, but it obviously created certain additional risks as well. Purposefully antagonizing their overwhelmingly more powerful neighbor in this fashion made it essential that the RCP elite reduce all possible avenues of Russian leverage. Limiting economic dependence on the U.S.S.R. was one important means of doing so.

Among the most pressing problems impelling Romania to trade with the West was the necessity of obtaining oil. Initially, possession of substantial domestic oil resources (over 80 percent of Eastern Europe's total) and other natural resources enhanced Bucharest's capacity to seek independence from the Soviets. But complete energy autonomy soon became impossible. Domestic production began to level off, growing by only 1.6 percent annually between 1966 and 1973 while the ambitious expansion of Romanian petroleum industry increased demand at a much greater rate (Joyner 1976: 498). Oil refining industry was considered crucial because it provided goods for the hard currency market, and was intended to play a key role in future development. Romania's problematic status within the CMEA, however, made it impossible to obtain low priced petroleum products from the Soviet Union under the conditions that applied to the other East Europeans. As a result Bucharest was forced to seek outside sources, and soon established a cordial relationship with members of OPEC.[7]

The progress of its industrialization effort compounded the RCP's problems, since reshaping Romania's domestic economic base concomitantly transformed the country's requirements in international trade. In the earlier period Bucharest's international trade served primarily as a vehicle for obtaining capital equipment from the West, but over time an expanded industrial base significantly increased the country's ability to supply itself from its own domestic machine industry, while at the same time stimulating demand for imported raw materials. This pattern was far from coincidental. Rather, it reflected the political elites' continual preoccupation with promoting industrial sovereignty. Despite the growing overall importance of Western trade the share of Western machine imports in total equipment investments was a mere 10 percent in 1975. As Marvin Jackson (1981a: 271) concluded, this level of independence could only have resulted from the conscious application of a policy of industrial autarky.

Romania's "autarkic" development strategy eased the demand for imported equipment, but on the negative side it simultaneously increased requirements for industrial raw materials. It also affected exports, most immediately by facilitating production of light consumer goods and semimanufactures for the external market. Between 1960 and 1970 this sector's contribution to foreign trade rose from 5.8 to 18.1 percent, while the relative share of raw materials in total exports fell. The U.S.S.R.'s importance in overall trade also continued to decline, from approximately 38 percent in 1965 to 26 percent in 1970, while the share absorbed by the developed Western economies steadily increased.[8]

Since the mid-1960s continued commitment to a policy of rapid industrialization, coupled with increasingly hostile relations with the Soviet Union, created pressures on the RCP that led it to further expand the foreign trade links already established with the noncommunist world under Dej. Attractive and relatively safe opportunities to obtain financial support presented themselves in the world market. The growing exploitation of these opportunities played an important role in the combination of factors that allowed the Ceausescu regime to resist succumbing to a longer term commitment to the accommodationist strategy that was briefly evident in the late 1960s transition period. Without the economic and political resources provided by the world economy remobilization would have been a much more problematic, although not necessarily an impossible, proposition.

TRADE AND FOREIGN POLICY THROUGH THE MID-1970s

Between 1950 and 1975 the growth rate of Romania's overall industrial production was among the highest in the world.[9] But even by the late 1960s its economic mechanism was on the way to becoming the dinosaur of the state-socialist world. Despite the increasing cost of bottlenecks, consumer shortages, and massive resource misallocation due to lack of information, the Ceausescu regime could not bring itself to relinquish its Stalinist heritage and accept the reduction in direct administrative control that would result from decentralization. Romania was last among the East Europeans to experiment with decentralization, and even then its attempts were halfhearted. Bucharest's "reformist" trend was quickly reversed, and the country experienced a slow but steady recentralization. As a result, by the 1970s the Romanians were approaching the limits of effective development within their existing "extensive" framework. Simply increasing inputs of labor and raw materials could no longer provide the large increases in growth rates that they had in earlier years.

Consequently, while the RCP leadership was intent on continuing rapid development through investment in heavy industry and increased accumulation continued to be their primary response to questions of economic strategy, other means were sought to ensure that economic progress would continue.[10] In addition to its innovations in the political realm the RCP ultimately fell back on further integration into the international market for economic support. By expanding its foreign trade Romania sought to procure technologically advanced producer goods as well as industrial raw materials from the developed capitalist economies. In exchange, planners intended to market the industrial goods it was now producing in sizeable quantities in the developed Western economies (Tsantis and Pepper 1979: 117). Financial demands played a considerable role as well. Implementation of the 1971–1975 Five-Year Plan required approximately $21 billion in total investment: $4 billion of this amount was sought from Western sources (Braun 1978: 24).

In order to promote its domestic economic agenda, as well as its more purely foreign policy goals, the RCP launched a determined program of "bridge-building" to the West under Ceausescu. Long-term technical cooperation and trade agreements covering the period of the Fifth Five-Year Plan were signed with both France and West Germany. In 1971 Romania became a member of the General Agreement on Trade and Tariffs (GATT), and in 1972 it became the first state-socialist country to join the International Monetary Fund. The Romanian government also permitted a number of new joint ventures with Western firms to join the Renault plant (begun in 1966) in operating on Romanian territory. Finally, the United States extended Most Favored Nation (MFN) status to Romania in 1975.

During the late 1960s and early 1970s the "infatuation" between the Ceausescu regime and the West reached a peak. The reformist politics of the transition years raised hopes among Western observers that another "moderate" alternative was about to emerge in Eastern Europe. Furthermore, it was obvious to Western governments that, all other considerations aside, a more independent Romania was a valuable asset in their ongoing competition with Moscow. The RCP's outspoken divergence from the Soviet Union on matters such as the Sino-Soviet rift and supranational planning in the CMEA broadened to include Romania's extension of diplomatic relations to West Germany, its failure to take a strong stand against Israel in 1967, and its withdrawal from active participation in the Warsaw Treaty Organization. Unlike more loyal allies, Romania voted with the Soviet Union on only 76 percent of all ballots cast in the United Nations from 1970 to 1976, while the remaining bloc members voted over 97 percent in its support (Zimmerman 1980: 435).

The value of Ceausescu's public stance in defense of self-determination in such forums as the United Nations and the opportunity that Romania presented for developing relations with the East outweighed any reservations that Western leaders might have had concerning its domestic affairs. Western appreciation of Bucharest's changing international status was symbolized by Richard Nixon's 1969 state visit, which made Romania the first East European country to receive a U.S. President in the postwar period. Despite the ideological remobilization and purge of the intelligentsia that dispelled some of the optimism of the transition period, Western benevolence toward the Ceausescu regime failed to erode substantially.

This favorable evaluation was reasonable in consideration of a generally, if not entirely, positive domestic sociopolitical image that endured into the mid-1970s. Improved consumption coupled with populist rhetoric and Ceausescu's ostentatious nationalism ensured general passivity if not active support among the vast majority of the Romanian population, apparently outweighing the regime's marked failure to reduce domestic political suppression. In fact, the Western economic connection was in itself an essential factor in the maintenance of domestic harmony, allowing RCP leaders to steadily if slowly increase consumption during the early 1970s, even while the rapid pace of industrialization was maintained, and to do so without economic reform (Tsantis and Pepper 1979: 175).

TRADE AND FOREIGN POLICY REDIRECTION IN THE MID-1970s

Initially Romania's trade strategy for the 1970s progressed as planned. Between 1970 and 1973 imports grew by 8.2 percent, and exports climbed by 10.8 percent (Tsantis and Pepper 1979: 120). Simultaneously Bucharest succeeded in shifting its trade into what was considered a more acceptable area from the perspective of national security. By 1973 the total CMEA share of its trade was reduced to 45.5 percent of exports and 40.7 percent of imports; Western commerce had moved in to fill the gap, and foreign policy links compatible with these trade relations had been established.[11] These successes allowed RCP leaders to maintain their chosen course, despite clearly signaled Soviet dissatisfaction. But future economic difficulties were already presaged by the failure to find a sufficient market for Romanian industrial consumer goods, whose share in exports increased by less than 1 percent from 1970 to 1973, and upon which planners were depending to produce growing amounts of hard currency in succeeding years (Tsantis and Pepper 1979: 578).

In the last two years of the 1971-1975 Fifth Plan period the foreign trade situation deteriorated as a result of both Romania's internal economic problems and the international climate. The beginning of the international oil crisis in 1974 not only increased the cost of imports, but also softened the market for Romanian exports, turning what had been a substantial trade surplus into a huge deficit practically overnight, with the previous positive trade balance transformed into a 1.3 billion lei deficit (*Anuarul Statistic* 1980: 498-501). Initially the trade deficit was met by restricting Western imports, shifting goods intended for export to the CMEA into the hard currency market, and by limited borrowing. Imports grew by only 4 percent in 1975, while exports rose by 14 percent, bringing overall trade back into balance (*Anuarul Statistic* 1980: 498-501). But the curtailment of imports could not be kept up without damaging the development effort, and there was an end to the supply of hard currency products that could be squeezed out of Romania's CMEA trade. As the problem continued unabated, RCP leaders were forced to begin searching for more permanent solutions.

Rather than limiting development, reorganizing internally, or turning back into the CMEA, planners pinned their hopes on a changed international posture. The RCP's new strategy relied on expansion of industrial exports to developing countries to generate the hard currency needed for offsetting increased oil imports. This move into the Third World was coupled with restriction of imports from the developed economies. Redirection was achieved with striking speed: the LDCs' share in Romania's total trade rose from 7 percent in 1970 to almost 25 percent in 1980.[12] The increase in imports over the course of the decade was accounted for in large part by the rise in oil import magnitude and prices, but exports to the Third World rose dramatically as well, from $68 million to $2,121 million over the same period (Droker and Martens 1982: 242; Central Intelligence Agency 1982: 106). Planners also succeeded in restraining imports from the industrialized West while Romania continued to market industrial raw materials and consumer manufactures to its developed trading partners. Between 1970 and 1975 total imports had expanded at approximately 38 percent annually, from 1975 and 1980 this rate dropped to 15 percent. Imports from the developed West declined from a peak of 42 percent of the total in 1975 to only 27 percent in 1980. This reduction helped to at least partially ameliorate the huge deficit that was emerging in trade with OPEC (CIA 1982: 106-7).

The effort to make economic inroads among LDCs also led to the formation of joint ventures abroad for the first time in the postwar period. By 1980 Romania was participating in at least 30 joint production enterprises outside its borders, concentrated in the Middle East, Africa, and Asia (Radu 1981: 253-56; Tsantis and Pepper 1979: 125).[13] In order to further promote friendly economic relations Bucharest also provided foreign aid to its less developed trading partners. From 1970 to 1975 this averaged $350 million per year, by far the highest level among the East Europeans (Linden 1981: 234). Much of Romania's financing was, however, provided in the form of loans for the development of raw material production, and must be repaid over time with the output of the completed projects.

As was the case with Bucharest's opening to the West, the mid–1970s shift in economic relations was matched by new foreign policy initiatives. Beginning in 1972 Romania identified itself as a "Socialist Developing Nation," and has since progressively strengthened this identification. By 1978 Ceausescu was emphasizing the need "to intensify our links with all developing countries" (quoted in Radu 1981: 242). In essence, RCP diplomacy sought to equate Romania economically with less developed countries (LDCs), and to establish it politically as a member of the nonaligned movement. This status was advantageous in a number of ways. First, it provided Romanian diplomats with added leverage in their attempt to obtain tariff advantages from the industrialized West. Bucharest's efforts in this direction met with considerable success: it obtained treatment as a developing nation from the United States under the terms of the General System of Preferences (GSP), and similar concessions from the West Europeans (Droker and Martens 1982: 223).

This new international posture also served as a means of convincing LDC leaders that Romania was a more politically appropriate trading partner than the developed capitalist states. In its new incarnation the Ceausescu regime became a vocal supporter of the New International Economic Order, which was promoted by Bucharest as a means of creating an environment in which all small and medium-sized states could be developed "multilaterally." Often to the dismay of the Soviet Union, the RCP became a strong advocate of disarmament; calling for the dissolution of military blocs, the formation of nuclear free zones, and the worldwide reduction of arms expenditures.

Romania also suggested reforms to increase the power of the General Assembly in the United Nations, and took a much more active interest than other state-socialist countries in establishing diplomatic links with the Third World. Between 1973 and 1980 its leaders signed treaties of friendship and cooperation with ten developing countries, in addition to Portugal, a NATO member (Radu 1981). By 1976 President Ceausescu had made state visits to over 30 LDCs (Braun 1978: 37). Romania joined the Group of 77, and participated with "guest" status at conferences of the nonaligned movement (Madsen 1982: 302; Linden 1981). Not entirely unrelated from the oil situation, the PLO was recognized as the legitimate representative of the Palestinians, and allowed to establish a quasi-official embassy in Bucharest. Romania also began to vote consistently with the Arab states on issues that concerned them in the U.N., and supported the Arab boycott of Israeli businesses (Braun 1978: 28).

Romanian economic planners thus sought to create a niche for themselves in the exchange of their surplus machine and engineering products for raw materials in the Third World, while agricultural goods and industrial raw materials were traded to the developed West for industrial commodities beyond their own technological capacity. With the realization of this policy shift Romania moved into an intermediary position in the world market. The absence of substantial internal restructuring made international redirection of this sort inevitable. Unlike Hungary, which chose a course of economic reform, Romania's enterprises were simply unable to compete effectively with those of the developed capitalist countries. The quality of its industrial output was too low to find a positive reception in the more sophisticated markets of Western Europe and the United States. On the other hand, its own recent experience with the problems of early industrialization and the relative simplicity of its production techniques could be turned to positive advantage in relations with the developing nations. RCP leaders also showed themselves to be quite adept at exploiting their limited diplomatic assets in developing an international political posture conducive to their economic strategy.

Participation in the international market thus increased Romania's autonomy from the Soviet Union, as required by the Ceausescu leadership's pursuit of a course of "nationalist" regime legitimation. It also facilitated the political elite's chosen strategy of sustained rapid industrialization without abandonment of economic and political centralism. When developed Western markets proved inappropriate to their country's competitive strengths, Romanian planners responded by moving, quite successfully, into the semiperipheral role initially predicted for it by world system analysts. All too soon, however, cracks appeared in the facade of economic well-being they had constructed only by drawing heavily on international, as well as domestic, reserves. Most of the Party's priority economic goals were met up to the mid-1970s, but at the expense of beginning a process of debt accumulation which ultimately proved unmanageable.

ECONOMIC DETERIORATION AND STATE RESPONSE

Dramatic as it was, trade restructuring in the mid-1970s did not resolve the foreign exchange problem. While remaining within tolerable limits, Romania's hard currency debt approximately doubled during the 1970-1975 plan period, from $1,227 to $2,449 million (CIA 1982: 54). But petroleum imports rose from approximately 10,000 barrels per day to over 16,000 barrels per day between 1976 and 1980, turning the country into a net oil importer in 1976, with a shortfall that continually grew (Droker and Martens 1982: 277). Coupled with sluggishness in the export market this added burden turned the balance of trade against the Romanians. Their hard currency debt grew by an average annual rate of over 36 percent of the second half of the decade, reaching $6.7 billion by 1979 (Droker and Martens 1982: 242).

In a very real sense sustaining growth during the late 1970s through borrowing had only exacerbated the unfolding crisis by increasing demand for imported raw materials to feed industries in which labor productivity was low even by East European standards, and whose products could not find adequate foreign markets. It has been estimated, for example, that by 1980 Romania was losing as much as $900,000 per day on its exports of refined petroleum products

(Droker and Martens 1982: 249). Under these conditions even accelerated borrowing could not stave off deterioration in the long term.

By the beginning of the 1980s Romania's economy had reached a point of near collapse. Its hard currency trade deficit climbed to $2.4 billion for 1980 alone before being brought back under control (Wharton November 9, 1982: 7). As planners struggled to find the funds to cover their import needs indebtedness rose dramatically. When total debt increased from $6,700 million in 1979 to $10,350 million in 1981 Bucharest had reached the end of its financial rope (CIA 1982: 54). Repayment proved impossible in late 1981, and loan restructuring agreements had to be negotiated for both 1982 and 1983 (Radio Free Europe Research Romania/Situation Report, January 13, 1983: 6). The effect of the debt crisis on trade was immediate. Between 1980 and 1981 imports from the industrialized West were reduced by 17 percent (CIA 1982: 106-7). In the following year this slide became an avalanche; 1982 imports were reduced by another 45 percent, and exports declined sharply as well, largely as a result of shortages in raw material imports for export producing industries. Overall trade with LDCs also fell off, but it remained above 1980 levels, and its relative share continued to increase.[14]

While external conditions were extremely adverse, the severity of their impact on Romania is clearly attributable to the inadequate organization of its domestic economy. Just as in the late 1960s, the 1978 reforms announced by the RCP were not fully implemented. The regime opted to retain close control of the country's economic processes as part of its more general endeavor to dominate social life as a whole, and appeared willing to accept whatever costs this might entail. Gross inefficiencies had been subsidized by capital inflows from the West, which in the final analysis had the effect of increasing the vulnerability of the economy to the international environment. Under the impact of external disruptions the irrationalities of the system became painfully obvious.[15] In 1980 Romania showed its second worst economic performance since World War II, and problems continued to grow in the following years.[16]

Romania's party elite responded to economic decline in their country with an austerity program analogous to those undertaken by the leaders of noncommunist LDCs caught up in the same cycle of debt accumulation. As a result of the RCP's investment policy the level of personal consumption in Romania has never been high during the postwar period, but those advances which had been made were quickly eroded by the Party's response to the foreign exchange crisis. Many goods that had only recently become available to the population disappeared from shops. Official reports showed a 1.9 percent decline in 1982 consumption; but in fact the situation was far worse than this figure would suggest (Wharton April 1, 1983: 5). It was typical of Ceausescu's policy that exports of food were increased and imports limited in order to generate hard currency, and that the burden of the shortfall was borne by the population. In 1982, for example, food exports rose by 12.3 percent while imports decreased by 66.8 percent (Wharton April 4, 1983: 4). Long lines appeared as consumers struggled to obtain such

basics as flour, potatoes, corn meal, oil, and sugar. In 1981 rationing was reintroduced for the first time since 1953.

Three effects of these increasingly difficult economic conditions became almost immediately visible in Romanian foreign policy. The first of these was
intensification of efforts to cement its association with the Third World as an
alternative to the industrialized West, with whom relations were clearly entering
a period of decline. Despite its own obvious difficulties, Bucharest maintained its
policy of supplying low cost industrial goods and technological aid to its less
developed trading partners. By 1981 LDCs accounted for 30 percent of Romanian imports and 25 percent of exports. While absolute declines appeared in
both categories in 1982 due to foreign exchange shortages, their relative importance in total hard currency foreign trade continued to grow (CIA 1982: 106-7).

The regional differentiation of trade, which reflects Romania's current intermediary position in the world economy was also reinforced. In its exchange with
the industrialized West, Bucharest has become an exporter of processed petroleum
products, basic industrial products (simple iron and steel products, yarn and
fabrics, etc.), agricultural commodities, and light consumer manufactures. Exports from Western developed countries to Romania are dominated by basic
industrial raw materials, and machines and equipment. In contrast, its position
with respect to LDCs became that of a developed nation. Exports were led by
industrial goods, machines, and more recently refined petroleum products, while
imports consisted largely of raw materials.

Efforts to establish Romania as a leading representative of LDC aspirations
have also been intensified. Bucharest launched a propaganda crusade against
international economic exploitation and the "brain drain" to the industrialized
West and the Romanian President's already busy schedule of visits to Third
World capitals expanded, as did his rhetorical denunciation of the arms race and
emphasis on Romania's independence from superpower military blocs. Both
Ceausescu's five-nation Asian trip in November 1982 and statements at the 1983
New Delhi conference of the nonaligned movement were used to underscore
Romania's LDC status and call for a more just international order. These pro-
nouncements have drawn attention not to issues that divided the world between
socialist and capitalist camps, but rather to those separating the rich from the
poor.

In particular, renewed efforts were made in the Middle East, where Ceausescu
became involved in the diplomatic exchanges intended to resolve the Lebanese
civil war, and carried on an ongoing connection with the heads of state of Jordan,
Syria, Libya, and Egypt (Bacon 1984: 363). This side of Romanian diplomacy
was clearly a consequence of its increased petroleum dependence. The same consideration was undoubtedly responsible for an increase in Romanian arms traf-
ficking. Between 1978 and 1982, Bucharest exported approximately $2 billion
worth of arms, of which two-thirds went to non-WTO nations. Military hardware
worth $825 million was sold to Iraq, from which it received very large amounts
of crude oil in return (US Arms Control and Disarmament Agency 1984: 95-98).

Second, the problems of the international economy led Romanian leaders to begin a reevaluation of their relationship with the socialist bloc, seeing it as a possible alternative source of badly needed industrial raw materials. Grudgingly, Romania did partially shift its trade back toward the CMEA. By 1985 trade with the state-socialist countries, with which Romania could take advantage of barter agreements, had increased to 57 percent of total foreign trade. But this was clearly treated by the RCP leadership as a short-term expedient. In commenting on the Seventh Five-Year plan, introduced in 1985, Prime Minister Dasculescu made it clear that reducing the level of CMEA trade was an important goal of the RCP's current economic program (Radio Free Europe Romanian/Situation Report 8, July 17, 1986).[17]

Bucharest refused, however, to alter its position on surpanationality, and in fact added even further demands, claiming special concessions as a developing country. In commenting on the CMEA's Comprehensive Program in December 1985, Ceausescu obliquely criticized the Soviets for failing to provide sufficient raw materials and energy to Eastern Europe. Romania was also the last of the Soviet Union's economic partners to conclude a long-term bilateral accord on economic cooperation; and in reporting on its signing clearly signaled dissatisfaction with the document (*Scinteia* June 4, 1986). Hence strained relations with Moscow made the political cost of gaining more favorable terms within the CMEA trade system unacceptable, and little progress was made. The RCP's recent foreign policy initiatives could hardly have been expected to win endearment within the CPSU. The Soviets were alienated by the RCP's criticism of rich rather than capitalist rich countries, and imperialism rather than capitalist imperialism, and they were irate over Romania's growing identification with the nonaligned movement. As a result they proved far from willing to lend a fraternal helping hand. Although in a position to do so, the Soviet Union provided Romania with little aid in dealing with its economic problems (Droker and Martens 1982: 238).

This cold shoulder from the East elicited an outpouring of polemic against the CMEA for the problems it has supposedly caused the Romanian economy. The Soviet Union, in turn, called for a closing of the ranks among all WTO countries in response to increased hostility in the West, and only thinly veiled references toward Bucharest. On an only slightly less overt level Soviet and Romanian theoretical journals entered into a heated debate concerning the primacy of "class character" as opposed to the interest of the "nation" in international affairs. Thus the economic crisis, which initially appeared to be forcing the Romanians back toward closer ties with the rest of the Soviet alliance system has in fact resulted in a marked cooling in relations.

Finally, relations with the industrialized West to a certain extent soured as well in the wake of Bucharest's economic debacle. Romanian diplomats made it more than clear that they lay primary blame for their problems, and those of other developing countries, squarely at the door of Western capitalist governments and the international financial community. Official Romanian statements concerning the sources of the international economic crisis became both more frequent and more harsh after 1979. During 1982 criticism of developed countries (particularly the United States) for their role in causing world poverty became an ubiquitous element of Romanian mass media and also made their way into the Western press.[18] They denounced unjustifiably high interest rates, the arms race, and an unfair international trading order as general causes of the global recession. On a more pragmatic level, Romanian leaders expressed growing dissatisfaction with the failure of their products to perform as expected in the developed Western economies, and with the credit terms that they have obtained from Western banks.

The question of emigration further complicated Bucharest's situation. Romania's preferred status in the West has always been predicated on at least minimal compliance on this issue. With the deterioration of economic (and, as far as the national minorities were concerned, political) conditions, however, there was a massive increase in the number of people seeking relief through departure to the West. Finally, in desperation Bucharest announced the imposition of an "education tax" on those wishing to leave the country, in late 1982 (*Scinteia* November 6, 1982). The tax, which demanded payment in hard currency, was interpreted in the West as a political barrier to emigration. Western reaction was swift, and its severity was apparently unexpected. The United States announced its intention to revoke Romania's MFN status in June 1983. Pressure was also brought to bear by the Federal Republic of Germany through delay of debt rescheduling talks, and discussion of the possibility of refusing to extend the existing Romanian-FRG cooperation agreement.

The effectiveness of this economic threat was increased by the fact that the crisis occurred at a time when maintaining the balance of trade was considered crucial by Bucharest. It is estimated that the loss of MFN in itself would have cost Romania from one-half to two-thirds of its exports to the United States, or approximately 3 to 4 percent of its total exports to the West (Wharton April 4, 1983: 8). Perhaps more importantly, the loss of preferential treatment by major Western governments would have damaged Bucharest's relations with the private sector, particularly Western banks, as well.

This confrontation placed the Romanians in an extremely uncomfortable position. Strained relations with the Soviet Union foreclosed the possibility of aid from that direction, except at an unacceptably high political price, and while the connection with the LDCs had become increasingly important, it could not serve as a replacement for the role played by the developed capitalist economies. Therefore, when faced with a strong response from the West, Bucharest was forced uncharacteristically to back down on an issue with which President Ceausescu had been personally identified. Following an extended round of negotiations involving visits by Romanian Foreign Minister Stefan Andrei to both Bonn and Washington, an agreement was reached whereby the education tax 'would not be enforced and Romania undertook "not to create ecomomic or procedural barriers to emigration." In return, Romania's trading relationship with its most important Western partners was not disrupted. MFN status was renewed, loan rescheduling with the Germans completed, and the hard currency payment by Bonn per emigrant to the FRG raised.[19]

The immigration issue thus highlighted the consequences that entanglement in the international economy presented for Bucharest. Closer integration into the CMEA, but only on Soviet terms, would necessarily undermine the Ceausescu regime's domestic position. On the other hand, Romanian leaders bitterly resented being pressured into compliance with Western demands regarding what they considered to be a purely internal political matter. It may have been theoretically possible to reject both the East and West and accept the domestic consequences, but this would certainly have devastated the RCP's economic development plans. On consideration the RCP's leaders prudently chose to maintain their Western economic ties, at least in the short term. It thus seems clear that Romania had in fact come under a degree of political constraint as a result of its ties with the world market.

CONCLUSION

Maintaining its hard won if partial independence from the Soviet Union has been a fundamental foreign policy goal of Romania for at least the past two decades. While it was not feasible for a country of its size to cut off all foreign trade ties its leaders could, and did, reduce their vulnerability to Soviet economic pressure through trade diversification. On the other hand, the RCP's domestic policy has been guided by a determination to retain the pace of industrial transformation and its highly centralized economic mechanism, and to defend the Party leadership's near total domination of the country's nonpolitical social institutions. Romania initially became involved in the world market as the result of a conscious decision on the part of its political elite, based on the belief that these internal and external goals were mutually reinforcing, and that both would be served by such a course. Insulation from the Soviet Union permitted Ceausescu to keep up the nationalistic rhetoric that is a fundamental pillar of his rule. Participation in the world market provided technology and financing that allowed the Romanian's hypercentralized economic mechanism to survive longer than it otherwise could have. It thus played a crucial role in enabling the RCP to avoid reforms undertaken in other Eastern European countries, and to attempt a strategy other than that of social accommodation.

Yet the international economic ties that this policy brought into being became so interwoven into the pattern of interests permeating Romanian society that successes within the world economy became intimately related to the fate of the regime, and thus imposed a further structural constraint on state behavior. Once limited to responses compatible with continued participation in the world market, Romanian decision makers were inevitably led to behave in accordance with its rules. Consequently the nature of their reaction to economic crisis appears quite familiar to Western observers; and it is characteristic of the policies employed by many noncommunist developing nations faced with similar conditions. After the collapse of the balance of trade, imports were maintained through foreign borrowing which quickly got out of control. The resultant debt crisis further damaged the economy and ultimately led to implementation of a national austerity program. This caused political unrest which, not surprisingly, was met with an intensification of already existing proclivities toward repression, and some cosmetic restructuring at the top of the political system.

In its mediation between international economy and its own population (much more than in its more strictly domestic role) the Romanian party-state has taken on the role of a collective capitalist; forcing down wages and social overhead as a response to declining profits. The most apparent distinction between it and other developing countries caught in a similar economic position has been the Ceausescu regime's greater familiarity with, and possession of, the means of repression; and therefore the greater ease with which a plan of austerity could be introduced. Because the current leadership was so closely identified with the present policy configuration, no meaningful alteration of this course could be expected in the absence of a fundamental reorganization of the political system.

8 CONCLUSION

INTRODUCTION

This study has explored the nature of political life in a particular East European country, the Romanian Socialist Republic, in the hope that its experience would shed new light on the evolution of all state-socialist political systems. At the inception of the analysis it was argued that these societies represent a unique form of social political organization, that they are capable of their own self-reproduction, and that they express a common and consistent pattern of behavior differing from both modern capitalism and from their own prerevolutionary social systems. The countries in question are distinguished by the state's retention of the right to intervene arbitrarily in normally nonpolitical realms of social life, and to eliminate private property in favor of state ownership. Market relations are replaced by continuous bureaucratic intervention into the productive process, and it is the bureaucracy that serves both to allocate resources and extract ecomomic surplus value. As Feher, Heller, and Markus (1983) convincingly argue, this aspect of productive organization is fundamental to the structural determination of state-socialist societies. Not profit, as in all forms of capitalism, but the maximization of resources *under the control of the apparatus* is the "goal function" of the centrally planned economies. Its pursuit generates the interests and contradictions that condition all other aspects of social life.

In each of these countries political power remains more or less completely in the hands of a functional elite that retains monopoly control over the state. At the core of the pervasive complex of interlocking bureaucratic hierarchies that make up the state is the communist party apparatus, through which political

leaders seek to exercise as broad an influence as possible over all other social
institutions. During the initial phase of the revolutionary transformation intense
coercion was employed freely by party elites to collectivize productive property,
break down existing patterns of behavior, and lay the foundation of a postrevolutionary social order. While this task was being fulfilled the new revolutionary
states enjoyed nearly complete autonomy, at least with respect to domestic constraints. The new institutions and practices which they set in place during the
revolutionary interregnum fundamentally shaped the postrevolutionary political
economy, even decades after constraints on its actions had reappeared.

The aging of the revolution fundamentally altered this exclusively coercive
relationship between state and society. As the struggle against immediately
identifiable class enemies was won and party cadres moved into positions of
power, revolutionary zeal invariably cooled. Barring not uncommon efforts to
"remobilize" cadre synthetically, such as occurred in the Soviet Union in the
1930s and in China during the Cultural Revolution, as well as the experience of
contemporary Romania, ideological commitment has been supplanted by leaders'
understandable desire to enjoy the fruits of their victory and the population's
equally understandable inclination toward a return to stability. When this occurred the active political direction of social life by party leaders was progressively replaced by a defensive, and in general passive, state posture. In most cases
a modus vivendi, if not a reconciliation, was reached between the political elite
and society. The functioning of explicit rules and implicit but clearly understood
postrevolutionary social norms became more significant than the coercive arm of
state power in regulating behavior, and the society began to reproduce itself
automatically on the foundation of institutions introduced during the revolutionary transformation.

Consistencies also emerged in the economic development of state-socialist
countries. The "command economy" model proved itself to be a successful
vehicle for mobilizing resources for the transformation from agricultural to
industrial society. Where state-socialism exists in its mature form the extremes of
wealth and poverty have been eliminated, and the minimum economic security
of the population has been guaranteed. On the other hand, problems of scarcity
of consumer goods persist, and recurrent economic crises of greater or lesser intensity have plagued Eastern Europe and the Soviet Union. Each of these systems,
faced with the exhaustion of unemployed resources, was compelled to attempt
negotiation of a transition from extensive to intensive modes of production.
Similarly, economic progress along the state-socialist path has consistently generated the growth of a stratum of highly trained personnel which enjoys a life-
style that differs significantly from the rest of the population, and which constitutes the foundation of a potential socialist privileged class.

Despite these obvious common traits, the character of political life in state-
socialist societies varies widely, just as analogous behavior differs in industrialized
capitalist countries. Socialist economic transformation and imposition of Leninist
party institutions did not occur in a cultural/historic vacuum, but rather in con-

crete societies, each with its own preexisting resources, conflicts, and cultural traditions. The intensity of revolutionary upheaval, the nature of the postrevolutionary accommodation, and the ultimate possibility regime legitimation are all highly dependent upon particular national conditions. Consequently as the straight jacket of externally imposed Stalinist conformity was loosened, each of the East European states has taken on its own unique coloration. It has been the central theme of the preceding chapters that a particular confluence of domestic political and cultural factors, along with international conditions, resulted in Romania's emergence as an extreme type on the continuum of possibilities currently represented within the state-socialist mode of production.

ROMANIAN EXCEPTIONALISM

August 23, 1945, found Romania beset by problems associated with long-standing underdevelopment and marginalization in the European industrialization process. Like neighboring states in Eastern Europe and its similarly disadvantaged Mediterranean contemporaries Spain and Portugal, Romania generated little economic growth but a great deal of social hostility in the first half of the twentieth century. Despite massive land reform its peasantry lived at the edge of impoverishment while the minuscule proletariat lacked both organization and meaningful political rights. Bucharest's commercial bourgeoisie acted as an intermediary for foreign interests, and drained off a significant part of the country's economic surplus into nonproductive uses. A corrupt and outsized state apparatus was relied upon by members of the privileged minority to secure their positions in the social hierarchy. During the interwar period social conditions deteriorated, and a new and destabilizing force, in the form of a marginalized intelligentsia committed to development within the national framework, emerged upon the scene.

Like other countries that experienced broadly similar patterns of development, Romania was thus ripe for an etatist solution to the problem of overcoming national dependency. All indications lead to the conclusion that this task could just as easily (and perhaps more naturally, given the country's historical legacy) have been undertaken by a right-wing dictatorship of the sort seen in Latin America and elsewhere as by a state-socialist regime. Peter Sugar (1984), among others, suggests that the pattern of political repression was so strong in Eastern Europe as to justify placing the current communist party-states squarely in the tradition of interwar authoritarianism. The implacable flow of international events in the region, however, determined that Romania would become the site of a "Leninist response to national dependency," as Jowitt (1978) terms the state-socialist experience.

In addition to the trait of "underdevelopment" which it shared in common with other countries that adopted state socialism (or were subjected to it, as the case may be), prerevolutionary Romania exhibited nationally specific tendencies that conditioned its political evolution after 1945. Not least influential among these were the intense nationalism that developed out of its long and difficult struggle for territorial consolidation and independence, and the linking of nationalism to the goal of industrial development, at least among a significant part of the prerevolutionary intelligentsia. Furthermore, in Romania economic exploitation was popularly identified with the interference of foreign powers, and with the role of minority communities in the domestic economy. Ethnic hostility, in part as a result of these factors, was widespread among the Romanian majority. In this domestic environment right-wing movements flourished, while the left met with only marginal success. Those seeking to promote socialism after World War I confronted a second nearly insurmountable obstacle, since the outstanding example of that alternative was the Soviet Union, successor to Romania's traditional Tzarist enemy and a continued threat to its territorial integrity even after the revolution. The combination of these factors contributed to the notable weakness of the Romanian Communist Party, and a widespread attraction among peasants, workers, and the marginalized intelligentsia to the fascism that came to a head during the 1930s.

The legacy of Turkish rule left an enduring mark on Romanian culture as well. Far from being considered an expression of legitimate collective social interests, the state came to be perceived by the general (largely peasant) population as an alien and oppressive force in their communities. For marginal intellectuals, on the other hand, a sinecure within the government represented the means of securing a somewhat improved social position, and the possibility of obtaining an income without recourse to more onerous and socially distasteful commercial activities through the implicitly accepted practice of accepting "baksheesh." Under these conditions the Romanian state was reduced to little more than an oppressive and corrupt bureaucratic parasite that hindered more than it advanced the cause of progress.

Similar, though perhaps less extreme, characteristics are far from uncommon in the histories of other East European countries. What, then, accounts for Romania's deviation from the state-socialist pattern? The more potent expression of traditional political behavior in contemporary Romania is attributable to a combination of international and domestic circumstances that enabled the RCP to consolidate an important margin of autonomy from the Soviet Union almost immediately on the heels of the collapse of Stalinism. For this reason the period from 1945 to 1964 was truly critical in Romania's political evolution. The success of Gheorghiu-Dej's "worker faction" in not just consolidating control over the party-state, but in effectively eliminating every plausible rival group from the RCP leadership, stands out as a unique achievement in Eastern Europe. The Dej group's manifest commitment to a Stalinist political strategy undoubtedly played a decisive role in this success. In no other case were "national" communists allowed by the Soviet Union to establish an equally undivided grasp on state power.

When differences arose between the CPSU and the Romanian political elite after the death of Stalin, Soviet policymakers paid a substantial price for their lapse. Dej and his followers proved markedly recalcitrant on the questions of de-Stalinization and economic reform, and their unity of purpose dramatically improved their power of resistance. If one wishes to understand Bucharest's successful defiance, however, it must be seen in conjunction with remarkably fortuitous international factors. First, it occurred during a period of reduced Soviet capability, when factionalism within the CPSU was clearly and negatively felt in the international arena. Second, the RCP's ability to retain control of its own population, and even to act in support of Soviet interests outside its borders during the crises of 1956, made any interference that might have reduced its stability at best a counterproductive proposition for the Soviets. Whatever else Kremlin leaders might have thought of their counterparts in Bucharest, they did not require intervention to guarantee Soviet security interests in the region. Finally, China's withdrawal from the Soviet alliance, or more precisely the diplomatic meaneuvering leading up to it, provided the RCP with added leverage based on its role as a mediator in the conflict between Peking and Moscow, and with a potent ally in its struggle for enhanced autonomy.

The question of how Romania was able to undertake a deviant course therefore appears sufficiently clear. The direction in which that course would lead was also presaged during the Dej years. From its inception the nationalist element within the RCP elite was committed wholeheartedly to extensive industrialization as a teleological goal. While consistent with Soviet Marxism, this ideological preoccupation was just as much a part of the Romanian cultural heritage. Once Soviet designs for southeastern Europe shifted from rapid industrialization to a plan for regional specialization that would have relegated Romania to the status of a perpetual "bread basket," it became apparent that the RCP leaders' attachment to economic development emanated primarily from the latter source. The issue of supranationalism thus played a fundamental role in the parting of ways that was made explicit in 1964. Once taken, the decision to resist Soviet intrusion into their domestic affairs impelled Romania's political elite to seek more thoroughgoing popular support. Their status as domestic communists was a formidable advantage in this pursuit. It enabled them successfully to demand a commitment to their cause as a "national" imperative. No similar response could have been elicited by revolutionary ideology, even among the growing element of the population that had benefited by the Party's victory, and while feasible for the Dej faction, it would have been foreclosed to the "Muscovites" or any other less authentically "Romanian" leadership from the outset.

Divergence from the Soviet norm on the level of elite politics and industrialization strategy did not deliver Bucharest from the contradictions that materialized elsewhere as a consequence of the state-socialist mode of production. By the early 1960s Romania was visibly plagued by the problems of overcentralization and "hyper-accumulation" that appear to be inherent to all command economies. The increasing complexity of investment ultilization outstripped central planners' allocative capabilities, and labor productivity suffered the consequences of severe restriction of the consumer sector. Consequently in the years immedi-

ately preceding Gheorghiu-Dej's demise the "first wave" of extensive industrialization bogged down into a morass of uncompleted projects.

The social impact of rapid industrialization conformed with the experience of
other CMEA countries as well. Romania was rapidly transformed from a traditional backwater into a rapidly developing society by a party directed revolution
from above. Thousands of newly recruited and marginally trained workers
emerged from the historically predominant peasantry to populate the country's
soon overcrowded cities. A growing technical/professional stratum was called
into being by the requirements of economic development. Thousands of educated
administrators were needed to assume positions of authority in the all-pervasive
institutions of the bureaucracy. Simultaneously a postrevolutionary cultural
intelligentsia emerged to participate in the social reproduction process, legitimating RCP rule, and propagating the regime's conception of the new order.

The character of the interests expressed by members of this postrevolutionary
intelligentsia presented inextricably intertwined economic and political problems
for the RCP elite. Its existence, and indeed expansion, was an absolute necessity
if industrialization were to proceed. This rudimentary fact was never seriously
questioned by even the most obscurantist of party leaders. But in Romania, as
elsewhere, it quickly became obvious that the material and cultural demands of
its members were quite dissimilar from those of the worker/peasant majority.
The talents of growing numbers of skilled professionals could not be put to their
best use within the constraints of the existing social/political framework; a new
political formula was required through which they could be integrated into the
structure of command economy, but without undermining the party's political
monopoly.

This combination of economic and social impediments that confronted RCP
leaders is characteristic of the *structural* constraints that preceded introduction
of economic reform and partial civil/state accommodation by other regimes at
approximately the same point in their respective evolutions. De-Stalinization in
most of Eastern Europe was designed to overcome these constraints without
fundamentally altering the existing power structure. Postrevolutionary stability
was thus dependent upon establishing a workable modus vivendi between the
masters of the revolutionary party-state and members of the extended intelligentsia upon whom they had to rely to ensure the minimum functioning of the
command economies. Pursuit of this political course favored further consolidation of such individuals into a privileged class, while allowing the communist
party elite to retain its monopolistic grasp on the state, and thus on political
power.

A similar outcome was far from unlikely in the Romanian context during the
second half of the 1960s. It is certain that there were those in the society at
large, and also within the political elite, who favored committing the RCP to the
path of civil/state accommodation. There were also elements of real reform
present in the initial "ambiguous" policy mix of Ceausescu's transition years.
The possibility of a fundamental shift in direction was considerably enhanced by

the fact that the party leader most responsible for the early phase of socialist construction, Gheorghiu-Dej, was already out of office and safely in his grave; which normally makes such a change of course significantly less difficult to facilitate than otherwise.

The unique *conjectural* features of the Romanian case, however, were such that the political balance was swayed in favor of an authoritarian rather than an accommodationist alternative. Ceausescu's eminently successful tactical maneuvering to gain control of the RCP at the close of the 1960s in itself played an important role in the evolution of the political system as a whole. His chief adversaries were eliminated in short order, and without recourse to excessively violent or destabilizing methods. Ceausescu's personal stature during the transition years was high, and after the Tenth Congress his position as party chief became virtually unassailable.

Once the filtering process of the early transition period was completed it became clear, to the dismay of those Romanians who expected otherwise, that ruling institutions were firmly in the hands of individuals who, like Ceausescu, were committed to retaining tight party control. The new RCP leader's own origins and early life, like those of many who rose to power through the apparat, were not of the sort likely to enhance his empathy toward the intelligentsia or its values. In fact, he appears to have avoided forming close relations with its members, instead surrounding himself with colleagues whose backgrounds were similar to his own (Fischer 1983: 31–32). Gheorghiu-Dej's successors also retained an intense commitment to continuing along the former leader's "nationalist" course, and to heavy industrial development, which they successfully presented to the populace as a necessity for achieving national sovereignty. Popular receptivity to this argument was clearly heightened by a culture shaped by over a century of struggle to achieve unification and independence in the face of external interference. In particular, the credibility of the elite's efforts was (and continues to be) strengthened by the RCP's confrontation with the Soviet Union in general, and its behavior during the Czechoslovak crisis in particular.

Having already established a significant degree of autonomy from the Soviet Union by the time that the "structural crisis" endemic to state-socialism occurred in Romania, the RCP elite was relatively free from external pressures which might otherwise have limited its options. This added margin of autonomy was essential in permitting the Ceausescu regime to play upon the "nationalist" theme to a much greater degree than would have been possible if the CPSU had been entirely free to exercise its veto power. It also allowed Romania to avoid being forced into line with the other CMEA economies, and therefore enabled its leader to lay the groundwork for a new round of extensive industrialization.

Successful negotiation of the leadership transition was followed by consolidation of a new power structure encompassing both relations of material production and the hierarchical institutions centered on the communist party. In a first step toward restructuring those at the highest levels of the Party moved to reinforce their control over the coercive apparatus, and to insulate themselves from influences emanating from "civil" society. In particular, an assault was launched against the extended intelligentsia, whose gains of the transition years peremptorily reversed.

Thus the RCP elite both cut itself off from Soviet support, and rejected alignment with the extended intelligentsia. As an alternative to reliance on cooperation with the intellectuals, political leaders constructed new institutional channels of mass participation and sought to "repoliticize" the worker/peasant masses in the pursuit of extensive industrialization. Similarly, party theoreticians pursued a populist ideological course based on appeals designed to resonate with the latent cultural attitudes of the general population. In particular the RCP message was directed to the displaced worker/peasant majority which, lacking the increased material consumption enjoyed in neighboring states, was nourished on the glories of the nation. It also appealed to recently mobile members of the extended intelligentsia who remained amenable to the argument that even if the regime's current posturings and pronouncements were not entirely palatable, they were at least necessary to maintain the country's independence.

The internal coherence of this "Ceausescu" strategy is evident. Rapid industrialization in the Stalinist pattern was compatible with the authoritarian politics most congenial to the General Secretary and his immediate colleagues. It also required less cooperation from, and therefore less compromise with, the growing stratum of managers, administrators, and cultural elites, whose interests ran counter to those of the Romanian party-state. Finally, industrial development, when incorporated into the hegemonic ideology as an absolute value, could be invoked to rationalize the continued harshness of material life and the state's retention of a coercive stance toward Romanian society.

Initially the sociopolitical strategy embarked upon by Ceausescu and his supporters appeared to (and to a certain extent did) meet with substantial success. Economic remobilization began well; dramatic growth rates were achieved, and impressive strides were made in transforming Romania into an industrial nation. But in more recent years the contradictions inherent in "command" economic models, long since acknowledged and in part compensated for by other state-socialist leaders, have made conditions increasingly difficult for Romania's less flexible rulers. As evidenced by the fate of the Sixth Five-Year Plan, continually raising the rate of accumulation simply cannot overcome the effects of increasing complexity, declining incentives, and shrinking resources. The year 1985 found Romania's per capita GNP (at 33.5 percent that of the United States) the lowest among East European CMEA countries (Alton, Badach, Bass, Lazarcik, and Staller 1986: 23).

Thus, while RCP leaders effectively blocked nonpolitical elites' efforts to gain increased autonomy, they have yet to discover an alternative to the role played by the extended intelligentsia in managing other state-socialist societies. Without the active efforts of mid-level administrators and technicians a "planned" economy cannot be made to function above a bare minimum level of efficiency. Nor can such personnel be coerced into more than pro forma compliance with the requirements of their employment. Hence improvement even in those centrally planned economies where market directed reforms have not been introduced is premised upon partial accommodation to the interests of the "privileged class." This strategy was rejected by the Romanian political elite, but only at the cost of increasingly severe economic consequences.

Similarly, the Ceausescu faction's political design has encountered growing obstacles since the second half of the 1970s. The political elite has not been able to resist high levels of intelligentsia social reproduction, or the formation of a distinct social consciousness among its members that reflects quite critically upon the current social environment. Liberal application of the state's coercive power may have successfully suppressed open expression of common interests by members of the extended intelligentsia and limited their access to the institutions of power, but it has not eliminated the formation of those interests. This, it appears, occurs as an inherent consequence of the state-socialist mode of production as such. Workers have not proven to be significantly more supportive of the RCP program than the intelligentsia. Manipulated participation, paternalistic authoritarianism, and ostentatious nationalism may have been sufficient to gain popular support in an environment of economic growth, high levels of mobility, and at least the promise of improved consumption, but by the late 1970s these criteria no longer applied to Romania, and RCP appeals increasingly fell on deaf ears. Consequently economic decline was accompanied by increased political instability, and the late 1970s saw large-scale labor unrest for the first time during the Ceausescu period.[1]

Economic decline among state-socialist countries, as Stephen White (1986) has argued, need not be translated into political crises. Party elites can, as he suggests, adopt "Kadarist" strategies of accommodation to counter the pressures which they come under. But, in keeping with its established pattern, the increasingly narrow leadership around Ceausescu chose quite a different course. The RCP elite tightened its grip on Romanian society rather than seeking avenues of reform, and in order to do so it fell back ever more openly on the prerevolutionary political tradition. Thus the familialization that has become increasingly evident in Romanian political life represents more than simply the practice of nepotism by top leaders; it is one aspect of the widespread regeneration of traditionalistic political behavior in a "modern" Leninist institutional framework. Under Ceausescu the Romanian Communist Party has undergone a progressive metamorphosis from an agent of social transformation into a profoundly conservative vehicle, employed by its members to promote their particular interests. Those individuals located in favorable positions within the party/state bureaucracy could, and did, demand extralegal rewards for acting on behalf of others with less power than themselves. To the degree that formal regulation of the economy fell short of the demands placed on it (and this inadequacy has grown progressively more grave as economic complexity increased), rational allocation was displaced by informal corruption. These activities within the RCP and the constellation of collateral institutions surrounding it constitute a structural component in a new pattern of postrevolutionary social relations. They are essential to the extended reproduction of the contemporary Romanian political economy.

In pursuing its new strategy the RCP sought to establish its ideological hegemony on traditional grounds as well. Propagandists promoted an identity for the Party as the political embodiment of the nation, and the RCP noticeably played down its "proletarian" roots. Thus statutes adopted at the 13th RCP Congress in November 1984 no longer identified the Party as "the vanguard of the working class," but rather as the "vital center of our entire nation, the guiding political force of the Socialist Republic of Romania, the organizer and catalyst of the creative energies of all working people in our homeland, of the entire people" (quoted in Maier 1985b). As the Romanian political elite struggled to retain its dominance under increasingly difficult circumstances other, more extreme, borrowings from the precommunist past became manifest as well. The idolization of the *Leader* characteristic of today's Romania was a vital element in the ideology of populist fascists who were inspired by Corneliu Codreanu. Nor is there much doubt that in their intensified promotion of nationalism and pandering to ethnic hostility RCP leaders have purposefully tapped a deep-seated emotional root in the popular culture. As Fischer-Galati (1984) suggests, it was anything but surprising that the RCP, once shed of its "alien" leadership and constraining ties with the Soviet Union, should have come increasingly to resemble the right-wing extremists with whom it competed during the interwar years. Both derived, after all, from the same cultural milieu, and their developmental goals were similar. Not only does the current elite's perception of autarkic industrial development as an imperative of national survival mirror the attitudes of Manoilescu and his compatriots, but its state-directed design for development conform in its essentials with his vision of corporatism.

Ceausescu's political tactics, however, failed in the face of a general deterioration in social conditions that caused further dislocation of the system of material reproduction and an upsurge of popular alienation from the political elite and its goals. In particular, the state's imposition of a domestic austerity program and decline in the standard of living that followed upon the collapse of Romania's international trade position in the early 1980s aroused intense hostility. Reports of over 50 strikes and work stoppages as well as demonstrations by consumers and other antigovernment manifestations reached the West in 1980 and 1981 (*1982 Yearbook of Communist International Affairs*: 462; Braun 1982: 53). Although mild in comparison to the levels of unrest seen in other parts of the world, such active display of resentment toward the ruling party was previously unheard of in postrevolutionary Romania.

The reaction of the Romanian party-state to these disruptions underscored the pattern of behavior established over the past two decades. Lest hopes be raised that the regime might be pressured into a change of course, RCP spokesmen made continual and unambiguous statements in support of orthodoxy on all fronts. Hence accumulation at a rate of from 28–32 percent of national income was raised by Ceausescu to the status of "an objective law of socialist construction" (Bistriceanu 1985). Far from considering decentralization, it was pronounced that the difficulties encountered in the national economy "necessitated an intensification and even greater perfection of planned social economic leadership, a growth of the role of the unified national plan as a fundamental instrument in regulating the functioning of the economy" (Dragomirescu 1985: 2). Finally, Party theorists opened a polemic against the "thesis heard here and there" that the role of common property (for example, the property of the state) should be diminished. On the contrary, such views which "contradict socialist principles" would never, according to Ceausescu, be allowed to manifest themselves in Romania under any circumstances.[2]

Immediate steps were taken to insulate the political leadership from social pressure and increase party discipline, while the personality cult surrounding Ceausescu reached heights of personal glorification that can only be compared with the extravagances of Stalinism at its peak (Fischer 1983: 41). As an alternative to admitting the existence of fundamental contradictions arising from the mode of production, criticism was directed toward more limited targets. Since 1979 a larger number of high officials have lost their jobs than at any other time since Ceausescu consolidated his position. Over half of the country's *judets* Party First Secretaries have been removed (Fischer 1983: 41). The Prime Minister and Minister of Foreign Trade, Ilie Verdet and Cornel Burtica, were deprived of their positions despite the fact that both were Ceausescu family members, a group that has until recently been politically sacrosanct.

Along with individuals accused of failing to properly implement party directives, the privileged class as a whole served as a scapegoat for economic failures too obvious to be discounted. When the NEFM failed to produce the results promised for it, enterprise managers and central ministry personnel were accused of foot dragging and evading the law. Numerous cases of fraud in the preparation of statistics on production results were reported in the media, and Ceausescu attacked local officials for lack of determination in stamping out corruption, and for complicity in criminal activities (*Munca de Partid* February 1982: 58-61). Repeated calls were made for increased discipline among managers, and for the "organs of control," to show more firmness and vigilance in ensuring that resources were employed with maximum efficiency (Ciurileanu 1986). Just as during the "little cultural revolution," calls were made for the transfer of administrative personnel into "productive" work (*Scinteia* October 31, 1980).[3]

Subsequently, large numbers of research and academic jobs were eliminated and the individuals who held them shifted to positions in industrial enterprises (personal observations and interviews). In conjunction with this offensive, that element of the cultural elite which resisted the course embarked upon by the RCP was also subjected to increasing pressure. Moderates were attacked as purveyors of "decadent Western culture," and allusions to alien influences gained currency in discussions of artistic works. The seriousness of the political elite's hostility toward this sector was signaled in the spring of 1982 through the purge of intellectuals epitomized in the well known "transcendental meditation" scandal. Such widely publicized assaults in combination with increasingly acerbic criticism of the cultural establishment represent a less than subtle reminder that in Romania positions of privilege are secure only on party sufferance.

CONCLUSION

In Romania, where the political elite has been sufficiently free of Soviet inter-ference to pursue a social/political strategy largely of its own design, certain features common to state-socialist political systems appear in a more sharply de-fined form than elsewhere. Despite nearly continual attempts to suppress it, the extended intelligentsia has emerged as a culturally distinct element of the society. The weight of evidence suggests that its members do in fact share common inter-ests based on their structural position in the society, and that those interests represent a continual challenge to the political elite whose position depends on control over hierarchical party/state institutions. It therefore appears justified to conclude that in Romania members of the extended intelligentsia comprise a social class in the early stages of formation, despite the fact that political power remains in the hands of the party elite. Politics in Romania, as in other Eastern European countries, has been fundamentally shaped by the ongoing contention between this nascent class, the communist party-state, and the working class.

The consequences of RCP leaders' failure to reach an accord with this newly emerging social force are stark. Centralized direction cannot cope with the in-creasingly complex task of organizing an industrializing economy. The degree of coercive force required by those who control the party-state to resist devolution of decision-making authority once the inadequacy of their efforts becomes apparent continually increases. Yet suppression of the formation of formal alter-natives to the command economy through political coercion merely gave rise to informal practices that were equally outside policymakers' control. The "famil-ialization" that results is preferred to the former course, however, because while it presents no hope of fundamentally improving the economic situation, neither does it constitute a threat to existing relations of social domination. Hence in the Romania of the mid-1980s alienation between the party-state and society are greater than ever, and the "second economy" applies not just to the sphere of distribution, but extends into the allocation of productive resources, and com-prises a fundamental element of the mode of production.

While the RCP elite's obvious efforts, consciously motivated and otherwise, to secure its position by anchoring what originated as an externally imposed regime in the domestic social formation have thus done little to alter the basic forces at work in the society, they have significantly shaped the character of Romanian politics. The country's particular experience with nation building, proclivities toward xenophobia in the popular culture, and a "Byzantine tradi-tion" with regard to state/society relations explain in large part why state-socialism evolved toward its present "national communist" form in Romania. Whether the melding of revolutionary institutions and the domestic political traditions of other state-socialist countries will produce a more benign result once constraints on their further adaptation are removed remains to be seen.

NOTES

CHAPTER 1

1. While a variety of names have been attached to this type of social system, (totalitarian, state-capitalist, etc.), I have chosen, following David Lane, to call them state-socialist throughout this study as the most descriptive, while least prejudicial, alternative available.

2. This discussion of the evolution of the literature on the politics of communist party-states is, admittedly, abbreviated. There is, however, a substantial body of work devoted to examination and criticism of the alternative approaches that have developed over the years. See, for example, Bunce and Echols (1979); Bunce (1984); Korbonski (1977); Odom (1976); Shoup (1984).

3. Neither does Bahro's analysis discount the importance of the division between trained managers on the one hand, and workers, both skilled and unskilled, on the other. However, he rejects the idea that the former represent a "class," since the political structure itself retains the power of disposal of wealth. Bahro has suggested that the postrevolutionary regimes, which he terms "currently existing socialism," are analogous to the economic despotism practiced by the Incas (Bahro 1978: 76). Other Marxist theorists have likened them to the Asiatic mode of production.

4. Admittedly, the question of autonomy of the state is both difficult and controversial in examining state-socialist politics. At one extreme, the totalitarian theorists attribute absolute power to the state. At the other, several varieties of Marxist theory contend that the state is entirely without power, or that it has come to comprise in itself a "bureaucratic monopoly capitalist class" (Cliff 1964; Marcuse 1961). This outright rejection of the possibility of autonomous state power suffers from a number of drawbacks. Most importantly, it fails to provide

any convincing evidence to confirm its central proposition; namely that members of the bureaucracy are fundamentally differentiated as such from other members of the society, and that they share a common location in the structure of production. Furthermore, introduction of the concept of "state-capitalist" ruling class suggests that either such a class is analogous with the Western bourgeoisie, or that the dynamics that underlay state-socialist societies are the same as those of Western capitalism. Both alternatives are apt to be highly misleading. Somewhere between these extremes lies the Trotskiist "bureaucratic degeneration" thesis, which treats the current party dictatorship as a deviant condition. According to this view state socialism represents a transitional society that exists somewhere between defeated capitalism and not yet achieved socialism (Mandel 1976, 1980).

In fact, pervasive state power is perhaps the most striking characteristic of state-socialism. As a consequence any model that rejects a priori the possibility of an autonomous state acting in its own interests must be treated with caution, whatever its strengths might otherwise be. While state-centric paradigms obscure the importance of the complex forces at work within state-socialism, the charge of obfuscation is no less true of theories that treat the state purely as an epiphenomenon (Skocpol 1979: 26).

5. For those within the Marxist tradition the greatest stumbling block to analysis lies in the area of ownership and relations to the means of production. Some theorists have resolved this dilemma through reliance on relations of control as a criterion of class, and others by using extraction of surplus value as a key indicator. Among neo-Weberians the crucial problem is presented by the lack of market relations as a cause of class structure. Some, like Giddens, have turned to social closure as an alternative, others, such as Goldethorpe, reject the existence of class in state-socialist societies, for much the same reasons as orthodox Marxists.

6. He also argues, briefly, that despite the relatively high levels of social mobility the new "ruling class" can at least in part reproduce itself due to the inheritance of privileges in education and influence; and that such a "mixture of inherited privilege plus some upward social mobility appears to be not at all inconsistent with such terms as 'class'" (Nove 1983: 302).

7. Such a view has much in common with Karl Polanyi's conception of "models of economic intergration," which deemphasizes the dichotomy between structure and superstructure, rather than the common interpretation of the Marxist mode of production. For an example of the practical employment of a similar perspective see Andrew Martin (1977).

8. This perspective shares certain common elements with more abstract current interpretations of Marx; particularly those focusing on the extended reproduction of social relations rather than relying on traditional economic categories such as the criteria of class membership (Poulantzas 1973; Therborn 1982). Such "structuralist" theories treat class as a location within a broadly conceived mode of production, deemphasizing the distinction between ecomomic base and political superstructure. Thus, according to Poulantzas, "social class is defined by its place in the ensemble of social practices, that is, by its place in the ensemble of the division of labor which includes political and ideological relations. This place corresponds to the 'structural determination' of class, that is, the manner in

which determination by the structure (relations of production, politico-ideological domination/subordination) operates on class practices—for classes have existence only in the class struggle." (Poulantzas 1973: 101)

This approach is appealing on a number of counts. It provides a comprehensive perspective of the determination of class that is useful in dealing with situations (such as exist under state-socialism) in which economic and political power are closely intertwined. Structuralist methodology, however, is at bottom not empirical, but idealist, and must be rejected on that basis alone. A determinative role is attributed to the mode of production; within a given mode, relations between *classes* shape social consciousness and the direction of social change. Individuals merely serve as the recruits and agents through which classes reproduce themselves over time. Actually, existing relations between individuals are thus seen as at best secondary to the relations of exploitation embedded in a particular mode of production; they are truly epiphenomenal and can be understood only when they are interpreted in light of preconceived structures (Connell 1982: 140). The result is an intellectually satisfying argument, but one less scientifically compelling than others, less elegant and more proximate to actual phenomena.

9. The extended socialist intelligentsia could conceivably be considered a "propertied" class, if one takes a broad view of property, treating it either as "property in education and qualification," or, as Frank Parkin does, "exclusionary social closure" (Parkin 1979).

10. As such they were anything but a new phenomenon in Eastern Europe. Much as the Austrians governed in Prague, the Russian Grand Princes held court in Warsaw, or the Phanariot Hospodars routinely ruled Romania as Ottoman tax collectors, they transmitted to their populations decisions that originated elsewhere.

11. While, as in a system-defining sense, this elimination of capital can be said to have occurred across the board, specific implementation varied. Thus a "petty bourgeois" element exists in virtually all of the socialist countries of Eastern Europe, and in Poland and Yugoslavia, for example, the landholding peasantry was never eliminated.

12. This should not be construed, however, as suggesting that Stalinism mechanistically generated a systemic crisis. Its impact was conditioned by domestic conditions in each of the East European countries, and by the intensity with which the Stalinist program was implemented. Consequently instability has occurred asynchronously, and has varied in its expression.

13. Soviet toleration for regime modification was not, and is not, unlimited. Without explicit statement, definite boundaries can be discerned from the Soviet reactions to East European policy initiatives from 1956 up to the present. These experiences of intervention and nonintervention allow a rough estimation to be made of behavior that the leadership of the CPSU will accept among its allies. First and foremost, no action is permissible in the realm of foreign policy which might be construed as inimical to the security interests of the Soviet Union. Second, the political monopoly of the communist party must be maintained, and control within the party must be vested in a leadership which Moscow feels it can trust to maintain internal stability. Third, state control of the means of production must be maintained in some form. Finally, at least lip service must be

paid to orthodox Marxism-Leninism, as interpreted by the Soviets, and public criticism of the Soviet Union or its leaders must not appear.

14. The failure of the East European state-socialist regimes to achieve real legitimacy is manifest. Pakulski (1986) argues that political stability in these countries is based instead on "conditional tolerance" that derives from the population's recognition of the costs of noncompliance and benefits of continued obedience.

15. This is not to say that either the present social systems or political elites would remain if Soviet influence were removed from the scene. Rather, I would suggest that under current conditions it is no longer a simple matter of communist party leaders serving as the local agents of a foreign power. Their role is better understood as analogous to that of the "penetrated elites" who have from time to time acted as intermediaries between imperialist powers and their domestic societies in the Western capitalist context.

16. As Maria Hirszowicz suggests, even "if the Marxist concept of classes does not apply to Soviet society, it does not mean that the Marxist methodology does not" (Hirszowicz 1976: 263). This general approach to the problem, that is, employing Marxist analysis of social contradictions but shorn of its class basis, is used by Bahro, and a number of other "neo-Marxists."

17. See the argument on post-Stalinism developed by Brus (1975: 104–48).

CHAPTER 2

1. The destiny of the Romanians during this interregnum is a matter of intense debate among historians. It appears most likely that the majority of the population survived as seminomadic shepherds who kept out of the path of invaders as best as possible by moving themselves and their possessions into the mountainous regions of the Carpathians. Others migrated further south into the Balkan peninsula where they played an important role in the establishment of the Second Bulgarian Empire. The agricultural communities that remained north of the Danube constituted the lowest strata of the population, paid the tribute demanded of them by their transitory rulers, and otherwise maintained their way of life relatively intact. Whether they continuously occupied all of the territory claimed by contemporary Romanian state remains a mystery, and is of limited importance except for its role in the ongoing dispute between Romania and Hungary, and in the formation of the "National Mythos."

2. For both sides of the question see "the Multi-Ethnic Character of the Hungarian Kingdom in the Late Middle Ages," L. S. Domopknos, in *Transylvania: the Roots of Ethnic Conflict*; and Seton-Watson 1934: 17–24).

3. See Karl Polanyi's work in *Trade and Market in Early Empires* for a detailed treatment of states of this sort.

4. The judiciary was separated from the rest of the administration, taxes were consolidated and rationalized, and a national police force was established. A national system of roads was built; for the first time a national medical service was created; and steps were taken to stamp out starvation by establishing state granaries (Otetea 1970: 329; Seton-Watson 1934: 208).

5. In each province a Prince was to be elected by an assembly restricted to 150 delegates, 27 merchants and the rest *boieri*. The Prince was to serve for a

period of five years and share power with a smaller council, dominated by *boieri* of the highest rank, which could not be dissolved (Otetea 1970: 330; Seton-Watson 1934: 208).

6. In the period from 1835 to 1845 the almost exclusively agricultural exports from Walachia tripled, and those from Moldavia more than doubled (Otetea 1970: 336).

7. By the 1850s a substantial trade had grown up around the centers of Sibiu, Cluj, and Brasov, where the Transylvanian Saxons struggled against foreign interests to maintain their hold on the province's commerce (Vedery 1983: 143–46).

8. On the other side of the debate were the French, and surprisingly, the Russians. Following the conclusion of the war, Russian policy experienced a startling reversal. Previously the champion of reaction, the Tzar, bitter about the Austrians' failure to repay their debt of 1848, now became a fervent adherent of national self-determination in the Balkans (Jelavich, Vol. I 1983: 290).

9. In a first confrontation, Cuza secured state control of the so-called "dedicated monasteries" despite opposition of the richest of the *boier* families (Seton-Watson 1934: 307). These religious estates, nontaxed and operated by Greek Orthodox monastic orders, accounted for around 25 percent of all cultivated land in Walachia, and nearly 33 percent in Moldavia.

10. In a labor market which became progressively more disadvantaged as demographic pressure grew, the demands placed on tenant farmers continually escalated. The average size of peasant holdings declined from 4.6 hectares in 1864 to 3.2 in 1905 (Chirot 1976: 134). In 1870 tenant farmers, on the average, turned over to landlords one-fifth to one-third of their produce; by 1906 they were commonly required to give up one half (Roberts 1969: 15). Under these conditions little progress was made toward agricultural modernization. The massive landholdings of the nobility were not operated as large-scale enterprises, but rather were divided among peasant producers who farmed them much as they had in the previous century. The aristocracy's financial requirements were met by simply increasing the acreage under cultivation (which grew substantially) or increasing rents. Thus while exports rose substantially between the time of the reform and the beginning of this century virtually no increases in productivity were achieved.

11. Until after the turn of the century landlords took practically no steps to increase capital in agriculture. Peasants who held less than 47 percent of the farm land, owned 96 percent of the plows in the country.

12. By the turn of the century urban population was larger than 15 percent in only three counties in Walachia, and in most it was far less (Chirot 1976: 145).

13. In fact, 35 percent of the capital's population was foreign, and Jews alone accounted for 41 percent of all those active in industry (Chirot 1976: 146; Janos 1978: 91). When one considers the additional proportion taken up by Greeks, Armenians, and Germans, all of whom were active in the economy, it is clear that the role of Romanians in entrepreneurial activity could not have been particularly great.

14. See Jelavich, Vol. II 1983: 160. The 1930 census gives figures of: Romanians, 71.9 percent, Hungarians, 7.9 percent, Germans, 4.1 percent, Jews, 4 per-

cent, Ukrainians, 3.2 percent, Russians, 2.3 percent, and Bulgarians, 2 percent (Rothschild 1974: 284).

15. At the beginning of the century over 75 percent of the population was illiterate; during the interwar period this proportion dropped to around 40 percent (Weber 1965: 512).

16. In the 1926 elections, for example, General Averescu appointed military officers as regional prefects, disallowed travel, prohibited "exciting the population," and arrested opposition delegates. The "siguranta," or state security police, employed less gentle means as well (Roberts 1969: 105; Nagy-Talavera 1975: 255). New constitutional stipulations introduced in the mid-twenties awarded a "bonus" to any party gaining a plurality consisting of half parliamentary seats plus an additional number proportional to its share of the vote. The monarch was charged with summoning a government; under the new rules its leaders could easily "make" an election using the state administration, with the result that democratic rule was severely undermined (Roberts 1969: 102).

17. Popular traditions were denigrated by all but a small minority among the elite. In "better" families French language was spoken not just in society, but also at home. This form of emulation became so widespread that the hordes of degree holders inhabiting the capital and seeking professional employment came to be known popularly as "Bonjourists" on the grounds that their sole qualification for employment was the ability to say that one word in French.

18. As reported in Weber (1965), Mihia Eminescu, the national poet, wrote before the turn of the century:

> He who takes strangers to heart
> May the dogs eat his part
> May the waste eat his home
> May ill-fame eat his name!

Similar sentiments were expressed, less eloquently, by leading educators and politicians of the time (Nagy-Talavera 1975: 248).

19. On moving to Moldavia the elder Codreanu, a school teacher, became a virulent nationalist (he named his daughter Irredenta), and an associate of the notorious anti-Semite, A. C. Cuza (Nagy-Talavera 1975: 252).

20. Its basic form of organization was the "nest," groups of from 3-13 members. Members were committed to six rules (discipline, work, silence, self-education, mutual aid, and honor). Meetings began with orthodox religious services, and continued to discuss selected topics, dependent on whether the membership was predominantly peasant or intellectual (Nagy-Talavera 1975: 271).

21. In its early years the Legion was successful almost exclusively in these provinces, where, in addition to ethnic tensions, the proximity of the Soviet Union heightened tensions, and the Romanian state administration was particularly corrupt and inefficient (Bessarabia was reputed to be the worst-governed province in Europe).

22. The Legion was aided by having formed an electoral pact with the National Peasants intended to ensure the honesty of the elections which were in fact the least corrupt in interwar Romania, and the only occasion on which the governmental party failed to win a majority (Roberts 1969: 192).

23. The Death Commandos managed to assassinate Minister Calinescu, which precipitated a crushing retaliation by the security forces. The rest of the imprisoned leaders were summarily shot, and in every province of the country a quota of Guardists were rounded up and hung from lamp posts (Nagy-Talavera 1975: 304).

24. In a single incident at the Jilava Prison, 64 ex-agents of Carol's government were murdered in their prison cells, while Professors Iorga and Madgearu were assassinated by the Death Squads for their past anti-Guardist attitudes (Roberts 1969: 234). The brutality of the Legion's retribution and the massive demonstration organized to commemorate its dead heroes terrified the Romanian bourgeoisie. Legionary publications took on a continually more radical and menacing tone, declaring finally that "There can be no place in the Legionary terminology for the bourgeoisie. . . . In its essence, the bourgeoisie is nothing. It is the expression of a way of life hostile to the Legionary existence: individualism. The legion will resolve radically the problem of the bourgeoisie." (Buna Vestire January 10, 1941; quoted in Nagy-Talavera 1970: 323) In contrast to its reception among the elite, this extremism apparently gained widespread support among the poorer population. Fascist leaders were forced to restrict enlistments into their organization two months after taking power because new recruits became too numerous to be accommodated.

CHAPTER 3

1. Ionescu (1964) remains the most useful work on the politics of the early period, while Jowitt (1971) adds significantly to understanding the evolution of the Party's political strategy.

2. Among those who played a critical postwar role elected at the 1932 Congress were Stefan Foris, Iosef Chisinevischi, Lucretiu Patrascanu, and Iosef Ranghet. Constantine Parvulescu and Ana Pauker were added to this group somewhat later (Ionescu 1964: 44–45).

3. In this sense the Romanian experience is similar to that of Hungary, where the Rakosi/Gero group chosen by Moscow to take command was also non-Hungarian.

4. This argument runs counter to the account given by Fischer-Galati (1967: 21–22) who contends that Dej and Bodnaras were in fact acting jointly against the wishes of the Soviet leadership.

5. Lucretiu Patrascanu and Miron Constantinescu were the most prominent among the "moderates," and both were to play significant roles in future developments. Complete membership of the 1945 central committee, including Nicolae Ceausescu for the first time, can be found in Ionescu (1964: 117–18).

6. The data above is drawn from a comprehensive table of Romanian Party membership gathered from various sources by Robert King (1980: 64).

7. With the ascent to power of the Groza government in 1945 the Ministries of Interior, Justice, and Economics became the responsibility of the communist representatives (Georgescu, Patrascanu, and Dej respectively). The RCP also took a predominant role in the leadership and expansion of the trade union movement, which it used to attract the growing numbers of industrial workers to its cause. The Plowmens' Front served a similar purpose with the peasantry, while

the Union of Democratic Women of Romania, and Union of Working Youth (Uniunea Tineretului Muncitoresc), under the guidance of Nicolae Ceausescu, were established to act as links with the female population and young people.

8. The new Politburo was reduced to 9 members, which included Gheorghiu-Dej, A. Moghioros, I. Chisinevischi, M. Constantinescu, G. Apostol, Chivu Stoica, E. Bodnaras, P. Borila, and C. Parvulescu; Ceausescu, A. Draghici, and D. Coliu were candidate members.

9. As has been noted by a number of commentators, the Party's inability to identify immediately a loyal cadre of 80,000 from its membership of over half a million can only be interpreted as a signal indication of its true weakness in these early years (King 1980: 75; Ionescu; 1964: 229).

10. See Ionescu (1964: 259–61) for a detailed account of the plenum and Dej's treatment of the Muscovites deviations.

11. For two very different interpretations of these events see Jowitt (1971: 172–75); and Fischer-Galati (1967: 67).

12. Daniel Chirot (1977) has applied this concept to the analysis of Romania specifically. For a wide selection of views on the applicability of Wallerstein's model to the East European states, see Christopher Chase-Dunn (1982).

13. For a detailed treatment of the war losses suffered by Romania and the magnitude of Soviet extractions, see Montias (1967: 16–23) and Ionescu (1964: 137).

14. According to Gilberg's estimates, between the first year of the plan and 1953, total investment rose from approximately 8.6 billion lei to 14.3 billion (Gilberg 1975: 143).

15. According to Montias (1967: 25), "only 872 new apartments were added to the housing stock from 1949 to 1952 [in Bucharest], nearly half of which were one-room dwellings; meanwhile the population increased by over 100 thousand inhabitants."

16. Many among the peasant population in Romania still remember this period quite vividly, and are willing to recount their experiences with the collectivization process. For such account see Vedery (1980: 34–39).

17. Fischer-Galati (1967) places the roots of the confrontation between the Soviet Union and Romania at the low end of the chronological continuum, suggesting that nationalism was part of the Dej leadership's agenda long before it could be openly expressed. Kenneth Jowitt (1971), however, concludes that no serious division was evident until the early 1960s. While no complete resolution of the question is possible, the timing of the conflict is important in understanding whether nationalism was truly a motivating factor, or one among many weapons used in what was at bottom a leadership struggle.

18. For the most comprehensive treatment of the Chinese role in the Soviet/Romanian conflict, see Madsen (1982); for more general discussions, Floyd (1970), Farlow (1971), and Braun (1978) are among the best.

19. For two quite different accounts see Ionescu (1967: 288–91), and Fischer-Galati (1967: 70–71).

20. The evolution of this debate is recounted in detail in Montias (1967: 187–230).

21. For a discussion of the Statement and its significance see Fischer-Galati (1967: 101–12). For the English text of the Statement see Griffith (1967: 269–96).

22. The total number of professional school students rose from 61,372 in 1948/49 to 182,391 in 1965/66, while the number enrolled in higher education climbed from 48,676 to 130,614 in the same years (*Anuarul Statistic* 1980: 544–45).

CHAPTER 4

1. I have utilized (Maxwell 1983) as the source for information concerning Ceausescu's prewar career given in this chapter. There are, in addition, a number of other official biographies of Romania's current leader, but the essential and limited facts provided by all of these are in general agreement with the account above.

2. I have not included a detailed discussion of the progress of the leadership struggle, since the fate of those involved in the ruling circle at the time is of only peripheral interest to the main theme of this dissertation. The most recent and complete review of the transition from "Dej" to "Ceausescu" leadership groups is found in Shafir (1985: 69–84).

3. While it is true that the number of technically trained professionals within the upper reaches of the leadership increased under Ceausescu, it should also be noted, as pointed out by Trond Gilberg (1975: 42–46), that most of the specialists who attain top positions were in fact co-opted into Party work early in their careers. Their status as anything other than "apparatchiks," as representatives of extraparty interests, must therefore be questioned.

4. The intensity of the postwar Romanian leaders' reaction against internal opposition groups has been noted and commented upon by nearly all analysts or Romanian political affairs. In his recent work on the subject, Michael Shafir (1985: 66–67) has dubbed this preoccupation with maintaining elite cohesion "faction-anxiety." He convincingly argues that it derives from the experience of the Dej generation with the nearly unending factional manipulation by the Comintern in the interwar years, which was subsequently transmitted to the Ceausescu leadership group.

5. Professor Cazacu's study was the only research of its kind done in Romania until quite recently. The sample which she employed was large; 919 respondents from Bucharest, and 197 from Calugareni, a rural commune not far from the capital. While the choice of individuals with the two sites was random, the sites themselves cannot be counted as typical of the country as a whole, as Walter Connor (1979), who used the study for his comparative analysis of social mobility under socialism, suggests. For his purposes Connor combined the two samples, weighting them to match the rural/urban balance of the country as a whole. For most of the analysis above I have used the Bucharest proportion of the sample. The pace of change in the capital was undoubtedly more rapid than in other areas of Romania, and the concentration of intelligentsia respondents is

certainly greater there. Despite shortcomings in the data, I would argue that the pattern indicated by the study is generally correct. Outside higher rates of intelligentsia reproduction, Cazacu's findings are generally in keeping with the experience of other East European countries, and with data collected in Romania in more recent years.

6. According to Cazacu's rural sampling the pace of social mobility within the rural population increased to an astonishingly high level. Beginning with the first generational transition, total mobility was 26.4 percent, rising to 46.7 percent for the transition from generation two to generation three, and finally to 77.7 percent for the final transition. The sites of her rural samples, however, are atypical; being geographically close to Bucharest and therefore subject to the strong attraction of the rapid industrialization of the capital.

7. The low level of peasant self-reproduction in the last generational transition is somewhat misleading. By generation IV, only 29 of the study's respondents remained in the peasant category, as opposed to 99 in the previous generation. Of those 17 came from peasant families, and 11 of the 12 remaining came from workers' families. While no substantiating data exists, it can in all probability be assumed that these comprised members of the growing number of "dual status" families, in which one parent worked in nearby industry while maintaining residence in the village, that were beginning to appear at the time.

8. A second indication that members of the intelligentsia were beginning to differentiate themselves from other social groups can be seen in the selection of spouses by its members. Even by the 1960s individuals holding positions within the group of occupations requiring higher education were characterized by a very high level of endogamous marriage (despite the fact that many among the progeny of the prerevolutionary elite are said to have resorted to choosing partners of worker and peasant origin in order to make up for their own negative class background). Within this category the rate of in-group marriage was found to be highest for those who were themselves of intelligentsia parentage (Cazacu 1974: 232). A similar analysis of data gathered by Cinca et al. (1973: 44–45) shows that over 60 percent of the parents of university students who occupy positions requiring higher education were married to spouses in positions with the same level of requirements. The somewhat lower figure derived from this data in comparison to that used by Cazacu can be accounted for by the deletion of housewives, whose social educational status is not noted.

9. The desire of newly established members of the intelligentsia to differentiate themselves from their worker or peasant origins, difficult to document, soon becomes apparent to anyone who spends substantial time in the country. Shafir (1985: 145) remarks appropriately that "those who climb the social ladder perceive the process in terms of *divorcing* themselves from their former social affiliations, rather than bridging the classes." Their disdain for manual labor has caused some of the more dogmatic Romanian sociologists to seek to convince the Party of the need to carry out a full-scale campaign to convince the intelligentsia of the superiority of "working class" occupations.

10. While no hard data on this subject are available for obvious reasons, the practice of employing special influence to reduce the strictures of the admissions process is widely commented upon by those involved in it. Even those who decry the practice as a general phenomenon will admit to aiding relatives of their

own without any sign of ill ease on the ground that helping "family" is a special case. The overall effect of outright corruption is probably quite small, since the chances for success of the children are already quite high because of their access to better early education and special tutoring if necessary. Hence, in the majority of cases resort to bribery or influence peddling is unnecessary.

11. See Fischer-Galati's analysis of the popular appeal of "Ceausescuism" in his "Romania's Development as a Communist State" (Fischer-Galati 1981).

12. This relatively contradictory combination of promises for continuity, implying on one hand tight central control and high levels of accumulation, and on the other hand increased consumption and managerial decentralization, is consistent with Mary Ellen Fischer's summation of the 1965–1967 period as one of policy vacillation. I would suggest, however, that it can be more usefully interpreted as a time of accommodation between group interests that lasted until internal contradictions in the interests involved made their further reconciliation impossible; and Ceausescu's political position had been consolidated to a degree that allowed him to resolve the situation as he desired.

CHAPTER 5

1. For a more general treatment of this issue, see Bacon (1984, 1981b); Alexiev (1977); and Volgyes (1982).

2. Ion Coman, another Ceausescu supporter, was made Secretary of the Higher Political Council, while his predecessor, Ion Dinca, moved into party work but retained responsibility for military affairs.

3. Replacement parts for some Soviet model weapons were obtained in Israel. Fast attack craft for its navy were provided from the People's Republic of China. Tactical fighter aircraft were developed working in conjunction with Yugoslavia. Bucharest also turned to the West for support. Alouette III and Puma helicopters were purchased from France, and BAC-111 air transports from Great Britain (SIPRI, 1983: 343; Radio Free Europe Research, Romania/Situation Report 4, March 1983; IISS, 1983: 24). Despite these measures, it remains true that the Romanian military has fallen visibly behind its neighbors in both the sophistication and quantity of its weaponry. This development could hardly have been looked upon with favor by professional military men.

4. See Ivan Volgyes (1982: 53) for detailed figures, or Mark N. Kramer (1985) for a discussion of Romania in comparison with other members of the Warsaw Treaty Organization. On a more general level, during the decade Romania's defense spending relative to that of its neighbors continued to deteriorate. According to officially published statistics collected by the International Institute of Strategic Studies (IISS), from 1971 to 1981 Bucharest's defense expenditure increased by 109 percent. The lowest comparable figure in Eastern Europe was 131 percent for Poland, while the GDR increased its spending by 322 percent (IISS 1983: 124–25). While these figures cannot be taken as completely accurate, they do provide a useful depiction of relative spending and the magnitude of change. Between 1982 and 1984 Romania's per capita military outlay increased only from $57 to $58. The lowest comparable 1984 figure in WTO was Poland's, at $160, while East Germany was spending $457 per capita (IISS 1986: 212). In November 1978 Ceausescu made this orientation explicit by announcing

that Romania would not comply with Soviet calls for increased WTO military expenditures, on the grounds that doing so would impede the country's socio-economic development program, and thereby undermine its defense capacity in the long term (*Scinteia* November 28, 1978).

5. The tenor of Ceausescu's criticism of the extended intelligentsia is reflected in his November 1971 remarks on improving ideological work:

Despite all these positive results some shortcomings continue to express themselves, particularly leniency and lack of firmness in the face of several retrograde manifestations. It is true that this state of things does not represent a grave situation, but however small the harm such manifestations might bring, we do not have the right to let them pass. . . . It can be said that a certain atmosphere of self congratulation has appeared, a decline in combativeness and revolutionary spirit, in some sectors a "bureaucratic" spirit is establishing itself, and here and there a misunderstood attitude of "intellectualism." (Ceausescu 1982 2: 157)

6. While the actual decline in the number of intellectuals within the RCP was probably less than indicated by the figures, with the rest being "transformed" into workers through changes in the occupational classification system, the officially acknowledged reduction in their strength remains a strong signal of the party leaders' increasingly negative attitude toward them.

CHAPTER 6

1. According to official figures, industrial workers receive an average of 2,056 lei per month for their efforts, compared to 1,957 for agricultural workers (*Anuarul Statistic* 1980: 124).

2. A significant side effect of state efforts to limit migration since the early 1970s has been the growth of the *navetism*, that is, the practice of retaining a household in the village and commuting for more or less lengthy periods to the city to work in industry. The prevalence of this phenomenon was reflected in the fact that while approximately 50 percent of the population was housed in villages in 1981, only a little over 29 percent were employed in agricultural occupations, with a very great part of the remainder employed in urban industry (Shafir 1981: 141). Evaluations of the effect of large-scale *navetism* on Romanian society during the 1970s vary widely. Unlike many Western analysts, Romanian social scientists have generally treated it as a difficulty to be overcome. Long-term commuters were found by researchers to be least likely to be well integrated into the urban environment, were most likely to have "comportment" problems, and were most likely to work at below average production standards (Mihut 1985: 117; Firuta 1978: Basiliade et al. 1982: 159–71).

3. The question of relative "standards of living" is admittedly a difficult one. The Romanian government's most recent statistics suggest that the difference between peasants' and workers' wages in recent years is approximately 100 lei per month. In fact, since the beginning of the 1980s it appears that minimum wage guarantees for agricultural workers have not been conformed with. Questions of remuneration aside, the villages are continually short of consumer goods that can be obtained in the cities. On the other hand, housing is probably better in the countryside than in the cities, as is access to many food items.

4. It is among the workers that the politically stabilizing role ascribed to continued links between rural and urban Romania by Cole has been most important. On a material level maintenance of close relations with the villages provided an alternative source of scarce food items that the official consumer sector failed to produce, and a standard of comparison by which urban life appeared superior. Perhaps just as importantly, continued identification with rural extended families has retarded the development of a strong working class consciousness in the cities that might otherwise be translated into more active opposition to the regime.

5. Workers' relative satisfaction is clearly attested to in a recent study of the "quality of life" coordinated by Catalin Zamfir. The survey, carried out nationwide between 1979 and 1981, included nearly 2,000 respondents from all walks of life. Over 200 questions were asked, ranging from the respondents' actual material conditions and their participation in social activities, to their hopes for their children and attitudes about the future. Respondents were separated into four social categories: industrial workers, service workers, mid-level personnel, and intellectuals.

6. This estimate is arrived at by reconstruction from data provided by the Zamfir study (1984: 160, 174), which suggests intellectuals enjoy an approximate mean income of 2,915 lei, as opposed to 2,005 per month for workers. Their acquisition of consumer durables was, as a consequence, somewhat greater as well, though it does not compare particularly favorably with other occupational categories. A comparison of families' ownership of various household items (by percent) is provided by the following table, from Zamfir et al. (1984: 83).

	Workers	Service Workers	Midlevel Workers	Intellectuals
TV	79.9	93.9	95.4	94.0
Washing Machine	56.6	79.1	79.5	74.4
Tape Recorder	25.7	47.3	50.9	62.0
Automobile	12.3	36.0	29.3	50.7

7. According to Petre and Stefanescu (1985), 57 percent of the children of intellectuals in their sample did not remain in the same social category. If this

figure represents the reality of the situation, intelligentsia reproduction is currently lower than that of either workers or intermediate level employees. The actual rate may well be quite different, since mobility into the intelligentsia during the course of one's career is substantially greater for the intelligentsia children than any others. A more complete understanding of the situation may be forthcoming with publication of additional data from the 1982–1985 Bucharest Sociological Center study on social mobility, of which the Petre and Stefanescu work is a part. Interestingly, researchers familiar with the topic have reported in informal conversations during 1985 that mobility rates do in fact remain lowest within the intelligentsia.

8. Suteu and Ozunu's study showed 77 percent of 172 students (in grades 7–12) questioned in various schools in Bucharest were planning to enter universities, and a further 14 percent chose professional or technical schools. The proportion of those choosing to enter nontechnical university faculties was even higher when the researchers focused just on the *liceu* (somewhat analogous to the gymnasium in the German educational system) in Bucharest, Cluj, and Ploiesti (Sutu and Ozunu 1977).

9. While a great deal of low-level bribery is assumed, in recent years scandal has reached the highest levels of power. In 1982 a First Deputy Minister of Foreign Trade and two Deputy Ministers of Agriculture have been dismissed for corruption, and even Ceausescu family insider Cornel Burtica was forced to relinquish his positions (Radio Free Europe Research/Romanian Situation Report 9, May 21, 1982). It has also become increasingly common of late for plant managers and personnel from the central economic ministries to collude in "fixing" production indicators to ensure that bonuses are forthcoming. In the countryside it has been reported that outsiders assigned to cooperative and state farms are often faced with the choice of entering into ongoing schemes to defraud the state or being forced to flee from the retribution of the local population.

10. Two such recent works on the importance of economic development to national defense are: *Economia si Aparaea Nationala*, Lieutenant Colonel Simion Pitea (Bucharest: Editura Politica, 1976), and *Factorul Economic si Rolul sau in Intarirea Capacitatii de Aparare a Patriei*, Lieutenant General Victor Stanculescu and Colonel General Gheorghe Anghel (Bucharest: Editura Militara, 1984).

11. The growing difficulty created by intensified Romanian nationalism is epitomized by the case of Karoly Kirily. Kirily was a member of the RCP Politburo until 1972, and remained on its central committee until 1975. He was active in the leadership of the Hungarian Nationality Council until he wrote and made public three letters to the party leadership condemning the state of minority relations in the country, at which point he was removed, harassed by the security services, and completely isolated from public media.

12. Shafir (1983) discusses the ease with which anti-Semitic literature seems to enter the country, despite extremely effective measures to keep other Romanian language material from crossing the border. The same is true of inflammatory tracts "documenting" the atrocities carried out by the Hungarians against Transylvanian Romanians prior to 1945. It is interesting to note in this context that a surprisingly cordial relationship seems to be developing between

right-wing members of the Romanian exile community and the Ceausescu regime.

13. For an extensive sampling of the lengths to which such eulogies can be taken, see Maier (1984b). Elena, for example, has been referred to as "the 'Woman-Mother' who has become the guarantee of the immortality of the nation," while Nicolae is the "brilliant founder of new Romania . . . fervently beloved by mothers and children."

CHAPTER 7

1. The effect of the international economy on domestic politics in developed, capitalist nations and in the "Third World" has long been a topic of substantial academic interest. See, for example, Alexander Gershenkron, *Economic Backwardness in Historical Perpsective* (Cambridge: Harvard University Press, 1962); Peter Gourevitch, "The Second Image Reversed: International Sources of Domestic Politics," *International Organization*, 32: 4 (Autumn, 1971); James Kurth, "The Political Consequences of the Product Cycle: Industrial History and Political Outcomes," *International Organization*, 33: 1 (Winter, 1979); Guillermo O'Donnell, *Modernization and Bureaucratic Authoritarianism: Studies in South American Politics* (Institute of International Studies, University of California, Politics of Modernization Series No. 9, 1973). Until relatively recently less attention has been devoted to the impact of the international economy on the political evolution of state-socialist countries. Primary among the reasons for this lack of interest has been the limited nature of past links between state-socialist countries and the international market. This situation began to change at a startlingly rapid rate in the early 1970s for Eastern Europe as a whole, and did so even earlier for Romania. International economic relations have been particularly salient in the Romanian case because of their role in promoting the country's real, albeit limited, autonomy from the Soviet Union, and because of the RCP's intense effort to establish a strong independent industrial base.

2. The preeminent statement of this position is found in Immanuel Wallerstein, *The Modern World System* (New York: Academic Press, 1974); see also Christopher K. Chase-Dunn, ed., *Socialist States in the World Capitalist System* (Beverly Hills, California: Sage Publications, 1982) for a debate on the veracity of Wallerstein's theory.

3. For example, Romania's per capita national income for 1937 was $81 as compared with $440 in Great Britain and Sweden, $265 in France, and $170 in Czechoslovakia. It was followed only by Yugoslavia, at $80, and Bulgaria, at $75 (Berend and Ranki 1977: 99).

4. For a discussion of Romania's postwar leadership and its policies, see Chapter 3 above or the following: Ionescu (1964); Fischer-Galati (1970); and Jowitt (1971).

5. See, for example, the discussions found in Fischer-Galati, and Ionescu op. cit.

6. See Chapter 3 above, or Montias (1967: 163).

7. Ceausescu's government signed trade agreements with Iran in 1968 and 1969 totaling $315 million (Braun 1978: 25). By 1970 Romania was importing 2.29 million tons of oil annually from the West, while its imports from the Soviet Union remained at zero (Joyner 1976: 516).

8. The West's share grew from 32 to 38 percent of Romania's imports, and from 23 to 29 percent of exports (Tsantis and Pepper 1979: 554–57).

9. Between 1950 and 1975 the growth rate of overall industrial production was among the highest in the world, increasing at approximately 13 percent annually. This increase breaks down into 14.5 percent in producer goods and 10.5 percent in consumer goods. If one looks at the more general indicator of per capita net national income, increases are less impressive but still quite good, at 5.3 percent annually (Tsantis and Pepper 1979: 192; Chirot 1978: 472).

10. During the first half of the decade accumulation absorbed over 35 percent of national income in order to maintain a growth rate of approximately 11 percent. The actual rate varied between 10.5 percent and 11.3 percent (*Anuarul Statistic* 1980: 91; Tsantis and Pepper 1979: 93).

11. The Soviet Union's share dropped to 22 percent of exports and 19 percent of imports while the developed Western economies accounted for 32.2 percent and 41.4 percent, respectively (Tsantis and Pepper 1979: 574–77).

12. In dollar amounts imports grew from only $117 million in 1970 to $4 billion in 1980 (CIA 1982: 106).

13. These included companies involved in extraction and production of minerals, chemical and wood processing facilities, tractor production and assembly, and power plants (Tsantis and Pepper 1979: 125).

14. Figures on trade with LDCs are from Wharton (April 4, 1983: 2). This was coupled with a tendency toward obtaining more industrial raw materials from within the CMEA than had previously been the case. Both imports from and exports to Eastern Europe declined somewhat between 1979 and 1981, though less than trade with the West and then saw an upturn in 1982 as Romania began to adjust to its new circumstances, increasing 6.0 and 11.2 percent respectively.

15. Energy consumed per dollar produced of Net Material Product, for example, was two to four times higher in Romania in 1982 than in advanced Western economies. The inadequacy of the state's response is exemplified by its energy conservation program. Beginning in 1979 a program of stringent energy conservation in both industry and private consumption was initiated. Although clearly a necessary effort, conservation in the context of Romania's political economy had a major disruptive effect. Under central pressure to reduce energy consumption local authorities overrode more general priorities in their attempts to comply. In a number of instances power supplies were cut off to factories while they were in full operation, damaging machines and wasting thousands of hours of labor. In some cases power to mines was cut without warning while miners were still underground, forcing them to climb to the surface and wait until it was renewed, or their shift ended (Radio Free Europe Research/Romania Situation Report, 18, 1983: 21; personal communications to the author in Romania during 1982–1983).

16. Official estimates put Net Material Product growth in 1981 and 1982 at 2.2 percent and 2.6 percent respectively; in fact even this estimate appears to be optimistic (Braun 1982: 51; *1982 Yearbook of International Communist Affairs* 1983: 461). For reports from Romania see Paul Gafton (Radio Free Europe Research/Romania Situation Report, March 7, 1983: 11). For a representative Western estimate see Wharton (April 1, 1983: 2).

17. Disagreement over trade was particularly acerbic with respect to oil sales. Replacements for Romania's Western supplies, disrupted by the Iran/Iraq war, were purchased from the Soviet Union at fairly high levels in 1979, 1980, and 1981 ($618 million dollars in 1981 alone) (Wharton April 4, 1983). While the proportion of these Soviet imports in Romania's overall oil trade was quite low, the cost was significant, since the Soviet Union has not allowed them to take place within the normal trade framework between the two countries. Unlike other commodities petroleum trade was carried out only at world market prices and only in exchange for Western currency or "hard" goods. News of the Soviet sales was first announced to Romanian listeners not by their own government but over Radio Moscow, along with the pointed comment that other CMEA members were obtaining Russian oil at 40 percent below world market prices (Radio Free Europe Research, Romania/Situation Report, 1980: 5).

18. See, for example, Ceausescu's interview in John B. Oakes, "Ceausescu on Romania, the West and East," *The New York Times*, August 4 and 5, 1982.

19. Details of the agreement are given in *The New York Times*, June 4, 1983, and George Cioranescu (Radio Free Europe Research Romania/Situation Report, June 7, 1983: 4).

CHAPTER 8

1. See Horvat (1982: 70–83) on the relation between political elites and classes in state-socialist countries.

2. On the strengthening of socialist property see Popescu and Balaure (1986); Floares (1986); Postelnicu (1986).

3. As recently as 1986 Party dogmatists were still calling for the elimination of "nonproductive" jobs. Thus according to Nasta (1985: 2), "In order to assure a superior quality of preparation and efficient use of the labor force, in strict correlation with the needs of the economy, improvement of the structure of the work force constitutes a major problem. Improvement is meant in the sense of increasing the proportion of those working directly in production, and the channeling of those who are specialists into technical activities, into direct management of production, and reduction to the absolute minimum of those employed in indirect production and administration."

REFERENCES

Abonyi, Arpad
   1982 "Eastern Europe's Reintegration," in Christopher K. Chase-Dunn, ed., *The Socialist States in the World System* (Beverly Hills, CA: Sage Publications), pp. 181–202.
   1978 "Internationally Diffused Innovation and Conditions of Change in Eastern Europe," in Andrew Gyorgy and James A. Kuhlman, eds., *Innovation in Communist Systems* (Boulder, Colorado: Westview Press), pp. 163–78.

Academia Republicii Populare Romine: Institutul De Cercetari Economice
   1958 *Dezvoltarea Economiei RPR Pe Drumul Socialismului: 1948–1957* (Bucharest: Editura Academiei Republicii Populare Romine).

Alexiev, Alexander
   1977 "Party-Military Relations in Romania," Rand Paper Series, no. P-6059 (Santa Monica, California: The Rand Corporation).

Alton, Thad
   1977 "Comparative Structure and Growth of Economic Activity in Eastern Europe," in *East European Economies Post-Helsinki: A Compendium of Papers submitted to the Joint Economic Committee* (Washington: U.S. Government Printing Office), pp. 267–88.

Alton, Thad, Krzysztof Badach, Elizabeth Bass, Gregor Lazarcik, and George J. Staller
   1986 "Economic Growth in Eastern Europe: 1970 and 1975–1980," *Occasional Paper No. 90*, Research Project on National Income in East Central Europe (New York: L. W. International Financial Research, Inc.).

Alton, Thad, Krzysztof Badach, Elizabeth Bass, and Gregor Lazarcik
  1984 "Eastern Europe: Domestic Final Uses of Gross Product 1965, 1970, and 1975–1983," *Occasional Paper No. 82*, Research Project on National Income in East Central Europe (New York: L. W. International Financial Research, Inc.).

Anuarul Statistic al Republicii Socialiste Romania: 1982
  1982 (Bucharest: Directia Centrala de Statistica).

Anuarul Statistic al Republicii Socialiste Romania: 1980
  1980 (Bucharest: Directia Centrala de Statistica).

Arendt, Hannah
  1958 *The Origins of Totalitarianism* (London: Allen & Unwin).

Bacon, Walter M.
  1984 "Romania," in Daniel N. Nelson, ed., *Soviet Allies: The Warsaw Pact and the Issue of Reliability* (Boulder, Colorado: Westview Press, Inc.), pp. 250–63.
  1981a "Romania: Neo-Stalinism in Search of Legitimacy," *Current History* (April), pp. 168–72.
  1981b "Romanian Military Policy in the 1980s," in Daniel N. Nelson, ed., *Romania in the 1980s* (Boulder, Colorado: Westview Press).

Bahro, Rudolf
  1978 *The Alternative in Eastern Europe* (London: New Left Books).

Barbu, Zev
  1981 "Romania," in Woolf, S. J., ed., *Fascism in Europe* (New York: Methuen & Co. Ldt).

Barth, Fredrick
  1979 *A Transylvanian Legacy: the Life of a Transylvanian Saxon* (Salt Lake City, Utah: Transylvania).

Basiliade, George, et. al.
  1982 *Resurse Calitative ale Fortei de Munca Tinere din Industrie* (Bucharest: Editura Politica).

Becker, David
  1983 *The New Bourgeoisie and the Limits to Dependency Mining, Class and Power in "Revolutionary" Peru* (Princeton, New Jersey: Princeton University Press).

Berend, Ivan T. and Gyorgy Ranki
  1977 *East Central Europe in the 19th and 20th Centuries* (Budapest: Akademiai Kiado).

Berindei, Dan
  1967 *Cucerea Independentei Romaniei* (Bucharest: Editura Stiintifica).

Bistriceanu, Gheorghe
  1985 "Cresterea venitul national—baza progresului economico-social al patriei," *Revista Economica*, nr. 18 (April 19), pp. 1–2.

Borstein, Morris
  1973   *Plan and Market: Economic Reform in Eastern Europe* (New Haven: Yale University Press).
  1977   "Economic Reform in Eastern Europe," in *East European Economies Post Helsinki: A Compendium of Papers submitted to the Joint Economic Committee* (Washington, D.C.: U.S. Government Printing Office), pp. 102–34.

Botezatu, Doina
  1984   "Constiinta si Participare," in Marinescu, C. Gh., and Constantin Vlad, eds., *Constiinta si Progress* (Iasi, Romania: Editura Junimea), pp. 278–89.

Braun, Aurel
  1982   "Romania's Travails," *Problems of Communism*, vol. XXXI. (May/June), pp. 49–55.
  1978   *Romanian Foreign Policy Since 1965: The Political and Military Limits to Autonomy* (New York: Praeger).

Brown, J. F.
  1969   "Romania Today I: Towards Integration," *Problems of Communism* Vol. XIII no. 1 (January/February), pp. 8–17.

Brus, Woldzimierz
  1975   *Socialist Ownership and Political Systems* (Boston, Mass.: Routledge & Kegan Paul).

Brzezinski, Zbigniew
  1967   *The Soviet Bloc: Unity and Conflict* (Cambridge, Mass.: Harvard University Press).
  1966   "The Soviet Political System, Transformation or Disintegration," *Problems of Communism*, XV (January, February), pp. 1–15.

Bunce, Valerie
  1985   "The Empire Strikes Back: The Evolution of the Eastern Bloc from a Soviet Asset to a Soviet Liability," *International Organization*, Vol 39, no. 1 (winter), pp. 1–46.
  1984   "The Logic of Elite Studies," in Ronald H. Linden and Bert A. Rockman, eds., *Elite Studies and Communist Politics: Essays in Memory of Carl Beck*, University Center for International Studies, University of Pittsburgh (London: Feffer and Simons Inc.), pp. 21–148.
  1981   *Do New Leaders Make a Difference?: Executive Succession and Public Policy Under Capitalism and Socialism* (Princeton, New Jersey: Princeton University Press).

Bunce, Valerie, and Alexander Hicks
  1987   "Capitalism, Socialism, and Democracy," *Political Power and Social Theory*, Vol. 6.

Bunce, Valerie, and John M. Echols, III
  1979   "From Soviet Studies to Comparative Politics: The Unfinished Revolution," *Soviet Studies*, vol. XXXI, no. 1, January, pp. 43–55.

Burke, David P.
    1980   "Defense and Mass Mobilization in Romania," *Armed Forces and Society*, vol. 7, no. 1 (Fall), pp. 31–49.

Cartana, Iulian, and Constantin Mocanu
    1986   "Conceptia tovarasului Nicolae Ceausescu privind istoria unitara a poporului roman—fundament al activitatii ideologice, politico-educative desfasurate de partidul nostru," *Era Socialista*, nr. 11 (June 10), pp. 21–24.

Cazacu, Honorina
    1974   *Mobilitatea Sociala* Teza de Doctorat (Bucharest: Universitate Bucuresti, Facultatea de Filozofie).

Ceausescu, Nicolae
    1982   *Opere Alese*, vols. 1–3 (Bucharest: Editura Politica).
    1979   *Raport la cel de al XII-lea Congres al Partidul Comunist Roman* (Bucharest: Editura Politica).
    1972   *Raport la Conferinta Nationala a Partidului Comunist Roman: 21 iulie 1972* (Bucharest: Editura Politica).
    1970   *Romania pe Drumul Construirii Sociatatii Multilaterale Dezvoltate*, Vol. 4 (Bucharest: Editura Politica).
    1969   *Romania On The Way To Completing Socialist Construction* vols. I–III (Bucharest: Meridiane Publishing House).
    1968   *Romania Pe Drumul Desavirsirii Constructiei Socialiste* vols. I–III (Bucharest: Editura Politica).

Ceterchi, Ion, Ion Florea, and Aristotle Cioba
    1981   *Democratia Socialista si Autoconducere Muncitoreasca in Romania* (Bucharest: Editura Politica).

Chase-Dunn, Christopher K., ed.
    1982   *Socialist States in the World System* (Beverly Hills, CA: Sage Publications).

Chelcea, Septimiu
    1979   "Satisfactia muncii industriale," *Viitorul Social*, Vol. VIII, nr. 1, pp. 91–100.

Chirot, Daniel
    1980   "The Corporatist Model and Socialism: Notes on Romanian Development," *Theory and Society* no. 2, pp. 363–81.
    1978a "Neoliberal and Social Democratic Theories of Development: The Zeletin-Voinea Debate Concerning Romania's Prospects in the 1920's and its Contemporary Importance," in Kenneth Jowitt, ed., *Social Change in Romania 1860–1940*, Research Series, No. 36 (Berkeley: Institute of International Studies), pp. 31–52.
    1978b "Social Change in Communist Romania," *Social Forces* Vol. 57: 2 (December), pp. 457–99.
    1976   *Social Change in a Peripheral Society: The Creation of a Balkan Colony* (New York: Academic Press).

Cinca, Elvira, Gheorghe Craciun, Roman Cresin, Fred Mahler, Vasile Miftode, Achim Mihu, Constantin Schifirneti
  1973   *Studentul si Societatea: Contributii la Studiul Profilul Politic si Socio-professional al Tineretului Universitar din Romania* (Cluj Napoca, Romania: Editura Dacia).

Ciurileanu, Radu
  1986   "Exercitarea cu inalta raspundere si evicienta a autoconducerii muncitoresti si autogestiunii," *Revista Economica*, nr. 8 (February 21), pp. 10-11.

Cliff, Tony
  1964   *Russia: A Marxist Analysis* (London: Socialist Review Publishers).

Cohen, Stephen
  1985   *Rethinking the Soviet Experience: Politics and History Since 1917* (New York: Oxford University Press).

Cole, John W.
  1981   "Family, Farm, and Factory: Rural Workers in Contemporary Romania," in Daniel N. Nelsen, ed., *Romania in the 1980s* (Boulder, Colorado: Westview Press), pp. 71-116.

Collier, David, ed.
  1979   *The New Authoritarianism in Latin America* (Princeton, New Jersey: Princeton University Press).

Coman, Ion, Lieutenant General Constantin Olteanu, Major General Ilie Ceausescu, Colonel Emil Burbulea, and Colonel Mihai Arsintescu
  1982   *Apararea Nationala in Conceptul Partidul Comunist Roman* (Bucharest: Editura Militara).

Congresul al IX-lea Partidului Comunist Roman
  1966   (Bucharest: Editura Politica).

Congresul al X-lea Partidul Comunist Roman
  1969   (Bucharest: Editura Politica).

Connell, R. W.
  1982   "A Critique of the Althusserian Approach to Class," in Anthony Giddens and David Held, eds., *Classes, Power, and Conflict* (Los Angeles, University of California Press, 1982), pp. 130-47.

Connor, Walter D.
  1979   *Socialism, Politics, and Equality: Hierarchy and Change in Eastern Europe and the USSR* (New York: Colombia University Press).

Croan, Melven
  1970   "Is Mexico the Future of East Europe: Institutional Adaptability and Political Change in Comparative Perspective," in Samuel P. Huntington and Clement H. Moore, *Authoritarian Politics in Modern Society*, pp. 451-83.

Crompton, Rosmary, and Jon Gubbay
  1977   *Economy and Class Structure* (New York: Macmillan).

Deac, A.
  1967   *Marea Rascoala A Taranilor Din 1907* (Bucharest: Academiei Re-
          publicii Socialiste Romania).

*Directivele Comitetului Central al Partidului Comunist Roman cu privire la per-
fectionarea conducerii si plani ficrea economiei nationale corespunzator conditii-
lor noii etape de dezvoltare socialiste a Romaniei*
  1967   (Bucharest: Editura Politica).

Dinculescu, Constantin
  1978   "Mobilitate si Dinamica in Structura Sociala a Judetului Vilcea,"
          Viitorul Social, Vol VII., nr. 4, pp. 688–95.

Djilas, Milovan
  1966   *The New Class, An Analysis of the Communist System* (London:
          Allen & Unwin, 1966).

Djordjevic, Dimitrije, and Stephen Fischer-Galati
  1981   *The Balkan Revolutionary Tradition* (New York: Columbia University
          Press).

Dobrescu, Emilian, and Ion Blaga
  1973   *Structural Patterns of Romanian Economy* (Bucharest: Meridian Pub-
          lishing House).

Douglas, G.
  1984   "Rewriting August 23," Radio Free Europe Research, Situation Re-
          port, Romania/7 (April 19).

Dragomirescu, Horatiu
  1985   "Conceptie novatoare privind perfectionarea conducerii economico-
          sociale planificate," *Revista Economica*, nr. 31 (August 2), pp. 2–3.

Dragut, Aurel
  1978   "Promovarea Profesionala si Satisfactia in Muncii," *Viitorul Social*,
          Vol. VII, nr. 3. pp. 490–94.

Droker, Linda S., and John A. Martens
  1982   "Romania: Performance and Prospects for Trade with the U.S. and
          the West," in *East-West: The Prospects to 1985* (Washington, D.C.:
          U.S. Government Printing Office).

Eidelberg, Philip G.
  1974   *The Great Romanian Peasant Revolt of 1907: Origins of a Modern
          Jacquerie* (Leiden, Netherlands: E. J. Brill).

Farlow, Robert L.
  1978   "Romania: The Politics of Autonomy," *Current History* (April), pp.
          168–71.

Feher, Ferenc, Agnes Heller, and Gyorgy Markus
  1983   *Dictatorship Over Needs* (New York: St. Martin's Press).

Firuta, Argentina
1978   "Schimbari in Modul de Viata al Clasei Muncitoare," *Viitorul Social*,
        Vol. VII, nr. 1, pp. 72–78.

Fischer, Mary Ellen
1983   "Nicolae Ceausescu and the Romanian Political Leadership: Nationali-
        zation and Personalization of Power," (Washington: National Council
        for Soviet and East European Research).
1981   "Idol or Leader? The Origins and Future of the Ceausescu Cult," in
        Daniel N. Nelsen ed., *Romania in the 1980s* (Boulder, Colorado: West-
        view Press), pp. 117–41.
1980   "Political Leadership and Personnel Policy in Romania: Continuity
        and Change, 1965–1976," in Steven Rosefielde, ed., *World Commu-
        nism at the Crossroads: Military Ascendancy, Political Economy, and
        Human Welfare* (Boston, MA: Martinus Nijhoff Publishing), pp. 210–33.
1979   "The Romanian Communist Party and Its Central Committee: Pat-
        terns of Growth and Change," *Southeastern Europe*, 6, Pt. 1, pp. 1–28.
1977   "Participatory Reforms and Political Development in Romania," in
        Jan F. Triska and Paul M. Cocks, eds., *Political Development in East-
        ern Europe* (New York: Praeger), pp. 217–37.

Fischer-Galati, Stephen
1985   "National Minorities in Romania, 1919–1980," in Stephan M. Horak,
        ed., *Eastern European National Minorities 1919–1980: A Handbook*
        (Littleton, Colorado: Libraries Unlimited, Inc.), pp. 190–215.
1981   "Romania's Development as a Communist State," in Daniel N. Nelsen
        ed., *Romania in the 1980s* (Boulder, Colorado: Westview Press), pp.
        4–16.
1971   "Fascism in Romania," in Peter F. Sugar ed., *Native Fascism in the
        Successor States: 1918–1945* (Santa Barbara, California: ABC CLIO).
1970   *Twentieth Century Romania* (New York: Columbia University Press).
1967   *The New Romania: From People's Democracy to Socialist Republic*
        (Cambridge, Massachusetts: M.I.T. Press).

Floares, Alecu Al.
1986   "Consolidarea si perfectionarea propietatii socialiste," *Era Socialista*,
        nr. 9 (May 5), pp. 32–35.
1978   "Trends in Socio-Professional and Territorial Mobility in Iasi County
        during the Present-day Scientific and Technological Revolution,"
        Viitorul Social Vol. 69, No. 7, supplement, pp. 121–29.
1977   *Mobilitatea Polulatiei* (Iasi, Romania: Editura Junimea).

Friedrich, Carl, and Zbigniew Bzrezinski
1956   *Totalitarian Dictatorship and Autocracy* (Cambridge, Mass.: Harvard
        University Press).

Friedrich, Carl, Michael Curtis, and Benjamin Barber
1969   *Totalitarianism in Perpsective: Three Views* (New York: Praeger).

Fulea, Maria, and Georgeta Tamas
  1982 *Modernizare si Structura Sociala in Comunitatea Rurala* (Bucharest: Editura Academiei Republicii Socialiste Romania).

Gershenkron, Alexander
  1962 *Economic Backwardness in Historical Perspective*, (Cambridge: Harvard University Press).

Gilberg, Trond
  1984 "Romania's Growing Difficulties," *Current History* (November), pp. 375–379.
  1981 "Modernization, Human Rights, and Nationalism: The Case of Romania," in George Klein and Milan J. Reban, eds., *The Politics of Ethnicity in Eastern Europe* (Boulder, Colorado: East European Monographs).
  1979 "The Costly Experiment: Collectivization of Romanian Agriculture," in Ronald A. Francisco, Betty A. Laird, and Roy D. Laird eds., *The Political Economy of Collectivized Agriculture* (New York: Pergamon Press), pp. 23–62.
  1975a *Modernization in Romania Since World War II* (New York: Praeger).
  1975b "Romania: In Quest of Development," in Ivan Volgyes, ed., *Political Socialization in Eastern Europe: A Comparative Framework* (New York: Praeger), pp. 147–49.
  1974 "Ceausescu's Romania," *Problems of Communism*, Vol. XXIII (July/August), pp. 29–43.

Gill, Graeme J.
  1975 "Romania: Background to Autonomy," *Survey* 21: 3 (Summer) pp. 94–113.

Gitelman, Zvi
  1970 "Power and Authority in Eastern Europe," in Chalmers Johnson, ed., *Change in Communist Systems* (Stanford, CA: Stanford University Press, 1970), pp. 235–63.

Glodeanu, Eugen
  .1979 "Integrarea Socio-culturala a intellectualilor din Mediul Urban (Cazul Orasului Slobozia)," *Viitorul Social*, Vol. VII., nr. 1, pp. 122–27.

Gourivitch, Peter
  1971 "The Second Image Reversed: International Sources of Domestic Politics," *International Organization*, 32: 4 (Autumn), pp. 481–912.

Grafton, Paul
  1984 "Ceausescu Lays Foundation Stone for Grand Bucharest Project," Radio Free Europe Research, Situation Report, Romania/11 (July 26).

Granick, David
  1975 *Enterprise Guidance in Eastern Europe: A Comparison of Four Socialist Economies* (Princeton, New Jersey: Princeton University Press).

Griffith, William
  1967 *Sino-Soviet Relations: 1964–65* (Cambridge, Mass.: M.I.T. Press).

Hagan, Trofin
    1985   *Teoria si Practica Socialismului Stiintific in Romania* (Bucharest: Editura Politica).

Haraszti, Miklos
    1978   *Workers in a Worker's State* (New York: Universe Books).

Hirszowicz, Maria
    1986   *Coercion and Control in Communist Society: The Visible Hand in a Command Economy* (New York: St. Martin's Press).
    1980   *The Bureaucratic Leviathian* (New York: New York University Press).
    1976   "Is There a Ruling Class in the USSR?—A Comment," *Soviet Studies* vol XXVIII, no. 2, (April), pp. 262–73.

Hohmann, Hans-Hermann
    1979   "The State and Economy in Eastern Europe," in Jack Hayward and R. N. Berki, eds., *State and Society in Contemporary Europe* (New York: St. Martin's Press), pp. 141–57.

Holzman, Franklin D.
    1976   *International Trade Under Communism—Politics and Economics* (New York: Basic Books, Inc.).

Horvat, Branko
    1982   *The Political Economy of Socialism: A Marxist Social Theory* (Armonk, New York: M. E. Sharp, Inc.).

Hough, Jerry
    1972   "The Soviet System: Petrification or Pluralism," *Problems of Communism*, vol. 12 (March-April), pp. 25–45.

Humphreys, R. J. E.
    1933   "Report on Economic Conditions in Romania," British Department of Overseas Trade (London: His Majesty's Stationery Office).
    1928   "Report on Economic Conditions in Romania," British Department of Overseas Trade (London: His Majesty's Stationery Office).

Hutira, Toma
    1983   *Calaficare Fortei de Munca Industriale: Concept, Nivel, Tendinta* (Cluj-Napoca, Romania: Editura Dacia).

IISS (International Institute for Strategic Studies)
    1986   *The Military Balance: 1986–1987* (London: The International Institute for Strategic Studies).
    1983   *The Military Balance: 1983–1984* (London: The International Institute for Strategic Studies).

Ionescu, Dan
    1985   "A Touch of Royalty," Radio Free Europe Research, Situation Report, Romania/2 (January 22).

Ionescu, Ghita
    1964   *Communism in Romania: 1944-1962* (London: Oxford University Press).

Iorga, N.
   1925   *Istoria Comertului Romanescu: Epoca Mai Noua* (Bucharest).

Jackson, Marvin R.
   1981a   "Perspectives on Romania's Economic Development in the 1980s," in
            Daniel N. Nelsen, ed., *Romania in the 1980s* (Boulder, Colorado: West-
            view Press), pp. 254–305.
   1981b   "Romania's Economy at the End of the 1970s: Turning the Corner on
            Intensive Development," in *East European Economic Assessment: A
            Compendium of Papers Submitted to the Joint Economic Committee*,
            Part II (Washington, D.C.: U.S. Government Printing Office), pp. 231–
            97.
   1977   "Industrialization, Trade, and Mobilization in Romania's Drive for
            Economic Independence," in *East European Economies Post-Helsinki:
            A Compendium of Papers submitted to the Joint Economic Committee*
            (Washington, D.C.: U.S. Government Printing Office), pp. 886–940.

Janos, Andrew
   1978   "Modernization and Decay in Historical Perspective: The Romanian
            Case," in Kenneth Jowitt, ed., *Social Change in Romania 1860–1940*,
            Research Series, No. 36 (Berkeley: Institute of International Studies),
            pp. 72–117.
   1970   "The One-Party State and Social Mobilization: Eastern Europe be-
            tween the Wars," in Samuel P. Huntington and Clement H. Moore,
            eds., *Authoritarian Politics in Modern Society: The Dynamics of
            Established One Party Systems* (New York: Basic Books), pp. 204–36.

Jelavich, Barbara
   1983   *History of the Balkans*, vols. I and II (New York: Cambridge Univer-
            sity Press).

Johnson, Chalmers
   1970   "Comparing Communist Nations," in Chalmers Johnson, ed., *Change
            in Communist Systems* (Stanford, CA: Stanford University Press,
            1970), pp. 1–32.

Jones, Christopher D.
   1977   "Soviet Hegemony in Eastern Europe: The Dynamics of Political
            Autonomy and Military Intervention," World Politics 29: 1 (January),
            pp. 216–41.

Jowitt, Kenneth
   1983   "Soviet Neotraditionalism: The Political Corruption of a Leninist
            Regime," *Soviet Studies*, vol. SSSV, no. 3 (July), pp. 275–95.
   1978   *The Leninist Response to National Dependency*, Institute of Interna-
            tional Studies, *Research Series* no. 37, (Berkeley, CA: University of
            California).
   1974a   "Political Innovation in Romania," *Survey* No. 4, pp. 132–51.
   1974b   "An Organizational Approach to the Study of Political Culture in
            Marxist-Leninist Regimes," *American Political Science Review* Vol.
            68, No. 3., pp. 1171–91.

1971   *Revolutionary Breakthroughs and National Development* (Los Angeles, CA: University of California Press).

Joyner, Christopher C.
1976   "The Energy Situation in Eastern Europe: Problems and Prospects," *East European Quarterly*, vol. X, No. 4, pp. 493–516.

Kassoff, Allen
1969   "The Administered Society: Totalitarianism without Terror," in Fredrick Fleron, ed., *Communist Studies and the Social Sciences* (Chicago: Rand-McNally), pp. 153–69.

King, Robert R.
1972   "Rumanian Difficulties in Military and Security Affairs," Radio Free Europe Research Romania/Background Report, no. 6 (March 6).
1980   *History of the Romanian Communist Party* (Stanford, CA: Hoover Institution Press).

Kolarz, Walter
1946   *Myths and Realities in Eastern Europe* (London: L. Drummond Ltd.).

Konrad, G. and Ivan Szelenyi
1979   *The Intellectuals on the Road to Class Power* (Brighton, Sussex: Harvester).

Korbonski, Andrzej
1977   "The "Change to Change" in Eastern Europe," in Jan F. Triska and Paul M. Cocks, eds., *Political Development in Eastern Europe* (New York: Praeger), pp. 3–29.
1976   "Leadership Succession and Political Change in Eastern Europe," *Studies in Comparative Communism* Vol. IX, nos. 1–2 (Spring-Summer), pp. 3–22.
1972   "Comparing Liberalization Processes in Eastern Europe: A Preliminary Analysis," *Comparative Politics*, 4: 2 (January), pp. 231–49.

Kornai, Janos
1980   *Economics of Shortage*, Vol. A (New York: North-Holland Publishing Company).

Kramer, Mark N.
1985   "Civil-Military Relations in the Warsaw Pact," *International Affairs*, Vol. 61, No. 1.

Kurth, James
1979   "The Political Consequences of the Product Cycle: Industrial History and Political Outcomes," *International Organization*, 33: 1 (Winter), pp. 1–35.

Lane, David
1982   *The End of Social Inequality?: Class, Status and Power Under State-Socialism* (London: George Allen & Unwin).
1976   *The Socialist Industrial State* (Boulder, Colorado: Westview Press).

Lawson, Colin W.
  1983 "National Independence and Reciprocal Advantages: The Political
         Economy of Romanian-South Relations," *Soviet Studies* XXXV, No.
         3 (July), pp. 362–75.

Linden, Robert H.
  1979 *Bear and the Foxes: The International Relations of the East European
         States, 1965–1969* (Boulder, Colorado: East European Quarterly).
  1981 "Romania's Foreign Policy in the 1980's," in Daniel Nelson, ed., *Ro-
         mania in the 1980s* (Boulder, Colorado: Westview Press), pp. 219–53.

Macartney, M. A. and A. W. Palmer
  1962 *Independent Eastern Europe: A History* (London: Macmillan).

Madgearu, Virgil
  1930 *Romania's New Economic Policy* (London: P. S. King & Son LTD.).

Madsen, Mark Hunter
  1982 "The Uses of Beijingpolitik: China in Romanian Foreign Policy Since
         1953," *East European Quarterly*, vol. XVI, No. 3 (September), pp.
         277–309.

Maier, Anneli
  1985a "Romanian Historians Discuss Controversial Hungarian Issues," Radio
          Free Europe Research, Situation Report, Romania/5 (March 13).
  1985b "RCP Adopts New Party Statutes," Radio Free Europe Research,
          Situation Report, Romania/2 (January 33).
  1984a "Nicolae Ceausescu and His Personality Cult," Radio Free Europe Re-
          search, Situation Report, Romania/2 (January 30).
  1984b "Elena and Nicolae Ceausescu's Birthdays Celebrated," Radio Free
          Europe Research, Situation Report, Romania/3 (February 14).
  1984c "Visitors and History Underscore Autonomy," Radio Free Europe
          Research, Situation Report, Romania/12 (September 4).
  1983   "Romanian-Soviet Polemics," Radio Free Europe Research, Situation
          Report Romania/9 (May 24).

Mallet, Serge
  1974 *Bureaucracy and Technocracy in the Socialist Countries* (Nottingham,
         U.K.: Spokesman Books).

Mandel, Ernst
  1979 "Once again on the Trotskyist definition of the social nature of the
         Soviet Union" *Critique*, No. 12 (Autumn-Winter), pp. 117–26.

Marcuse, Herbert
  1961 *Soviet Marxism: A Critical Analysis* (New York: Random House).

Marginean, Ioan
  1985 "Tendinte ale Evolutiei Structurii Sociale din Romania," *Viitorul
         Social*, (May-June) nr. 4, pp. 251–55.

Marinescu, C. Gh., and Constantin Vlad, eds.
  1984 *Constiinta si Progress* (Iasi, Romania: Editura Junimea).

Martin, Andrew
   1977   "Political Constraints on Economic Strategies in Advanced Industrial
          Societies," *Comparative Political Studies*, Vol. 10, No. 3 (October),
          pp. 323-54.

Matthews, Mervyn
   1972   *Class and Society in Soviet Russia* (London: Allen Lane).

Maurer, I. G.
   1969   *Report on the Directives of the Tenth Congress of the Romanian
          Communist Party* (Bucharest: Agerpress).

Maxwell, Robert, M. C., gen. ed.
   1983   *Leaders of the World. Nicolae Ceausescu: Builder of Modern Romania
          and International Statesman* (Oxford, Pergamon Press).

Measnicov, Ion, Ilie Hristache, and Vladimir Trebici
   1977   *Demografia Oraselor Romaniei* (Bucharest: Editura Stiintifica si
          Enciclopedica).

Melotti, U.
   1980   "Socialism and Bureaucratic Collectivism in the Third World," *Telos*
          No. 43 (Spring), pp. 175-81.

Miftode, Vasile
   1984   *Elemente de Sociologie Rurala* (Bucharest: Editura Stiintifica si
          Enciclopedica).

Mihut, Liliana
   1985   *Tineretul: Omogenizarea si Diferentiere* (Cluj-Napoca, Romania:
          Editura Dacia).

Mills, C. Wright
   1959   *The Power Elite* (New York: Oxford University Press).

Mitrany, David
   1930   *The Land and the Peasant in Romania: The War and the Agrarian Re-
          form (1917-21)* (London: Humphrey Milford, Oxford University
          Press).

Mlynar, Zdenek
   1979   "August 1968," in G. R. Urban, ed., *Communist Reformism* (New
          York: St. Martin's Press), pp. 116-43.

Moldovan, Toader
   1982   *Autoconducerea Muncitoreasca pe Coordonatele Democratiei Socialiste*
          (Bucharest: Editura Politica).

Montias, John Michael
   1978   "Notes on the Romanian Debate on Sheltered Industrialization: 1860-
          1906," in Kenneth Jowitt ed., *Social Change in Romania 1860-1940*,
          Research Series, No. 36 (Berkeley, CA: Institute of International
          Studies), pp. 53-71.

1967   *Economic Development in Communist Romania* (Cambridge, Massa-
        chusetts: M.I.T. Press).

Nadelea, Marin
    1985   "Partidul, forta politica conducatoare a societatii noastre socialiste,"
            Era Socialista, nr. 10, (August 15), pp. 9–13.

Nagy-Talavera, Nicolas M.
    1970   *The Green Shirts and Others: a History of Fascism in Hungary and Ro-
            mania* (Stanford, California: Hoover Institution Press).

Nasta, Eliza
    1985   "Conceptia tovarasului Nicolae Ceausescu privitoare la reorganizarea
            pe baza intensive a economiei," *Revista Economica*, nr. 2 (January 11),
            pp. 1–2.

Nelson, Daniel
    1981   "Workers in a Workers' State," in Daniel N. Nelsen, ed., *Romania in
            the 1980s* (Boulder, Colorado: Westview Press), pp. 174–97.
    1980   "Workers in a Workers' State: Participation in Romania," *Soviet
            Studies*, vol. XXXII, No. 4. (October), pp. 542–60.

Nove, Alec
    1983   "The Class Nature of the Soviet Union Revisited," *Soviet Studies*, vol.
            XXXV, No. 3 (July), pp. 298–312.
    1975   "Is there a Ruling Class in the USSR?" *Soviet Studies*, vol. XXVII, no.
            4 (October), pp. 624–35.

Nydon, Judith
    1984   *Public Policy and Private Fertility Behavior: The Case of Pronatalist
            Policy in Socialist Romania*, Unpublished Ph.D. Dissertation, Univer-
            sity of Massachusetts (September).

Odom, William E.
    1976   "A Dissenting View on the Group Approach to Soviet Politics," *World
            Politics*, vol. 28, pp. 542–67.

O'Donnell, Guillermo
    1973   *Modernization and Bureaucratic Authoritarianism: Studies in South
            American Politics* (Institute of International Studies, University of
            California, Politics of Modernization Series No. 9).

Olteanu, Ionitza, and Ileana Ionescu
    1980   "The New International Economic Order: A Romanian Perspective,"
            in Ervin Laszlo and Joel Kurtzman, eds., *Eastern Europe and the New
            International Economic Order: Representative Samples of Socialist
            Perspectives* (New York: Pergamon Press), pp. 45–63.

Olteanu, Colonel General Constantin, Lieutenant General Ilie Ceausescu, Colonel
Florian Tuca, and Colonel Vasile Mocanu
    1984   *Armata Romana in Revolutia Din August 1944* (Bucharest: Editura
            Politica).

Ossowski, Stanislaw
    1963   *Class Structure and the Social Consciousness* (New York: The Free Press).

Otetea, Andrei
    1945   *Tudor Vladimirescu si Miscarea Eterista in Tarile Romanesti: 1821-1822* (Bucharest).

Otetea, Andrei, ed.
    1964   *Istoria Romaniei Vol. III* (Bucharest: Editura Academiei Republicii Populare Romane).
    1970   *The History of the Romanian People* (New York: Twayne Publishers, Inc.).

Pakulski, Jan
    1986   "Legitimacy and Mass Compliance: Reflections on Max Weber and Soviet-Type Societies," *British Journal of Political Science*, 16 (January), pp. 35–56.

Parkin, Frank
    1979   *The Marxist Theory of Class: A Bourgeoisie Critique* (London: Tavistock).
    1971   *Class Inequality and the Political Order Social Stratification in Capitalist and Communist Societies* (London: Macgibbon & Kee).

Pascu, Stefan
    1982   *A History of Transylvania*, D. Robert Ladd, trans. (Detroit: Wayne State University).

Petre, Ioana, and Stefan Stefanescu
    1985   "Tineretul Urban In Procesele de Mobilitate Sociale," *Viitorul Social*, pp. 243–52.

Petrescu, Ion
    1977   *Psihologia Conducerii Colective a Interprinderii Industriale* (Craiova, Romania: Scrisul Romanesc).

Pitea, Simion
    1976   *Economia si Apararea Nationala* (Bucharest: Editura Militara).

Polanyi, Karl, Conrad Arensberg, and Harry W. Pearson, eds.
    1957   *Trade and Market in Early Empires* (New York: Free Press).

Polonsky, Antony
    1975   *The Little Dictators: The History of Eastern Europe Since 1918* (Boston: Routledge & Kegan Paul).

Popescu, Marin, and Florin Balaure
    1986   "Intarirea proprietatii socialiste—legitate a dezvoltarii noii orinduiri," *Era Socialista*, nr. 11, (June 10), pp. 5–8.

Popescu, Sofia
    1983   *Forma de Stat* (Bucharest: Editura Stiintifica si Enciclopedica).

Postelnicu, Gheorghe
1986 "Rolul si functiile proprietatii socialiste," *Era Socialista*, nr. 1 (January 10), pp. 13–16.

Poulantzas, Nicos
1975 *Classes in Contemporary Capitalism* (London: New Left Books).
1973 "On Social Classes," *New Left Review*, 78, pp. 27–39, 47–50.

Raboaca, Gheorghe
1984 *Retrebutia–Pirghie a Folosirii Eficiente a Fortei de Munca* (Bucharest: Editura Academiei Republicii Socialiste Romania).

Radio Free Europe Research
Radio Free Europe Situation Reports/Romania, various issues from March 1980 through March 1983.

Radu, Michael
1981 "Romania and the Third World: The Dilemmas of a 'Free Rider'," in Michael Radu, ed., *Eastern Europe and the Third World: East vs. South* (New York: Praeger), pp. 235–72.

Rakovski, Marc
1978 *Toward an East European Marxism* (New York: St. Martin's Press).

Ratner, Michael
1981 "Schools, Jobs, and Young People in Romania: An Anthropological Account," Studia Univer. Babes-Bolya, XXVI, 2, pp. 10–17.
1980 *Education and Occupational Selection in Contemporary Romania* unpublished doctoral dissertation, Washington, D.C., The American University.

Recensamintul Populatiei si Locuinte din 15 Martie 1966
1970 (Bucharest: Directia Centrala de Statistica).

Recensamintul Populatiei si Locuinte din 5 Ianuaria 1977
1981 (Bucharest: Directia Centrala de Statistica).

Rigby, T. H.
1972 "Totalitarianism and Change in Communist Systems," *Comparative Politics*, Vol. 4, No. 2 (April), pp. 433–53.

Roberts, Henery L.
1969 *Rumania: Political Problems of an Agrarian State* (Archon Books).

Rothschild, Joseph
1974 *East Central Europe between the two World Wars* (Seattle: University of Washington Press).

Roucek, Joseph S.
1932 *Contemporary Romania and Her Problems: A Study of Modern Nationalism* (Stanford, California: Stanford University Press).

Sandu, Dumitru
1985 "Continuitate si Schimbare in Cercetarile Romanesti Asupra Integrarii Socioprofesionale: in Model Explicativ," in Marie Stanciu, ed., *Semni-*

ficatia Documentelor Sociale (Bucharest: Editura Stiintifica si Enciclopedica).

1984   *Fluxurile de Migratie in Romania* (Bucharest: Editura Academiei Republicii Socialiste Romania).

Sarbu, Mariana
1978   "Conducerea colectiva si participarea la Conducere," *Viitorul Social*,
Vol. VII, nr. 3, pp. 482–89.

Schifirnet, Constantin
1979   "Motivatii si Conditii ale Alegerii Profesiei de catre Studenti," *Viitorul
Social*, Vol. VIII, nr. 3, pp. 515–23.

Schmitter, Philippe C.
1978   "Reflections on Mihail Manoilescu and the Political Consequences
of Delayed-Dependent Development on the Periphery of Western
Europe," in Kenneth Jowitt ed., *Social Change in Romania 1860–
1940*, Research Series, No. 36 (Berkeley: Institute of International
Studies), pp. 117–39.

Schopflin, George
1974   "Romanian Nationalism," *Survey* (Spring/Summer), pp. 77–104.

Seton-Watson, Hugh
1956   *The East European Resolution* (London: Methuen).
1963   *A History of the Roumanians* (London: Archon Books).

Shafir, Michael
1985   *Romania: Politics, Economics, and Society* (Boulder, Colorado:
Lynne Rienner Publishers, Inc.).
1983   "The Men of the Archangel Revisited: Anti-Semitic Formations
Among Communist Romania's Intellectuals," *Studies in Comparative
Communism*, No. 3 (Autumn), pp. 223–43.

Shoup, Paul
1984   "The Origins of Political Change in Communist Systems," in Ronald
H. Linden and Bert A. Rockman, eds., *Elite Studies and Communist
Politics: Essays in Memory of Carl Beck*, University Center for Inter-
national Studies, University of Pittsburgh (London: Feffer and Simons
Inc.), pp. 143–66.

Sik, Ota
1981   *The Communist Power System* (New York: Praeger).

SIPRI (Stockholm International Peace Research Institute)
1983   *World Armaments and Disarmament, SIPRI Yearbook 1983* (New
York: International Publications Service).

Skilling, H. Gordon
1976   *Czechoslovakia's Interrupted Revolution* (Princeton, N.J.: Princeton
University Press).

Sklar, Richard
1983 "On the Concept of Power in Political Economy," in Dalmas H. Nelson and Richard L. Sklar, eds., *Toward A Humanistic Science of Politics: Essays in Honor of Francis Dunham Wormuth* (Lanham, New York, London: University Press of America, Inc.), pp. 179–205.
1979 "The Nature of Class Domination in Africa," *The Journal of Modern African Studies*, Vol. 17, No. 4, pp. 531–52.

Skocpol, Theta
1979 *States and Social Revolutions* (New York: Cambridge University Press).

Slomczynski, Kazimierz, and Tadeuz Krauze eds.
1978 *Class Structure and Social Mobility in Poland* (New York: M. E. Sharpe, Inc.).

Smith, Alan
1980 "Romanian Economic Performance," in *Economic Reforms in Eastern Europe and Prospects for the 1980s*, Colloquium, April 16–18, 1980, Brussels (New York: Pergamon Press), pp. 35–57.

Spigler, Iancu
1973 *Economic Reforms in Rumanian Industry* (London: Oxford University Press).

Spulber, Nicolas
1966 *The State and Economic Development in Eastern Europe* (New York: Random House).
1957 *The Economics of Communist Eastern Europe* (New York: M.I.T. Press and John Wiley & Sons, Inc.).

Stahl, Henri H.
1980 *Traditional Romanian Village Communities* (London: Cambridge University Press).

Stanculescu, Lieutenant General Victor, and Colonel Gheorghe Anghel
1984 *Factorul Economic si Rolul Sau in Intarirea Capacitatii de Aparare a Patriei* (Bucharest: Editura Militara).

Starr, Richard, ed.
1983 *1982 Yearbook of International Communist Affairs* (Stanford: Hoover Institution Press, 1983).

Sugar, Peter
1984 "Continuity and Change in East European Authoritarianism: Autocracy, Fascism, and Communism," *East European Quarterly*, Vol. XVIII, No. 1 (March), pp. 1–23.

Sugar Peter, ed.
1971 *Native Fascism in the Successor States, 1918–1945* (Santa Barbara, CA: ABC-CLIO Press).

Suteu, Titus, and Dumitru Ozunu
1977 *Alegerea Profesiunii* (Bucharest: Editura Politica).

Sweezy, Paul M., and Charles Bettelheim
1971 *On the Transition to Socialism* (New York: Monthly Review Press).

Szczepanski, Jan
1978 "Early Stages of Socialist Industrialization and Changes in Social Class Structure," in Kazimierz Slomczynski and Tadeuz Krauze, eds., *Class Structure and Social Mobility in Poland* (New York: M. E. Sharpe, Inc., 1978).

Szelenyi, Ivan
1978 "The Position of the Intelligentsia in the Class Structure of State Socialist Societies," *Critique*, Nos. 10–11. (Winter-Spring), pp. 51–76.

Teodorescu, Alin
1985 "Indicatorii Integrarii: Modele in Evolutie," in Marie Stanciu, ed., *Semnificatia Documentelor Sociale* (Bucharest: Editura Stiintifica si Enciclopedica).

Therborn, Goran
1982 "What Does the Ruling Class Do When it Rules?: Some Reflections on Different Approaches to the Study of Power in Society," in Anthony Giddens and David Held, eds., *Classes, Power, and Conflict* (Los Angeles, University of California Press, 1982), pp. 224–248.

Tismaneanu, Vladimir
1985 "Ceausescu's Socialism," *Problems of Communism* (January-February), pp. 50–66.

Traistaru, Elizabeta
1975 *Mobilitatea Socioprofessionala A Populatiei Active* (Craiova, Romania: Editura Scrisul Romanesc).

Traistaru, Ion
1983 *Eficienta Economico Sociala* (Craiova, Romania: Editura Scrisul Romanesc).

Traistaru, Ion, and Elizabeta Traistaru
1979 *Omogenizarea Societatii Romanesti* (Craiova, Romania: Editura Scrisul Romanesc).

Trotsky, Leon
1958 *The Revolution Betrayed* (New York: Pioneer Publishers).
1979 *Classes Strata and Power* (London: Routledge & Kegan Paul).

Tsantis, Andreas C., and Roy Pepper
1979 *Romania: The Industrialization of an Agrarian Economy Under Socialist Planning* (Washington, D.C.: The World Bank).

Tuitz, Gabriele
1981 "Romania," *East European Economics*, Vol. VXIX, No. 4 (Summer), pp. 41–46.

Turczynski, Emanuel
  1971   "The Background to Romanian Fascism," in Peter F. Sugar, ed., *Native Fascism in the Successor States: 1918-1945* (Santa Barbara, California: ABC-CLIO).

U.S. Arms Control and Disarmament Agency
  1984   *World Military Expenditures and Arms Transfers: 1972-1982* (Washington, D.C.: Government Printing Office).

U.S. Central Intelligence Agency
  1982   *Handbook of Economic Statistics.*

Vasilescu, Ilie P.
  1985   "Inginerul: grad sporit de participare creativa in dinamica intreprinderii," *Revista Economica*, nr. 35 (August 30), pp. 15-16.

Vedery, Kathern
  1983   *Transylvanian Villagers: Three Centuries of Political Economic and Ethnic Change* (Los Angeles: University of California Press).

Volgyes, Ivan
  1982   *The Political Reliability of the Warsaw Pact Armies: The Southern Tier* (Durham, North Carolina: Duke University Press).

Wallerstein, Immanuel
  1979   *The Capitalist World Economy* (Cambridge, England: Cambridge University Press).

Weber, Eugen
  1965   "Romania," in Hans Rogger and Eugen Weber, eds., *The European Right: A Historical Profile* (Los Angeles, CA: University of California Press).

Weiner, Robert
  1984   *Romania's Foreign Policy and the United Nations* (New York: Praeger).

Wesolowski, Woldzimierz
  1979   *Classes, Strata, and Power* (Boston, Mass.: Routledge & Kegan Paul).
  1978   "The Influence of Technical-Economic and Historical Cultural Contexts on the Differentiation and Integration of Social Classes," in Kazimierz Slomczynski and Tadeuz Krauze, eds., *Class Structure and Social Mobility in Poland* (New York: M. E. Sharpe, Inc., 1978), pp. 37-47.

Wharton Econometric Forecasting Associates, Jan Vanous, ed.
          Centrally Planned Economies Current Analysis, Selected issues, November 1982-April 1983.

White, Stephen
  1986   "Economic Performance and Communist Legitimacy," *World Politics*, 38 (April), pp. 462-82.

Witness to Cultural Genocide
  1979   (New York: American Transylvanian Federation, Inc., and the Committee for Human Rights in Romania).

Woolf, S. J., ed.
  1981   *Fascism in Europe* (New York: Methuen & Co. Ltd.).

Yanowitch, Murry
  1977   *Social and Economic Inequality in the Soviet Union* (New York: M. E. Sharpe Inc.).

Zamfir, Catalin, et. al.
  1984   *Indicatori si Surse de Variatie a Calitatii Vietii* (Bucharest: Editura Academiei Republicii Socialiste Romania).

Zane, G.
  1970   *Industria din Romania in a Doua Jumatate a Secolului al XIX-lea* (Bucharest: Editura Academiei Republicii Socialiste Romania).

Zaslavsky, Victor
  1982   *The Neo-Stalinist State: Class, Ethnicity, and Consensus in Soviet Society* (Armonk, New York: M. E. Sharpe Inc.).

Zimmerman, William
  1980   "The Energy Crisis, Western "Stagflation," and the Evolution of Soviet-East European Relations: An Initial Assessment," in Neuberger and Tyson, eds., *The Impact of International Economic Disturbances* (Elmsford, N.Y.: Pergamon) pp. 409–44.

INDEX

ABOUT THE AUTHOR

WILLIAM CROWTHER received his Ph.D. from the University of California, Los Angeles, in 1986. He carried out research in Romania in 1985, and in 1982–83 as an IREX Fellow. He has previously written on Romanian and Philippine politics. He is currently an Assistant Professor of Political Science at the University of North Carolina, Greensboro.